STRANGE VAGABOND OF GOD

To John,
to whom I owe my vocation after God;
and to his lepers and their friends,
especially Pauline.

STRANGE VAGABOND OF GOD

THE STORY OF
JOHN BRADBURNE

FR JOHN DOVE SJ

First published in 1997

Reprinted 2001

Gracewing

2 Southern Avenue, Leominster
Herefordshire
HR6 0QF

ISBN 0 85244 383 8

Additional typesetting by Action Typesetting Ltd,
Gloucester, GL1 1SP

Transferred to digital press by
Antony Rowe Ltd, Eastbourne

Contents

Prologue

Mutemwa is a great dome of granite rock which rises to the east of Mutoko, a dorp in the north of Zimbabwe. Mutemwa, which in Shona means 'you are cut off', gives its name to a small hamlet where a community of lepers live. It is flanked on its northern side by a great whaleback of rock called Chigona, whilst to the east the Inyanga mountains grace the skyline.

September is the beginning of the summer heat with the African sun beating down upon the huts of the lepers. The great rock features of Mutemwa and Chigona shimmer in the heat while thermals swirl the dust around the settlement. Bush fires cause smoke clouds to dull the atmosphere. The parched land longs for the coming rains.

I thought of John sweltering in his tin hut, his hermitage, and wondered how he fared as he went on his daily rounds, ministering with so much love to his little flock of lepers. The situation was tense and dangerous. The war now encircled even Mutemwa with its poor community. I prayed for John's safety and was sad to be so far from him.

The Slyne Head lighthouse must be the most westerly point on the beautiful coast of Connemara in the West of Ireland. Not far from its warning light on the mainland my cousins and I were lent a cottage – a real Connemara cottage previously inhabited by men of the sea, now owned by Joe and Eleanor McFadden.

It was early September 1979, wet as wet could be, when we arrived. The cottage was by a small creek with the great Atlantic booming on the rocks a little way out. The cottage was snug with a welcome fire of turf. We were soon at home.

In Zimbabwe, land-locked and high, one longs for the sea and the cliffs and the gulls. It was all here with a wonderful coast – walk north to Mannin Bay and Clifden. One met only a shepherd or a man in search of driftwood. One could be alone with the ocean, the gulls and the sheep. I was on leave.

On the 3rd September I went to bed early. I woke at about half-past eleven and decided to say a rosary to send me to sleep. I was fingering my beads and thinking of Christ's agony when suddenly I had an inner experience of agony – deep and sure. I woke to the full and wondered what to do. Whose agony? It was not mine, nor did it appear to be the agony of Christ. Sleep overtook me but I woke again and again with the inarticulate experience vividly to the fore. The day dawned and I found myself only able to wander along the coast and the cliffs trying to fathom this mystery and at the same time to offer prayers for those in any agony.

The next day, 5th September, I went to Ballyconeely post office some five miles away to post a card to John Bradburne, addressed to him at the Mutemwa leper settlement in Zimbabwe. He liked pictures of the sea and coastlands. The postmistress eyed me and enquired of my doctor cousin, Patricia, whether it was Father Dove – if so, the Gardai had a message for me. At that moment a police car arrived at the post office. I was to ring a certain number in London. The call box outside this tiny post office responded to the urgency of the moment. I was through in three minutes. Tony spoke to me from Jesuit Missions. John Bradburne had been abducted in the early hours on Monday, the 3rd September. Zimbabwe was at war. All manner of bands roamed the country and people just disappeared. Tony had tried to find me over the past two days.

John's body had been found on the main road beyond Mutoko near Lot, very close to where Dr Luisa Guidotti had been killed. They had doubts as to whether he had been shot or bayoneted to death. Tony feared the latter was true. (Later I learned that he had been shot.)

The cause of my experience of agony was none other than my lifelong friend John. He was gone, gone to the Lord, through an agony and death.

There was a moon that night and the sea was silver calm. John himself wrote:

> To contemplate the motion of the sea,
> To see the ocean moving constantly
> Wakens in you as surely as in me
> Bold longings to endure and to be free.

'... to endure and to be free.' Poor John; bayoneted to death – gone. I was grief stricken.

> Alas the glory of Israel has been slain on your heights'...
> O Mountains of Gilboa let there be no dew or rain on your
> treacherous field for there the hero died ...
> O Jonathan in your death I am stricken.
>
> (Samuel)

I was so grateful to be alone with the sea and the gulls and the moon that night, alone to lament to God.

The glory of it all was to follow after, as these pages relate. John – Gurkha, Chindit, poet, mystic, 'martyr' – has a message for us all both in his life and in his death.

PART I

WORLD WAR II –
India, Malaya, Burma

*I love this age in which I am on earth
so blest be God who gives to no man
choice concerning when and where he'll
come to birth.*

(J.R.B.)

CHAPTER 1

The East: A Memorable Meeting

The train left Delhi at 9 p.m. We looked forward to the cool of the hills and a view of the Himalayas. Towards dawn the engine began to labour at the beginning of the climb up to Dehra Dun. I remember a stop at Hardwar on the River Ganges with the many pilgrims crowding the platform, and the cries of those selling drinking water. John used to love to mimic their cry, 'Hindhu pani walla how'. Then there were the beggars, the poor outcasts of India crowding round the windows of the carriages pleading for alms, 'baksheesh Sahib'. The train moved off and one began to notice trees, saw – mills, and hill folk. The sweltering plains of India were now below as one at last aproached Dehra Dun some 2,200 feet up.

A truck picked us up from the railway station for the 5½-mile journey to Birpur, the centre of the 9th Gurkha Rifles. On the way we passed the 'midan' of the 2nd Gurkhas with a lovely view up to Mussoorie, the hill station above Dehra Dun, standing at 6,600 feet. The truck then took one into the firs and deodars of Birpur Estate, home of the 9th Gurkha Rifles.

The centre is old and permanent with a fine officers' mess whose lawns look up to the Mussoorie heights above, now the refuge of the Dalai-Lama. There were officers' bungalows with their lawns and gardens and trees – overcrowded then because of the war. Nearby was a fine polo ground and beyond were the men's lines – all in a setting of mountain deodars and firs. One remembers the brightness of the dawn over the mountains, the cool of the evenings and the smell of wood-smoke from flickering fires.

The Gurkhas were mercenaries from Nepal, stocky, cheerful little men with Mongolian features. They were 'pahari log', hill folk, able to ascend and descend mountains with a natural ease and astonishing skill. The Gurkhas were divided into their different tribal groups. Sherpas from around Mount Everest, Chetris and Thakurs nearer to Katmandu. The 9th Gurkhas were made up mainly of those Chetris and Thakurs – the high-caste Gurkha who ate long-tailed goats' meat. One could not help liking these joyful people, childlike and full of fun, but to whom fear was a stranger. John loved their songs – mountain airs about far-off homes amid the great snow peaks of the Himalayas – and wrote a poem about them:

The Gurkhas

From mountain airs of Himalyas,
O sad departing!
From homes 'neath lairs of shaggy bears,
And we come laughing.

To sunbaked plains or jungle rains,
Or lonely dying,
Though great the pain, we follow fame,
Our loved ones sighing.

From lands of flowers and fresh'ning showers,
And cowbells ringing;
Near temple towers sweet peace was ours
With sadhus singing!

It was March 1942 when I met John Randal Bradburne at the 9th Gurkhas Regimental Centre. It was a memorable meeting. I was a brand new subaltern and he was already a hero. I had a gramophone record – light music. Someone said that John had a gramophone with a square solid wood frame complete with ancient horn. I knocked shyly at his bungalow door. Introductions over, he took one look at the record and firmly put it to one side. 'We will play Johann

Sebastian Bach,' he said, as he chose 'Jesu, Joy of Man's desiring'. Thus our life-long friendship began.

John was the son of an Anglican parson with a living first in Cumbria, where John was born, and then in Norfolk. He had two brothers and two sisters. Philip and Mary were older; Audrey and Michael came after him. Philip and John were both at 'Greshams' together; Michael went to Eton later on. All married except John, and all have outlived him except his parents.

When at his public school, Greshams, John had been a member of the OTC (Officers' Training Corps) and had acquired a certificate 'A' which gave a youngster the taste or distaste for military knowledge. He had also been a bandsman – wind instruments.

The war broke out in September 1939. John applied to join the Indian Army. He probably heard about the need for officers in the Indian Army whilst still at school, since all public schools received circulars requesting volunteers to go out to India at that time. They were desperately short of officers and anyone with John's background and Indian connections (John's mother was born in Lucknow) was snapped up.

John tellingly described his early experience of military life in the following lines written not long before his death:

Right on my nineteenth birthday I was found Dressed as a
   raw recruit at heart of Reading. An OTC at school had
   been my ground of back experience ... forth I was
   heading!
Three bedboards and three 'biscuits' were my bedding,
My brand-new boots encaged my feet like iron,
I hoped I'd soon be wounded for a wedding
With fairest of all Nurses: she's of Zion.[1]

They made me a lance-corporal and crowned
My ignorance by sending me from Reading
To something called an OCTU which was found
On Salisbury Plain, at Bulford – Deadening!

---

1. The line 'the fairest of all nurses: she's of Zion' refers to the Mother of God, to whom John had an extraordinary devotion.

After four months of that, under the heading
Of 'Indian Army Unattached', signed on
As Subaltern, I signed on for a wedding
With fairest of all Nurses: she's of Zion.

I had no 'jungle-sense', no feel for ground
Unless it was the bit where I was bedding ...
An undistinguished fellow, homeward-bound
After four years abroad, I thought me heading
Even for heaven ... Devon saw me shedding
All chance of being ever aught but John ...
Revered by none I steered towards a wedding
With fairest of all Nurses: she's of Zion.

John received his commission as a 2nd Lieutenant, Indian
Army Unattached, on 20 December 1940, by coincidence
on the same day as his elder brother Philip. They both
sailed for India on the same ship from Liverpool on 21
January 1941, reaching Bombay in April of the same year.
Philip did not detect any religious vocation in John at this
time; on the contrary, he often found himself the peace-
maker when John got at cross-purposes with his fellow
officers. John wrote a few lines about that memorable
voyage on the good ship *Mulbera*.

The first one he called 'A Ballade of the Crossing of the
Bar'.

> Our speed was rather slower than you'd run,
> Our aptitude for indolence increased;
> Supine, we studied Urdu in the sun,
> Dallied, played goat and gloated: going East
> Man did not then consider Pan the Priest
> Who is the Sun of Justice ... going South
> We duly crossed the bar ... Apollow-fleeced,
> We revelled in the message from his mouth!

The second, 'A Ballade of a very Slow Voyage':

> The taking in of six fixed ports took seventy slow-moving
>   days,
> The wakening of youthful thoughts for glory in the glowing
>   East
> Went off to sleep before the deep Pacific with its wide amaze

Beamed on the boys whose bouncing joys were seamy oft to
say the least;

Arrival at Bombay after an eight-week voyage was something never to be forgotten. All those who sailed in
wartime convoys to the Far East will vividly remember that
first sight of the Indian shore as the ship slowly made her
way into Bombay harbour. Unlike the first call at Freetown
on the West Coast of Africa, followed by Capetown or
Durban, this was journey's end and the beginning of the
unknown – India and the Far East.

One stood fascinated at the ship's rail as she edged into
the harbour amid the shouts of deck hands above and
coolies below.

CHAPTER 2

India and Malaya

Arrival and a fresh-water bath, a cool drink, and one's first taste of the East. Bombay is hot – sticky heat which varies little the year round. Air-conditioning was primitive in those days and mostly confined to the punkah or fan. The Taj Mahal hotel was air – conditioned and most young officers made a bee-line to this haven of cool with its luxurious fare.

John and his elder brother, Philip, learned of their postings on arrival in Bombay – John to the 2/9th Gurkhas, and Philip to the 1/10th Baluch. Both regiments were at Secunderabad in the state of Hyderabad at the time, so the two brothers were not far apart.

The early impressions India made upon John are evident in these lines:

Indian Bazaar

Sacred bulls of lumb'ring size,
Mooching 'mongst the stalls;
Varied smell of merchandise
This Englishman enthralls.

Shelves of food with flies aswarm,
Betel-nut and dust;
Heavy air and very warm
But stay to look I must.

Tongas[1] reeling through the crowd,
(Scarecrow ponies' task);
Cripples, outcasts, beggars bowed:
Old India's lifted mask.

Holy men in wailing trance,
Wand'ring on the road:
Money lenders seizing chance
And counting all they're owed.

Idler babus drinking tea,
Babbling empty news;
'British not worth ek rupee,[2]
Their naukri[3] we refuse!'

Pie-dogs slinking in and out
(Traffic, shops, and feet)
Feasts of garbage strewn about
Each fly-infested street.

Haughty camels: caravan
Bearing bales of straw;
Swearing, grumbling driver-man –
Here's nature in the raw!

In August 1941 John's brigade went to Malaya, and a month later his brother Philip departed for Iraq and the Middle East. From then on they went their separate ways.

John spoke little of his war experience. He seemed humiliated by it all, even though for most of us he was something of a hero. He did reveal to me a little of his Malayan adventure. Churchill, in his history of the Second World War, stated that the idea of trying to defend and hold the Malay peninsula, 400 × 200 miles at its widest parts, with only two divisions could not be entertained. It needed the strong backing of the fleet. On Sunday, 7 December 1941, Pearl Harbour was attacked. The Japanese then began their invasion of Malaya on 8 December at Kota Bharu. The 'strong backing of the fleet' suffered a severe reversal with the sinking of the *Prince of Wales* and the *Repulse* – two of the British Navy's finest battleships.

---

1. Horse and trap. 2. Local currency. 3. Employment.

Soon after this the Japanese, with holdings in the north, had cut off Malaya with five divisions. Officers and men of the 2/9th Gurkhas were told to pair off and to avoid capture.

John and an ex-Assam tea planter paired off and hid in the Malayan jungles, living off roots, wild fruit, and an occasional gift of rice from a friendly village. Finally they made for the coast and captured a sanpan in an attempt to reach Sumatra and safety, but they hit the tail end of a typhoon and were shipwrecked and washed ashore in true Pauline style. They lay up for a while until they were able to capture another sanpan. Then, in the company of a few 'Jocks' from a Highland regiment, they set sail for a second attempt. This time they forced the Malay seamen to sail the sanpan for them. Thus they reached Sumatra.

John was suffering from heat stroke, sun stroke, and terrible malaria. His companion literally carried him aboard the last British destroyer out of Sumatra, brushing aside the sailors on the gangplank who said, 'Sorry, chum, we're full.' Listing with her overweight of refugees, the ship managed to ferry them out to a British cruiser, which eventually took them to Bombay and the safety of India. After treatment and rest in Bombay John made his way up to Dehra Dun in March 1942. It was there that I met him.

CHAPTER 3

Gurkha Days

A wartime army gathers together strange companions in arms. John and I moved into the same bungalow, number 9 Birpur, where we shared a room. In an inner room there was an ex-bank manager from Kenya; in the front room a burly Scot from a Highland regiment. The other half of the bungalow housed a 'box wallah', an old Wellingtonian, and a tough tea planter. In a nearby tent a talented pianist composed his own concerto.

Each bungalow had an array of servants. We all had a personal bearer whilst we shared a 'dhobi' (washerman), 'bhisti' (water carrier for our baths), sweeper, and a 'mali' for the garden.

John's bearer Dhil Bahadur was a hillman. The bearer had to provide one daily with starched shorts and shirt, along with a shining belt and boots. The bearer also marshalled the communal servants.

John's bearer's son, a chokra (little lad), woke us every morning with a cup of tea to the sung lament 'paune che, Sahib' – 'quarter to six, Sir'. Thus the day began often accompanied by some music from John's square gramophone. I remember in the first light of morning listening to the Pastoral Symphony, the Appassionata Sonata and, of course, Bach. Then parade.

In the afternoons we were required to study Gurkhali. This we did in our bungalow, tutored by a Munshi Sahib or teacher. The afternoons were very hot in India and so, more often than not, we lay on our beds while the poor teacher attempted to take us a step further in the vernacular. After ten minutes John would be up. 'Enough of that. Now, Sahib, you must learn to appreciate some Bach.' The rest of the lesson consisted in musical appreciation, in spite of the fact that we were paying for our lessons.

In the early evening after parade, we rode or walked. There was a great stillness before sunset over the mountains, and we used to enjoy riding over to the Forestry Research Institute, passing through the Gurkha lines and Indian villages into the great deodar forests which surrounded the Institute with its lovely lawns and shrubs.

At night we dined for the most part in the Mess. Such evenings could be formal or informal. On formal Mess nights the Colonel dined with us, dressed in his 'number ones'. Gurkha pipers (Himalayan Scottish) piped as we dined. There was then the toast to the King.

The Colonel always retired discreetly after coffee to leave the young bloods to dress up in tiger skins and to play Mess rugby. John and I were quite astonished after one such "formal" Mess gathering, when a young parachutist lad brought home to our bungalow our elder companion from Kenya, slung across his shoulders.

There were Mess guest nights at other times to which one could invite ladies. Our elder companion saw to it that John and I did not embark upon such occasions unaccompanied. He was a type of social magician who soon got to know all and sundry in the little hill station of Dehra Dun.

A most dangerous task was to be the Orderly Officer in charge of issuing rum to the men. Gurkhas drank rum and, in more of a naval tradition, they were issued with a tot on some evenings, a dangerous task because one was always obliged to sink a tot and a half under the vigilant gaze of a Gurkha Subahdar Sahib. John enjoyed such occasions, bringing back a little 'rukshi' to our Highland companion who was always out-of-pocket when in Mess.

On occasions we went to the Dehra Dun Club. We normally travelled the $5\frac{1}{2}$ mile by tonga (a horse and trap). The passengers were supposed to sit with their back to the horse and driver. John always climbed in next to the driver in front and, when the driver beat the horse, John beat the driver. Great arguments ensued and, on one occasion, even the horse gave up.

John was the life and soul of a party with his antics and ready wit. At the same time, he was a very affectionate person who enjoyed the company of the young belles who lived with their families in the cool of the hill stations. He was seldom fully understood and always gave more than he received, often to his cost in heart and spirit, and even in material goods. He would give his all to those he loved, as indeed he did at the end with his life.

What of religion? In those days all nature spoke to him of God – the Indian sunrise and sunset, the hills, the forests, the birds, the sadhus and holy men. He read poetry and loved music and beauty in people whom he came across. Later, his love for the Himalayas, for India and the East found its way time and again into his poetry. He loved to recall the silence, the contemplative spirit which pervaded those heights, and the chant of the sadhu at prayer. He wrote these lines when at Mutemwa:

> I well recall one morning as I went
> Up that long avenue in Hindoostan
> I heard a Sadhu chanting (sweetly blent
> With jacaranda's fragrance): Lindesfarne,
> Cluny and Quarr, look eastward! praise there one
> Singing alone, entempled in the sun.

Lindesfarne, Cluny and Quarr – how he loved the Western chant, too, of monks in choir. So often he reached out to that high form of prayer in his heart, expressing his joy for all creation himself in sung chant. He sang sad things, too, and later mastered by heart the 'Lamentations of Jeremiah' by Francois Couperin.

John was seeking in those days; he sought anything which captured the spirit. When on week-end leave in Mussoorie, he wrote:

> Once in Mussoorie on the foothills high
> Of higher, hymning Himalayan snows
> I walked into an Indian shop to buy
> Not anything but everything that rose

Up with my heart when, dusty, did disclose
From hid for many moons that Hindoo man
A record made by monks: High Anglican.

On one side Nunc Dimittis, Will Dufay,
And, on the other, glad I am to say,
'Gloria in Excelsis Deo' dating
back to King Henry Sixth I'm celebrating.

High Anglican he was at the time but one did not notice
any formal or institutional approach to religion in him. He
was like the woman who met Christ by the well of Jacob.
'Believe me, woman, the hour is coming when you will
worship the Father neither on this mountain nor in
Jerusalem. The hour will come ... when true worshippers
will worship the Father in spirit and truth" (John 4.21). It
seemed that the Spirit had touched John's inner being,
causing him to search everywhere for the meaning of that
inner message. Thus any beauty, be it in music, in nature,
in people, in song, in prayer, moved him further in his
search. The monks at Quarr or the sadhu in his solitude,
all that reached beyond, attracted him. They disturbed
him, too, as is reflected in the following verse:

I heard a sound of singing, saw a sole
Sadhu at praise ... into the fane did stroll
And felt myself a fool and vain, no role ...
Back I did go to Bach and Bacchus mixed
And barked up trees of wrong where song was lost.

In the regiment we had two missionaries – non-
conformists; both married men. They were older than
John and one in particular, although 'non-conformist', did
try to make John conform to a churchman's way. John
declined with courtesy. I remember him asking me about
the Church of Rome. In those days 'Rome' was still something of the 'scarlet woman' to public school men. I, too,
had been at a public school, somewhat Low Church – C. of
E. Being a Roman Catholic boy I was 'odd man out' and
excused from chapel and taught religion. Thus, starved of
dogma and doctrine, I was left with a simple devotion to
the Mass and the Sacraments. I remember, at school and in

the army, instinctively finding my way to Mass on Sundays. For the life of me, I could not give the 'why'. For me, too, this was an inner secret of faith, inarticulate. Thus I could not answer John's question. I directed him to the parish priest, a missionary Franciscan I believe, at the Roman Catholic Mission in Dehra Dun. This good father welcomed John and lent him a book by Arnold Lunn: *Now I See*. I do not remember if John read the book or whether he was led any further in his search. He spoke kindly of the interview but continued to seek as the Spirit directed him then, which was to no particular Church but using all Churches' literature and prayer which made appeal to his inner soul.

The East attracted him greatly. He felt its spirit upon him not knowing the reason or the source. High Brahmin or low-caste village Hindhu all seemed to contain a secret as yet unknown to him. The climate added to the mystery with its dramatic changes of heat, monsoon and cold. The blood-red sunsets and bright dawns; the arid, desert-like, dry season, suddenly transformed by the torrential rains into a green morass of life, producing numerous varieties of shrubs, trees, wild flowers, birds and bees; all of this made a deep impression upon him and was recalled in later years at Mutemwa leper colony:

> Five hundred yards of jacarand' and more
> Measures this vista fair from North to South
> And teminates but slightly past my door
> In other kind of tree that minds its mouth
> Singly, resembling Oriental tree
> Called Peepal and recalling East to me.

John was never attracted to yoga. He did not seem to need to quieten his body or his mind. He had already acquired, as though by natural gift, the ability to find God in almost all things. In what is termed the first world of today – the industrialised technological world – many seek to quieten their minds and hearts amidst the noise and mad rush of this jet age. They often turn to the East for modes of prayer – yoga, transcendental meditation; and more often they return sadly disillusioned, mistaking the means or method for the end. The quiet they experience at first is taken to be union with God, not merely a preparatory quiet in which to approach God. John, the true guru, had an early gift of discernment; his spirit seemed to need no formal method of prayer. I remember John's amusement when a bungalow companion practised yoga after parades, similar to my own on discovering a young Jesuit practising yoga after lectures in moral theology, seemingly just to clear his head.

One mode of prayer did attract John, a method often despised by church folk, who will quote holy scripture in their defence. He wrote:

> Need never be vain
> Repetitive prayer.
> The Queen of the Rosary's reign is fair:
> Domine Deus in Christendom dumb
> Et reus sum ego
> While easterly wheels are a hum?

Eastern prayer wheels and the repetitive plaint: 'Om mani padme hum' quite fascinated him. Later he delighted in the opinion that 'Om mani padme hum' was a corruption of 'Domine permane mecum'.

This autobiographical poem was written soon after the war:

OM

> A Buddhist pilgrim sat beside the way:
> All day he sat, and all he did was pray:
> He came at dawn; at eve he had not gone,
> He sat and stayed and simply murmured 'OM'.

> A certain missionary passed by chance
> With comrades twain; he gave a rapid glance:
> 'You see, such vain existence does not do:
> He merely murmurs, 'OM' the whole day through!'

> A person, seeming wise as he was rich,
> Beheld with scorn the pauper near the ditch:
> 'There's work a-plenty, progress to be made,
> And all he does is idle in the shade!'

The night time came, the moon in silence shone,
And still the Buddhist sat and murmured, 'OM':
The world had hurried by with scarce a nod,
This mighty fool remaining, near to God.

An outcast, ragged, old and bowed with woe,
Along the road alone that night did go:
'O holy man' he cried, 'please pray for me!
That when I die, more happy I may be!'

The Buddhist spoke to Heaven: 'Om', he said,
And gave the man his only piece of bread.
A fortnight afterwards, the outcast died,
And blessed the pilgrim from the other side.

***

A voice I heard: 'Well done, how keen your sight!
We cannot know which creed is fully right:
Cast off your shackles, make a broader search!'
'Not so,' I said, 'my King doth build his Church.'

This poem underlines John's love for the destitute poor.
Time and again his writings make reference to the outcasts
of this world dying alone in poverty, unwanted, unnoticed
save by God.

'OM' – He often used to say that one needed a 'prayer
wheel' as a background to prayer: something to occupy
the mind, whilst the spirit reached out to God. He used
the rosary in this manner with the 'Aves' adding the backcloth to his inner deep, reaching out to God. He would, of
course, discount the impious Eastern man who would
turn the prayer wheel for the public to behold. 'Two men
went up to the Temple to pray.' Worse, the man who sent
a servant to turn the prayer wheel for him. John was quick
to distinguish between the man who found God when
turning the prayer wheel, or when fingering his beads, or
when repeating an ejaculatory prayer, and the one who
did not. For John it was a matter of common sense: one
should find the mode of prayer which led one to God. He
never really understood the mind of the Pharisee, the man
who would outwardly pray when inwardly he was an

empty sepulchre. John was too naturally super-natural to fathom such people or, indeed, those who condemn repetitive prayer which is genuine.

Just as he loved 'Om' he loved 'El', the sacred word name of God. He wrote this of 'El':

> Simple ejaculation, single dart
> Piercing with love the heart of love our King,
> Whose thought our Father is, whose word I fling
> Straight into Godhead by his hand and art ...
> Monosyllabic nothing, winging all
> The deepest content of the deepest call!

This form of ejaculatory prayer, whether 'Om' or 'El' or the longer prayer of 'The way of the Pilgrim', would lead him into silent commune with God.

Continuing his appraisal of 'El', he is moved to flow on:

> Eloquent silence, sweet unsounded praise,
> Cloud of unknowing got at as she sways
> Encompassing ... cloud of forgetting ... plays
> Lightly, as with a child:
> Immaculate, enisled.

One could say that John in those early India days was well on the way in his search for God, uncluttered by dogma or denominations. Later he strongly upheld the need for a true Church with true sacraments. If anything he became rather conservative about belief in and respect for the Blessed Sacrament, for the Holy Eucharist, and the other sacraments. He had a simple devotion to 'confession' too. He hated a 'progressive' attitude which belittled the real presence of Christ in the tabernacle, of Christ in the particles of consecrated bread.

I remember him coming to me in his early Mutemwa days saying that he had the Blessed Sacrament in his hut and what should he do? A certain priest used to say Mass for the lepers using a very crumbling form of bread. After Mass, large bread crumbs were in evidence everywhere. John collected all of these devoutly and put them into a sacred place in his hut – there was no tabernacle at Mutemwa at the time. This worried John very much.

Eventually he was persuaded to consume these particles in Holy Communion one morning.

In his Gurkha army days, then, he had already attained the ability to raise his mind and heart to God without so much as knowing it. Although he thought he was nowhere, yet he was already a pilgrim in heart on the long climb towards higher union with God. He knew not that search led to God – 'Seek and ye shall find; knock and it shall be opened unto you'. His path was still unclear and, as can be imagined, the war confused his questing heart with its message of violence and hate. God was leading him into another warfare which would require even greater moral and physical courage.

CHAPTER 4

In The Hall of a Mountain Queen

In 1943 we took what was to be a final three weeks' leave together before our ways parted until the end of the war.

We decided to go to Naini Tal, the lake of the goddess Naini, situated on the borders of Almora within trekking distance of Nanda Devi, a snow-capped peak of great beauty rising 25,645 feet above sea level. The Tal or lake of the goddess Naini was 6,346 feet up, cool even in the summer heat.

The train from Dehra Dun took us right down to Bareilly junction and then back up to Kathgodam at the foot of the Naini Mountains.

Train journeys were an adventure in those days. Officers travelled first class, and all first-class compartments were 'sleepers' plus toilet and shower. One booked into a four-berth or two-berth. At the station the one in charge of reservations always played the same game. He said that some Major Sahib had a priority booking on our compartment but added that it was just possible that he might be able to make other arrangements for the two young Captain Sahibs. Some rupees were exchanged and very suitable arrangements were soon made. The fictitious name of the Major Sahib was removed from our compartment door.

Sometimes there were no dining cars on Indian railways. One stopped at a suitable station for a time long enough to enable the Sahib 'Log' to eat in comfort in the station restaurant. At the end of a good meal the train would depart, but not before one had tipped the punkah wallah. John loved this whole 'liturgy'. A small boy sat outside the restaurant with a cord wrapped round his big toe. The cord disappeared through a hole in the wall to attach itself to a punkah inside the restaurant. By moving his leg back and forth, he also moved the punkah (a long bamboo screen slung from the ceiling of the restaurant) which caused a movement of air within the restaurant to the satisfaction of the Sahib 'Log'. If the punkah stopped swinging there would be angry retorts from the diners. The poor lad duly received his few annas tip at the end of the meal to his and John's delight. In 1971 John wrote:

> My mind throws back full twenty year
> To Lucknow lack of a medium year
> And the locked-up in heat and the random fan
> Tied with a string to the toe of a man.

At one such stop John peered into the station master's office. The station master, an Indian, was sitting at his desk writing with a reed pen. Above him was a hornets' nest. The hornets flew in and out, apparently oblivious of the station master and he of them. John was intrigued and questioned the station master as to how he could sit so calmly beneath an hornets' nest? Years later he captured the incident in verse:

Nota Bene

> I said at last, past passing time of day,
> 'Do hornets in such close proximity
> Not worry you at all?'; a blissful ray
> 'Of soft ironic humour marked his glee:
> He answered, 'Sahib, there is no need to fuss,
> We do not speak to them nor they to us!'

Indian train journeys always seemed to require one night or longer in the train. We slept a night and finally reached Kathgodam at midday following. Kathgodam was at the foot of the Naini ascent. We still had to climb another 4,000 feet before reaching the Lake Naini. There were buses and there were taxis. The journey covered about twenty miles of hairpin bends in quite steep ascent. At the top one suddenly came upon the lake through a narrow entrance, since Naini Tal was encased in mountains which reached down to her shore. There were hotels, shops, and the club by the lakeside, but most residences were cut into the side of mountains overlooking the lake.   '

We had sent a telegram to the officers' hostel requesting two beds. Our baggage was duly loaded on to small ponies or 'tats' for the journey. Only mountain paths led up to the residences. We, too, rode upon ponies with the owner running alongside. The caravan set forth. At the hostel we were met by a charming 'grass' widow, the wife of a Gurkha officer, who was then in Burma. She explained that one could not book by telegram since the hostel was already booked up six months or so in advance. However, she had approached the wife of the Commissioner of Police for the United Provinces, who was delighted to put us up. She was a 'Lady' and he was a 'Sir', and we were only young officers. John enquired whether this meant that we would have to sit bolt upright on the edge of Chippendale chairs, to which our kind hostess burst into laughter and said, 'Go and see'.

We had to cross to the other side of the lake on our ponies and then climb 800 feet to a lovely house named Dwarkastan. Our 'Lady' hostess was quite charming; no Chippendale chairs but relaxation and every comfort and good will. We were at home.

Our hostess had horses, tennis court, and a fine cuisine. She knew everyone and what to do and where to go. One could sail on the lake, dine at the club, ride out towards Almora, climb China peak, and above all see Nanda Devi, one of the great mountain peaks of the Himalayas.

John was in paradise in this lovely mountain kingdom. He was full of joy and boyish adventure. We rode out to Sat Tal, the seven lakes, and had early morning breakfast of bacon and eggs, scones and honey, at a dear little cottage which could have been transplanted from Devon. We climbed China peak and gazed at Nanda Devi – an unforgettable sight. Years later John sent me a small water colour of Nanda Devi when I was a Jesuit scholastic. We were so sad not to have had the time to have made the trek to the foot of the mountain through the valley of flowers to the Pindari glacier.

The nights were full of fairy lights rising up to the heavens all around and above the lake. At our end of the lake there was an Hindu temple whose bell called the faithful to prayer at dawn and dusk. John loved this temple which we passed daily on our way to the shops or the club.

Some nights we went to the club, always by pony down the 800 feet and up again. In those days, ladies wore long evening dresses and could thus not ride back on ponies. For them a 'dandy' was available, a type of sedan chair with a hood carried by four mountain folk.

One night John decided to hire a dandy but, instead of being carried himself, he put one of the mountain men into the dandy and shouldered the weight with the other three up the long 800 foot climb. He was very sensitive of the burdens laid upon others, whether they be coolies, dandy wallahs or even tonga ponies. His inner spirit always reached out to the overburdened in this life:

Burdens

Luggage-laden coolie
On Orient station, ˗
Bowed beneath bauble of civilisation;
You from afar!
Look well on your brother;
The burden he carries
Is that of another.

Labouring coolie
As lean as he's tired,
Drawing a rickshaw by heavyweight hired;
You from afar!
Look well on this runner;
So quick with the burden
Which deadens his brother.

O European!
These lines are not written
Merely for purpose of preaching a sermon;
People are all

Bound one to another,
And each of us somewhat
Depends on his brother.

Therefore, all people!
For sake of the hired,
May his employer observe when he's tired;
Let each respect
The lot of the other,
For all are God's children
Regardless of colour.

The time to return was all too soon upon us. We bid a
fond farewell to our 'Lady' hostess, who had been a real
mother to us. The descent to the train at Kathgodam was
breathtaking. One saw the plains of India 6,000 feet below
sweltering in a heat haze. The taxi screeched around the
hairpin bends to reach the train an hour before departure.
We left sadly at 3 p.m. to reach Dehra Dun next morning.
Back to the business of war.

CHAPTER 5

Burma 1943: The Chindits

The war in Burma was now well under way. The Japanese were in Upper Burma and the problem of dislodging them was yet to be solved.

The lost 2/9th Gurkhas were being replaced by a new battalion, the 5/9th Gurkhas. John, the hero and escapee from the 2/9th, was offered the post of Adjutant to this new battalion – a feather in his cap. However, he declined the offer, preferring to stay with the more humble mortar platoon. There were no Gurkha King's commissioned officers in those days. We had Viceroy commissioned G.Os – Subadhars and Jemadhars. The men saluted the G.Os. They were a very efficient breed of men. John had a Jemadhar Sahib under him in the mortar platoon who was well able to run the platoon himself. This left John free for other more exciting events – bird-watching, singing psalms and even tending to the wounded.

The 5/9th Gurkhas moved to the forests around Saharanpur, South of Dehra Dun, for jungle warfare training. I remember John writing to me about those forests – the trees and the animal life. I subsequently spent a short while there myself. It was a real tented jungle camp amid the mountain firs, close to the Jumna River. John wrote about this river country in later years:

River Jumna

Jumna river's jungle country
Chital's fastness wild;
Skipping range of heights Siwalik –
Himalaya's child.

Whitest domes of Hindu temples
Palaces of peace;
Happy herdsmen homeward sending
Cattle, goats and sheep.

Many birds of many voices,
On the forest's rim;
Flutes and cowbells, songs and madals;
India's evening hymn.

Wisps of woodsmoke steeply rising
High in stillest air;
Creatures drinking at the waters
Watchful and aware.

River gliding past the gladelands,
Talking to the trees,
Soon the sun will vanish swiftly,
Sink with splendid ease.

Jumna! lovely is your country,
Kingdom near the hills,
Round your islands flow for ever,
Fed from rains and rills.

Eventually the 3/9th Gurkhas moved to assembly areas prior to the move into Burma. John had joined them.

Churchill appointed the young Major General Orde Wingate as an O.C. in Burma. Wingate had made his mark as a leader in Abyssinia and had greatly distinguished himself in jungle fighting in Burma. In some circles he was nicknamed the 'Clive of Burma'. Churchill noted that the Jewish Zionists had their eye on him as a possible future commander-in-chief of an Israelite army. John believed that Wingate was a convert to Judaism. He loved the Jews both because Christ was from their stock, and also because they were an oppressed people. He so often prayed that they might become one with Christ.

Wingate became famous for his long-range penetration groups which were landed behind the Japanese lines by air. They were known as the Chindits.

In early 1944 the Japanese were preparing to attack Imphal in Assam, the gateway to India – a crisis indeed. The Chindits were to drop behind them with a view to cutting off their supply routes around Indaw. John's brigade was to be crash-landed into this operational area by gliders. Landing strips had been cut in the thick of the forests where these gliders could land.

Prior to take-off Wingate himself inspected the brigade of which John was a member. Wingate walked down the line of officers stopping in front of John. John was taken aback. Wingate looked him straight in the eye, shook him by the hand and said: 'Congratulations, Captain Bradburne, on your escape and upon your M.C.' (Military Cross). He was never given his M.C. It was conveniently overlooked, but John never forgot Wingate. Shortly afterwards Wingate himself crashed to his death: Churchill said, 'With him a bright flame was extinguished.'

John never spoke much about his war. He told me a little of their landing in Burma. A large force was in fact crash-landed behind the Japanese lines – men and mules. John said that the air strip cut amid the jungle trees looked mighty small from up aloft. The glider in front of him crashed into the trees, killing some mules; theirs got down alright. Thus he arrived in Burma.

He spoke even less of the year or more that he spent there with the Chindits. A mutual friend told me that John had to be forced into a slit trench in the thick of battle. He loved to watch the birds and be about his sung 'office'. A badly wounded British soldier on one occasion asked John to shoot him. He could not do it. Who could? The severely wounded feared to be left behind as prey to a Japanese patrol.

John had to be flown out on two occasions for treament of recurrent malaria. Malaria drugs were in their infancy in those days. I myself spent three weeks in hospital with a bad bout, receiving only quinine as the remedy.

In 1945 John was flown out to Poona for extensive rest and treatment. He did not return to the front again but was sent home for eventual release and demobilisation. He told me that he had to go before an army medical board who passed him A1 fit. He was now a civilian.

It is hard to assess the effect of the war upon John, nor did I question him as to when he first experienced the finger of God upon him. He was both a hero and a misfit. War demands courage and expertise in killing. The latter was quite foreign to John.

Perhaps the experience of war helped his eventual detachment from the world, his withdrawal from conventional society. Grace builds upon nature. I believe that God called John to an inner life and the beginnings of a withdrawal from 'the world' as early on as the Malayan Campaign. At that time, and later in Dehra Dun and Burma, the seed thus sown began to urge him on in his search – 'O Beauty so ancient and yet so new'.

I was out of touch with John at the time of his homeward journey since I was in Greece with 1/9th Gurkhas. We did not return to India and to the beloved Dehra Dun until as late as February 1946. On arrival a letter awaited me from John. He was home and contemplating a job with the Forestry Commission on the Quantocks in Somerset. This was my home country – roll on demob. I eventually got back in September 1946 and we were soon to meet.

PART II

PEACE – RETURN TO ENGLAND 1945

Rarely not have readers seen
Rural England rolling green
Undulating over land
More divine through human hand.
(J.R.B.)

CHAPTER 6

Home Again

Oh, to be in England ... five years is an eternity to the young. John was only twenty-four when he returned. To his dying day he loved England, steeped as he was in her high culture. He remained an Englishman to the end, spoke much of her in his poetry, but always adapted with graceful courtesy to the ways of others.

Sailing the coast towards Southampton Water
As far from shore as ships show near to land
I gloated for my country, and I thought her
The fairest sunlit isle where one may stand;
I strolled her in my soul, did hold her hand
As lovingly as five years exile thence
Can prove it, and I moved in recompense.

Returning home I lacked that glint of glory
Which glows upon the brows and prows of some;
No hint heroic dints unshielded story
With scars to stir the martial trump and drum:
Writ on my heart, 'Om mani padme hum'
Sounded less strongly than the gongs of war,
Yet was the getting of its worth much more.

Her chessboard map of broad and happy fields
Clapped England's name for glee as sailed we by;
Those glimpses of her vistas and her yields
Wielded no jingoistic battle-cry;
Her woodland sang wild boars that know no sty
And rang with echoes of her silven past
Until on silent joy goaled at last.

At home now, away from men's rough ways and even rougher language. Away, too, from an endless foreign routine from 'reveille' to 'last post'. V.E. day and V.J. day left behind. Demobilisation – 'demob', the casting off of coarse uniforms as one returned to the leisure of home clothes, the trip to Aldershot to acquire a suit, the last formality, with quite a good raincoat and hat into the bargain.

John had already started work with the Forestry Commission on the Quantocks before I reached Somerset and home. We were soon in touch and our first meeting, since Dehra Dun in 1943, was in Bridgewater. John and his fellow foresters used to go to a small club in Bridgewater and so I drove in the long evening light to meet him. He was wearing a roll neck, breeches, wool stockings, and forester's boots. He looked fine, well and strong. We spent a while at the club and ended with a cool draught of bitter at the inn close by. He told me that he had taken this job with the Forestry Commission to enable him to clear the cobwebs of war from his mind. He loved the hills and the trees and the clean air. He could think here and pray a little.

We met intermittently in Bridgewater or at my home – an old country house which had been a manor, with mill and farm. It was a long, rambling old place set in a valley with wooded hills rising to the front. One end of the house used to be the children's large playroom-cum-schoolroom and a night nursery. This was to be ours. The night nursery was named, by John, the Trappists' dormitory. It had a large window overlooking green lawns, fields, and the wooded hills. On the mantelpiece stood a little statue of St Anthony holding the child Jesus. It had been there since childhood days. Later it was to be with John in the hut from which he was abducted.

A mutual army friend and I wanted him to come to Switzerland for a final 'fling' before we, too, had to take up a civilian career. John could not get leave from the Forestry Commission.

On my return just before Christmas in 1946 I went to stay two or three nights at John's home, 'Fir Grove' in Ottery-St-Mary, Devon. We travelled down together by car. It was to be my first meeting with his family. I do not remember rightly who was there – his father and mother certainly and one sister, probably Mary. Philip and Michael were away, and Audrey too. I remember being conscious of the fact that I was amongst a family who were High Anglican, and highly educated. I suppose I was shy and remember well the kindly welcome by John's father and the homeliness extended by his mother. His father had by now retired from the ministry. He was a keen gardener and loved the countryside; a quiet man with much courtesy. Later he was to blame me for John's crossing to Rome. Little did he know that John was 'guru' and I his 'disciple'.

After a happy stay I returned to my family for Christmas, my first at home since I left for the war in 1941.

The New Year of 1947 brought an exceptional cold spell with snow lying almost uninterrupted from January to March. It was cold on the Quantocks; nevertheless, John worked on.

I had to go north for a job. It was not until Whitsun that we met. By this time the winter snow, the open air life and hard exercise had done their work. The cobwebs of war had been blown away. With the coming of spring the spirit stirred within John and in the full of summer he moved further west, this time to Buckfast Abbey.

He took this step not without a grave and searching decision. On his return home he was not a monk, nor hermit, nor religious; he was John, young, strong and good-looking. He was still very sociable, cheerful in a unique manner. He met a lovely lass or two who came from fine homes, blending with the new-found loveliness of the English countryside. At one stage he was greatly attracted to marriage and even travelled along the path to that goal for some time. What made him stop? There are practical considerations before one can take such a momentous step: a job; somewhere to live; a future. He had no such equipment since he lived for the present, God's present. For John, the past had gone and the future was in God's hands. The present required decision; to follow the gentle but firm invitation of the hound of heaven, or to follow a natural inclination to love, to marriage, to the natural joys of the family and the world about us? The deep inner call – deep calling to deep – seemed to make it clear that human marriage was not for

him. His call was, in some way, to transcend the near horizons of this world to a beyond. It was a special call to him,
John; a special invitation to belong to God. The decision
was his: like the good young man in the gospels, he could
choose either way. John chose to walk with God.

Monasteries and religious houses are not filled with
eunuchs or soured rejects from the world's marriage
markets. They are peopled, for the most part, by those
who know the joys of human love but have opted for a
higher love – a transcendental love. St Augustine experienced both loves: 'Our hearts are made for Thee and shall
not rest until they rest in Thee,' he wrote. The human
heart longs for infinite love, to be fulfilled. Some who
enter the married state are disillusioned when they
discover that they are wed to finite love. The longing for
the infinite is always there and, like the woman by the well
in St John, chapter four, some seek it in many human loves
until, like her, they meet Christ, or die disillusioned.

John was endowed with great natural affection. He
responded warmly and generously to human affection and
love. It was not because he was incapable of human love
that he pursued his unique vocation, nor because he
regarded human companionship with distaste. Neither was
he jilted in love. No, he followed his way because for him it
was God's way. This demanded a great sacrifice from him, of
home, of family, of a wife-to-be and, in the end, even of his
own life. The call to follow the Spirit of God in such a
unique bond does not erase the demands of nature. It gives
strength to sublimate these natural desires. Nevertheless
there is a price to pay. John knew the bite of the flesh, the
attraction of beauty in the body and soul of a woman, but he
put aside the temporary joy of a human companion in order
to seek God alone and to the full. The Holy Spirit brooks no
rivals to the divine call. In return John enjoyed inner
converse with God with a corresponding attraction to solitude. 'O beata solitudo' he so often quoted. Later he wrote
these lines which he named 'Lovesong':

> Love is a short disease, a long desire
> And an eternal healing, love is odd
> Only if matched unevenly, the fire

Of love and not the ire of lust is God;
Stronger than death because its breath is life
Love wrongs itself if shelves it unfulfilled,
Either it seeks a husband or a wife
Or mounts towards the founts whence it is willed;
Met physically love ignites, it flows,
It blows upon the furnace of the heart;
It heats itself by starving as it goes
Feeding on freedom with angelic art;
In elemental trappings love is fair
As lapping waters: light, it walks on air.

At the same time he was always extremely sociable, right to
the end. People sought his company, drove miles to see
him to seek the joy and other-worldliness he imparted.
But he himself opted to be alone with God.

One has to remember that he was never under religious
vows; unlike the monk or the religious, assisted as they are
by their Rule, John vowed freely of his own accord. He
used to say that he had wed Miriam, the mother of God, so
that she might lead him into the sanctuary of the Spirit. He
had a great love for Our Lady and much of his poetry
reflected this devotion. At first, in his Anglican days, she
was a stranger to him, but later she seemed to take him
over and lead him to her Son.

Loneliness is the lack of what you long
To live with in this life and not to lose,
But solitude is company so strong
As mutual love with wife or living muse
Or even with them both, as in the case
Of anyone who weds the Queen of grace.
Some think it may be well if they but dream
All their lives long how strong they'll never get
Whilst others follow, as it were, a stream
They know will find the sea although not yet:
Truly the stream that leads towards the sea
Is warm reform in faith and feeling free
Flowing into Maria, Maid of Glee.

Thus it was with great generosity of heart that John went
his solitary way to Buckfast Abbey in 1947.

CHAPTER 7

Buckfast Abbey

In 1947 one took the train to Newton Abbot and then a bus to Dart bridge close to Buckfastleigh in Devon. Today a motorway passes close to the River Dart only half a mile from the Abbey. John describes the scene:

In Devonshire, the shining Dart
Comes swiftly from the moor;
A-lazing in its sunlit pools
The dappled trout I saw –
'Twas a memory of Eden.

Saint Mary's Abbey flourishes
Beside that river clear,
'Mid woods and meadows, once a haunt
of Devon's wild red deer: –
There walks God in Mary's garden.

One follows this rivulet for half a mile to the Abbey.

John looked upon Buckfast as his first real spiritual oasis after a long search during the war. It was here that he began to write in verse.

Each stone of this amazing Abbey – Church
Passed through the shaping hands of Brother Peter,
Into this fane I went to end my search
And to begin my pilgrimage in meter.

He told me all about the Abbey, quoting from Dom Norris's booklet. Buckfast Abbey can trace its history back a thousand years and more. As Dom Charles Norris's booklet relates, Buckfast was absorbed into the Cistercian Order in the year 1147. The ancient foundations upon which the present Abbey Church is built belong to this period.

In 1539 the Reformation caused the dissolution of the Abbey. From 1539 to 1882 there were no monks at Buckfast and so its beauty began to fade into ruin. The lead was stripped off the roofs and the bells removed to the Protestant church in Buckfastleigh. Finally, in 1806, the ruins were levelled and a pseudo-gothic mansion was created on the site. The desecration was complete.

Dom Norris goes on to tell us that in 1882 the resurrection began. A French Benedictine community, expelled from France, acquired the mansion and the site. In 1902 Buckfast was raised again to rank as an Abbey and, in 1906, Anscar Vonier became its great scholar-builder Abbot. It was he who saw to the building of the present Abbey by Brother Peter and his fellow brothers in Christ. He said in an article that the Brother Gardener discovered, quite by accident, the original foundations of the Abbey Church. Upon these the new Abbey was raised and completed in 1937, a year before Abbot Anscar's death.

It was awe-inspiring for a young man responding to the Spirit's urge to visit such a House of God in which a contemplative community lived – in fact for two young men, neither of whom had ever entered such a holy precinct before. With John as a guide it was a profound joy. On the panelled ceiling of the Lantern there is an inscription 'Great shall be the glory of this last house more than the first saith the Lord'. The whole Abbey seemed to be filled with glory and praise. John took me everywhere and in particular to the belfry. There hangs the great bourdon bell, 'Hosanna', weighing $7\frac{1}{2}$ tons. It was Pentecost and so we heard the whole peal of fourteen bells, the sound passing up the Dart valley to the hills beyond.

> Jubilant bells, to the glory of Christ
> Steep all the green valley in praise;
> And the watchmen who work in this beautiful place,
> Pure chords of thanksgiving shall raise.

Then there was the sung Divine Office, the 'Opus Dei'. We attended all we could and one remembers Vespers in particular when the monks, red in the face from haymaking, gathered in choir. John truly loved the melodic chant – Plainsong (Gregorian chant) – accompanied by the princely organ. 'I think that out of Plainsong cometh peace,' he wrote.

John arrived at Buckfast Abbey in the summer of 1947. Dom Raphael Stones OSB was in charge of the parishioners who came to worship. He had lost an eye in the first war, and it was to him that John went – a meeting of two war veterans.

For a while John helped Dom Raphael in the garden and in the cemetery while undergoing instruction, which would eventually lead him to his reception into the Church of Rome.

He then found a job and lodgings in Buckfastleigh, the village close by. The job was exacting. He became a builder's mate. At first his fellow builders resented his educated accent – 'ee baint one of us'. Some of them had also been in the war. They all took to John when they came to know him. they even "covered up for him" when he lost his balance on the rafters and let the bricks fall through a newly built ceiling.

In the evening he retired to the Abbey for instruction and prayer. It was after Compline that he met his future godfather, Hugh. They became deep friends. Hugh was a good twenty years older than John but not so far ahead of him in the Church. He had been 'received' at Buckfast in 1942, and was now the local bank manager. They met regularly after Compline for a chat in the long summer evenings over a glass of ale in an inn beside the Dart.

Hugh was a true godfather to John – a real old-world gentleman, quaint in the kindest sense, full of fun and the grace of God. I remember Hugh saying to us: "Now, you two, behave yourselves in the Monastery, and do not drink too much cider in front of my dear friend the Abbot.'

Abbot Bruno Fehrenbacher was a most dignified man, tall and princely, but with a great charm and simplicity. He was originally from South Germany and was very kind to John and myself. We did not drink too much cider. The cider, incidentally, was of Somerset's best – rough and powerful. It was possibly seasoned at the Abbey. Buckfast is, of course, famous for its tonic wine and honey. John wrote in memory of the Abbey bees:

> In a pub, I was told that a message had come,
> Marked 'Urgent! From all Abbey bees' ...
> 'Twas as follows: 'Dear Bard, tho'; we sing not, but
> hum,
> Our life is not given to ease.
> If you look in the Sanctuary, you will observe
> There burns near the Altar a flame:
> 'Tis fed buy a pillar of flowers and herbs –
> A wax candle – our title to fame!
> To us, lest the world think bees wanting in praise
> The Lord gives this work for a sign;
> And while others sing canticles marking the Phase,
> We cause His memorial to Shine!
>
> Alleluia

With the turn of the leaf heralding autumn, John's reception drew near. It was arranged for the feast of Christ the King, the last Sunday in October 1947. I was not able to get down from the North and so Hugh took John to the crypt chapel of St Mary's Abbey, Buckfast. There he was received into the Church of Rome with Hugh, his godfather, and some few friends, monks and parishioners in attendance. John was delighted that his baptism by his father was not called into question, but John's father, Anglican Minister as he was, obviously had misgivings about John's passage to Rome.

John's reception into the Roman Catholic Church was a great joy to Hugh and myself. I had played little or no part in this deep decision. As mentioned, John's father blamed me for John's crossing to Rome. In those days this was a serious matter for an English gentleman. Now no one would raise an eyebrow. My own father, a good low Churchman (C. of E.), blamed John for my entry into the

Society of Jesus. No one blamed the Holy spirit!

Later, in an interview for *The Shield*, a magazine of the Archdiocese of Salisbury (Zimbabwe), John said this about his crossing to Rome:

> The influence of India and four and a half years in the East stirred my mind a good deal. I wanted to be sure of salvation. I came to the conclusion that there could not be more than one true church that Christ had founded and by the grace of God I got there. There was in me a great desire to belong to a society which could embrace a maximum, and not an exclusive minimum of people on their way to heaven.
>
> I did not become a Catholic [he goes on to add] until after the war in 1947 on the feast of Christ the King. That is part of the whole Jewish idea which leads me to say that my concern for the Jews dated chiefly from my thinking about the gospel of that feast – 'Art thou the King of the Jews?'

It was a joy to me indeed. Now we could share the Body and Blood of Christ together. In the past we had shared a good many natural joys and some sorrows; now we could share those supernatural joys more fully in the measure that God gave to either or to each. We could go to Mass and receive communion at the same altar at Buckfast, Lourdes, or elsewhere. We could push each other into the 'Box', as John would call the Sacrament of Penance. John, the convert, had vast regions of knowledge about the faith gleaned from his recent instruction by that holy monk, Dom Raphael of Buckfast Abbey, of which I, a born Catholic, had little or none. These we could share too. Finally, it was John who introduced me to Buckfast Abbey – a memorable milestone.

John longed to enter Buckfast as a monk. Everything seemed to lead up to this decision: his love of the divine office, plainchant, monastic silence and his yearning for a measure of solitude. He really felt that he had reached his journey's end after the long search which had started in Malaya, India, Burma, the Quantocks, and now at last Buckfast. St Mary's Abbey, Buckfast seemed to be the answer to his deep inner prayer.

The Novice Master, Dom Placid, who later became Abbot, had doubts, according to John's godfather. Hugh said that all three, Abbot Bruno, Dom Placid and Dom Raphael, did not discern in John a vocation to the rule of St Benedict and the life in a Benedictine monastery. On the other hand, John, a war veteran and a genuine seeker, was quite certain that this was his calling at that time. What to do? The Benedictine rule says that one should keep knocking on the door. John did just that. He went to his godfather, Hugh, to beseech him to intercede with his friend the Abbot. This resulted in a provisional acceptance as a postulant, but in those days it was customary to wait for two years after one's conversion to Rome before entering religious life. One had to let the dust of conversion settle a little and find one's feet in a new universal community of worship.

At any rate John had come a long way. He was now in the barque of Peter, as he put it, and, further, he was provisionally accepted as a postulant in the Order of St Benedict at St Mary's Abbey, Buckfast. Praise be to God!

CHAPTER 8

Decline and Fall

What was he to do for two years? It must have been Dom Raphael or other friends of that time who introduced him to Gaveney House preparatory school near Exmouth. He was duly accepted as a prep school master. In later years he used to love to read Evelyn Waugh's *Decline and Fall*, in no sense of criticism of Gaveney House but in wonder at his own appointment. It would be interesting to know what the boys made of him. One master, Rupert, became a close friend.

He said that he began writing poetry during his first spring in the Church, which was in 1948: 'I never wanted to write, I never felt the impulsion to put thoughts into verse until that first spring. I also believe that anyone who has a talent, however small or great, once he is a Catholic should use it for the sake of the Kingdom.'

He wrote a lot during that first spring and summer at Gaveney House. There is a freshness, an inner joy, about his early poetry which is enchanting. He wrote about the beauty of nature, about the seasons, birds and bees. I treasure an early poem which summed up his frame of mind, his expectancy, his vocation at that time. It was written in holiday time and prefaced as follows: –

I went for a long walk yesterday in lovely Sussex, and at first felt depressed. But then I remembered that true joys are to be found only in Him who made all things, so I wrote this for you.

No more, my Lord, to dream away Thy time
Among the fading blooms on pleasure's lawn,
No more to slumber heedless of the chime
Which keeps untiring watch from dawn till dawn.
No more the quest for this world's fairest views
Which can but fill the eye with fresh desire,
No more the crowding vanities and news
That keep from souls Thy Holy Spirit's fire.
No more the wanderer way, the wide unrest
And weary search for joys that will not cease;
No more, good Lord, to turn from Thy behest,
No more! we know Thy will to be our peace.
To Thee we tread the road that Christ has trod,
So rest our hearts in His: Thy Heart, dear God.

John never read a newspaper or listened to a news broadcast in all the days I knew him. That kind of worldliness
never attracted him – neither political, nor social, nor
economic, nor even bat and ball. He had other tempta-
tions, though: a crisis was in the offing.

At this time the firm which was kind enough to employ
me decided that a little sun in the southern hemisphere
might improve my desire for business. One went by ship
in those days but John was not able to get away from the
summer term to boost my morale. Instead he wrote me an
anthology of his best-loved lines in a red school exercise
book.

One madrigal was to the forefront, which he quoted and
sang to his dying day:

The silver swan who living had no note,
When death approached unlocked her silent throat;
Leaning her breast against the reedy shore,
This song she sang, her last, then sang no more:
Farewell all joys! Now death come close mine eyes,
More geese than swans now live, more fools than wise.

Time and again he played this madrigal on recorder or
organ (with music by Orlando Gibbons). Probably while at
Gaveney House, certainly at this time, he wrote, after spot-
ting four flying swans:

Silver swans what seek you
Over land and sea?
Whither do you journey
So beautiful and free?

We desire a water
Higher than the sky;
Voiceless, still we're searching
To praise it as we die.

I went to Exmouth to bid him farewell since I had no notion how long I would be at the Cape of Good Hope. We met at a hotel close to the estuary. It was a lovely, long summer evening, whose beauty John captured:

Opalescent twilight
Tide at lowest ebb;
Single seabird calling;
Ocean's voice ahead.
Wind-signed sky for starlight
Hills in silhouette;
Estuary waters
Quieter, lovelier yet.

We parted. I paid a visit to Buckfast and sailed south.

John continued at his task of schoolmaster, teaching English certainly; probably all subjects. He never mentioned the boys to me. His sensitive heart went out to the homesick child:

I'll never be a scholar, Lord,
So slow am I to learn.
Yet, by Thy grace, dear Lord, to me
Death's naught but end of term.

This is an early reference to his outlook on death. Life for him was a search for God; death was the gateway to eternal life – the 'hols' and home in its truest sense.

I was back again for Easter in 1949 en route to Osterley – the ante-room for late vocations. John met me at Southampton and we drove back to Somerset on an April, spring and gusty day. It was good to be back. Easter was the following week and we both went to Buckfast for

happy reunions, with 'Hosanna' booming the Easter joy.
After Easter the Osterley term began. John saw me safely
into the hands of the 'gentle tiger' – Fr Clement Tigar SJ.
He then departed for Gaveney House to face an initial
crisis in his planned religious life.

St James says, 'My brothers, you will always have your
trials but, when they come, try to treat them as a happy
privilege; you understand that your faith is only put to the
test to make you patient, but patience too is to have its
practical results so that you will become fully-developed,
complete, with nothing missing' (James 1. 2–4).

One has to experience a vocation – a call to serve God in
an unique way – to understand the inner conflict. The
Greek word 'agony' means contest. A contest is present for
some. Sheila Cassidy in her autobiography puts it very
well: 'How can one convey the agony and the ecstasy of
being called by God? At one moment one is overawed by
the immensity of the honour, the incredible fact of being
chosen, and in the same breath one screams, 'No, no,
please not me, I can't take it!' That which seconds ago was
a privilege becomes an outrageously unfair demand. Why
should I be the one asked to give up marriage and a
career?'

John's final marriage crisis occurred while he was at
Gaveney House. His sensitive, human heart responded in
unequal measure to affection offered, often to the embar-
rassment of the lady of his choice. This lady was much
older than himself. He fell in love. The muse was upon
him, too, and that summer was blessed with many balmy
nights. This was a crisis indeed.

Many a priest, religious and monk has left his vowed life
to the Church or cloister in such a moment as this. John
the layman acted very differently, assisted by his lady. He
remained loyal to what he believed was God's call.

He did what he so often did in a spiritual crisis: he withdrew, leaving it to the Lord to heal wounded feelings. This
was often prefaced by the spin of a coin: heads I stay, tails
I go. He went! – right at the busiest time of the summer
term. May Gaveney House forgive him.

Buckfast were unwilling to accept him as a postulant
now. They were quite right. John, as it proved later, had

no vocation for the cloister. One could say that the Lord used a human crisis to push John along his true path. Perhaps, too, the scrutiny given to candidates for the cloister or the seminary tends to shy away from real characters and plump for moderation. John himself, in a letter written three years later about this crisis, said: 'You will recall that almost exactly three years ago I 'quit' a Prep. school on account of being in love – a seeming 'catastrophe', an 'outrage' and a 'cowardly escape' with no excuses: Yet it was the means of reaching the Charterhouse (the Carthusians) and Dom Andrew Gray and Jerusalem.'

However, godfather Hugh was furious. He wrote recently saying: 'John had badgered me to facilitate his acceptance as a Postulant at Buckfast Abbey. They somewhat grudgingly agreed to give him a trial as a Postulant. Shortly before the agreed date John turned up.' The crisis was laid at Hugh's feet. 'I blew up,' said Hugh, 'and gave him one of the biggest 'dressings down' of his life – I really let him have it.' Hugh suggested that he should go to sea as a member of crew – to sort himself out under sea-discipline and conditions. He loved John very much, and John would not now be near him 'at home' in Buckfast Abbey.

It is easy in retrospect to detect in the completed pattern of John's life the finger of Providence in all of this. Buckfast was right; Hugh was right – John had to be shunted on. He went to sea. The Lord had other designs.

CHAPTER 9

Lourdes 1949

He did not go to sea at once, but waited until he had seen me properly launched in the safe waters of the novitiate of the Society of Jesus.

Before this event we both decided that we would go to Lourdes, so we pooled our resources and booked on a pilgrimage – a sort of Cook's tour pilgrimage, not a real pilgrimage on foot, which John would make in later years.

Our decision sprang from different motives. Devotion to Our Blessed Lady was foreign to John at that time and he knew very little about St Bernadette. Nevertheless I do remember that he both had and said the rosary. He used to question me a good deal about devotion to Our Lady. There is no ready-made answer to such questions. It is very much like faith or love, an inner experience flowing from an inner gift. A good deal is said about Our Lady in theology, and theologians discourse learnedly about the Immaculate Conception and other titles of Our Lady, although it is alleged that she herself (in a private revelation) said that one does not theologise about a mother; one loves her. The apostles neither idolised her nor bypassed her. They simply loved her as His Mother and their Mother, and went to her when they needed her guidance or her loving care. John had no prejudices. He had an open heart and a desire to do just that which God desired.

We assembled at Victoria Station, spending one night in the hotel, which inspired John to write these telling lines:

O tippler-women, human geese
That cackle in this pub!
No doubt you seek a sure release
In beery waters, wat'ry beer,
No doubt you find a haven here
In alcoholic glow;
But what dismay at closing time
When homeward you must go.
This land, diluted like its ale
Through lawbound licence, does not fail
Its temperance to show!

And yet, O ladies, little I
Can tell about your thoughts.
I know not whether song or sigh
Or woe or laughter sways your minds,
If you your households soon may find
Contented or at strife.

We went by train and boat to Paris. John was in great form
and had the other pilgrims in stitches of laughter. He wore
a pink deer-stalker hat, complete with Gladstone bag and
recorder. The Paris-Bordeaux Express was a great experience. The French had gone electric very early on and so
we sped down through France at eighty miles per hour.
After steam trains this was a great thrill. John was never a
reader on a journey. He spent a good deal of the time in
the corridor drinking in the scene, pondering and telling
his beads. The vineyards of Bordeaux gave way to the
mountains of the south. We approached Pau and then
were soon in sight of Lourdes, a small town ringed by
mountains with a medieval fortress and swift flowing river,
the Gave. Not much of ancient Lourdes remains today, but
Bernadette would have known the castle and the river and
the long meadow.

The train edged its way into the station with a glimpse of
the Gave and even the heavy rock called Massabieille
where the grotto is to be found. We were all in the corridor by now, looking in silence.

On arrival we went straight to our hotel. Lourdes hotels
always seemed to double book. John and I were found a
small attic room with a fanlight, 'the maid's bedroom', as
he said.

After a quick supper we were soon out to explore. Neither of us minded the streets of open-fronted shops selling souvenirs. It reminded one of an Indian bazaar as people pushed to obtain their choice 'memento' of a happy experience. The grotto was protected from the noise and bargaining of commercial Lourdes. It was mercifully unspoilt, set into the great Massabieille rock with the River Gave swift-flowing to its front, and the meadow beyond. It was a sanctuary of peace amid this lovely mountain country.

Our pilgrim group was led by a Benedictine monk, a schoolmaster. However, he did not dragoon us too much, nor did he take offence if we absented ourselves from this devotion or that. We both made for the grotto whenever we could and we were happy just to be there, taking in the scene, the River Gave, the pilgrims, the rock, the invalids, the peasants of the world at prayer. Lourdes is not a place for the rich: they go further south-east to the resorts along the coast. Lourdes is mostly for the humble of this world – seekers of the Kingdom. John was quite fascinated by Eastern European pilgrims, displaced folk for the most part, carrying out their devotion unconcerned about what others thought. Fashions were not in evidence – simple dress, genuine hearts, suppliant prayer.

It was the feast of the Assumption. The weather was glorious and there were big crowds – over 200,000. The evening torchlight processions made a lasting impression upon John. All nations were gathered and all sang the 'Credo in unum Deum' and the 'Salve Regina' with one voice. John never lost his love for Latin, the universal tongue as he called it. As an ex-Anglican he was deeply moved to be with, and pray with, all nations.

He drank gallons of the waters of Lourdes and made straight for the baths where the sick, diseased, halt and lame bathe in the holy grotto waters hoping for a cure. No half measures for John, he went in and under, head and all. It is one of the miracles of Lourdes that people are not infected from these baths; some are even cured; many get relief from sickness of the soul. John remarked later: 'Lourdes worked a miracle in my body and soul: of that I am now sure. Our Lady has done the same for countless others, but that does not lessen the miracle, it increases its wonder.'

At the same time John was worried about devotion to Our Lady. Recent convert that he was, he found so much ceremony in her honour rather overbearing, to say nothing of the crowds. He sought advice from the good Benedictine Father, chaplain to our group, and was delighted with the reply: 'Allow her to show herself to you in her way.' This he did, and it later led to a close and extraordinary bond.

One could not help being fascinated by the history of Bernadette. Her poverty attracted John very much. She came from a destitute family and suffered greatly from asthma. The family lived in one room looking out on to a tiny courtyard which contained a manure heap and a cess-pool. The small window was barred since it had once been used as a prison cell. It was airless and lightless – a terrible 'home' for an asthmatic child. Bernadette got some relief when she stayed with relatives at Bartres, herding sheep. She was not clever and found it impossible to learn the catechism, but she loved her rosary. Back in Lourdes on 11 February 1858 she went out to collect some firewood on a bitterly cold day. In her own words she said:

> I had gone with the two girls to collect wood by the bank of the river Gave when I heard the sound of wind like a storm. I looked up and saw a grotto. And I saw a lady wearing a white dress with a blue sash. On each foot she had a yellow rose; her rosary was the same colour. When I saw her I rubbed my eyes. I thought I must be mistaken.

This was the first of eighteen appearances to Bernadette. It was the beginning of 'Lourdes' for the world at large.

Many have been cured at Lourdes but Bernadette herself was never cured of her physical sickness. She died after a most painful illness proclaiming that her illness was her 'job' for the Lord. A most consoling thought for those who have to endure ill health – negative disease becomes a positive 'job' for God. Lourdes gives, also, the grace of compassion for the sick and the poor, and an insight into

the dignity of the destitute in the eyes of God. There is so
much to learn in that mountain townlet.

On one day we went to Gavarnie, passing by the historical Knights Templar church at Luz. Gavarnie is close to the
Pyrenees, a place of great beauty. John wrote briefly of this
visit, noticing both the beauty of the Pyrenees and a
passer-by:

> I went to Luz and Gavarnie
> And caught a passing glimpse
> Of a graceful lass who seemed to me
> More than a Queen of Nymphs.

We left Lourdes, as most do, with deeper thoughts about
Christ and His Way, His Truth, His Life. Our Lady does just
that – brings to birth her Son in our poor human hearts.

On the way back we stopped off in Paris. John
contracted severe toothache and was prevented from
going to Lisieux to visit the Shrine of St Thérèse. We did,
however, visit the Convent of the Sisters of Charity in the
Rue du Bac where Our Lady appeared to St Catherine
Labouré whose body lies still incorrupt. We also visited
the big Church of the Sacré Coeur in Montmartre.

In the Madeleine John decided to go into the 'Box' as he
called Confession. I followed him. We chose one with
'English speaking' written on it. John was delighted with
the good old priest who obviously did not speak much
English. Thus he adopted the question and answer
method – did we go to Mass on Sunday? Did we go on the
feast of the Assumption? Having just come from Lourdes
we passed that examination pretty well!

Back in England we were soon to part again, with an 'au
revoir' to Buckfast and some days in Somerset where we
walked in the long summer evenings, stopping on occasion to listen to the 'enchanting music' of the nightingale.
John said the rosary daily and frequently at that time, and
we both drank a fair measure of Somerset cider, playing
skittles as was the custom in Somerset's country inns.

On my last night at home we sat down to dinner with my
parents. During the meal John produced a bottle of wine.
He proposed a toast to wish me Godspeed. My father
turned to John and said, 'but he is walking out on us.'

John tried to put the matter into perspective but my father felt that he was much to blame.

It goes to show how personal an inner vocation is and, if it involves sacrifice, then this is shared, too, by those 'left behind'.

John was always a man for signs, signs from heaven. He helped me to pack that night. I was leaving home for good. He started to tear up old letters and when disposing of them into the fire, a last small fragment fell to the ground and upon it was inscribed the sole word 'God'. John would refer to the mystic properties of this fragment time and again.

On 7 September 1949 we left for London. There John carried Adine, an eight-year-old niece of mine, shoulder high down the Mall. He then gave me a final shove into the novitiate. This done, he headed south-west and prepared to go to sea.

CHAPTER 10

Going to Sea

A week later he wrote, 'Adrian and I pushed off to Plymouth three days ago, and are staying at a seaman's home awaiting a posting which may materialise tomorrow, on a deep-sea tug that is coming in. I shall write again at my first opportunity at sea to tell you all about it. It is going to be tough but we look forward to it very much.'

After some time he wrote again to say that the venture was off and they had moved on to Southampton. There he had hopes of being taken on as a member of crew on a ship going East, in the direction of the Holy Land. But John was not a member of a seaman's trade union and so he was not recommended for the job.

Undaunted he headed north-east to Lowestoft. There he managed to sign on as an assistant stoker on a coal burner of the North Sea fishing fleet. He said that he had many thoughts about hell as he shovelled coal into the furnace! It was a backbreaking job in infernal heat, made all the harder by the pitch and toss and roll of the little fishing trawler in the October gales. He wrote vividly of this experience:

Hauling Time – October Night

Moves the great Spirit o'er all these wintering waters:
Glide, go restfully, birds, e'er wild winds blow;
Wave-crests show white upon this darkening ocean,
Strongly seas flow.

Heaves a lone trawler along these turbulent waters:
Watch, watch patiently, gulls and solan-geese;
Hark for the winches, hauling the night catch nearer,
Engine throbs cease.

Drawn is the trawl-net from out these gathering waters:
Wait most warily, gulls and solan geese;
Follow the ship and dive for what fish are out-flung, then
Shorewards to peace.

Stands a stray landsman, amid these wide northern
    waters:
Watching wearily gulls and solan-geese;
Musing of quiet green fields in Devonshire valleys,
Dreaming release.

Breaks the full moon from clouds as black as these waters;
Saints and angel ones! watch o'er souls below:
Star of the Sea, blest Mary, Queen of creation,
Christlight bestow.

He returned to port, was paid and signed off. He
wondered if he had been to sea enough to satisfy his
godfather, Hugh. He did what he was to do time and again
– a sign of the cross, a hail Mary and the spin of a coin.
Tails – to sea once more!

It was even rougher on this trip, freezing on deck and a
furnace below. Yet he managed to write about a small
inner Hebridean harbour on the north-west coast of Scotland:

Tobermory

Tobermory, Tobermory!
Hebridean harbour town;
From a trawler, Tobermory,
I behold the night come down.

Moor and mountain, Tobermory,
All surround your sheltered place,
Crowned with stars and northern light-shine,
I could feel your silent grace.

Tobermory, there is written:
'GOD IS LOVE' upon your shore;
Thus His name in clearest legend
Signs your beauty evermore.

He added a footnote: "A little girl fell from a high cliff there, but was unhurt. Her parents had the words "God is Love" set on the cliff-face.'

Thus ended his seafaring for the time being.

CHAPTER 11

A Carthusian Interlude

John returned from his seafaring episode in early 1950. What next? The door of Buckfast Abbey seemed to be closed, yet he was still attracted to the cloistered life. The Carthusians offered more solitude, most austerity, perhaps more contemplative prayer. How about it?

John delved into the history of the Carthusians to discover that the Order was founded by St Bruno at the Grande Chartreuse (from which derives the name Carthusian) in the early eleventh century. At the beginning there was no special rule but a great emphasis on the contemplative life. The monks lived rigorously and austerely, eating no meat, fasting frequently and wearing hair shirts. They lived in individual cells vowed to silence. Gradually, customs or a rule of life emerged and received papal approval. The monks devoted several hours daily to mental prayer, coming together only for the sung office and the conventual Mass. Lay Brothers tended to their physical needs, bringing them one meal a day to their individual cells. Only on big feast days did they meet their brethren for meals. The Carthusians thus combine the solitary life of the desert hermit with the discipline of a monastery.

This greatly attracted John and so at about the time of Lent (1950) he made his way to the English Charterhouse – the only Carthusian monastery in England, situated at Parkminster, a village in Sussex. This

Charterhouse was established in 1883, but prior to the Reformation there was a famous Charterhouse at Witham founded by the Carthusian St Hugh of Lincoln in the late twelfth century.

John was given a warm welcome at this Charterhouse and was allowed to stay for four months or so as a working guest. This gave them time to look at him and for him to look at them. In fact he was put under the care of the Sub-Prior, Dom Andrew Gray, and assigned the task of door-keeper. He kept the hours with the monks attending the sung divine office. I remember him telling me how hard it was at first to cope with broken sleep, rising in the middle of the night to sing Matins and Lauds in an unheated church, and then retiring again for a short while to rise again at dawn for Prime and the conventual Mass. He got used to one meal a day – fasting was never a problem for him. He did remark on the cold. The monastery was unheated, but the monks did have little wood stoves in their cells. However, there was nothing in the gatehouse. John's godfather, Hugh, noticed that his knuckles were scarred after leaving the Charterhouse. Upon asking him how they had become so, John replied that they were the result of chilblains, but he made nothing of it. In later years he loved the heat of Africa and could not abide the cold.

Hugh also mentions that John was much loved by the community at Parkminster. I remember meeting the Sub-Prior, Dom Andrew Gray, on one occasion. He was very fond of John and had great hopes that he would stay with them.

The reason for his departure is given by himself in a letter to me dated 14 September 1950. It read as follows:

There is a good deal to tell you. My enthusiasm for the Jews and desire to bring them their King has culminated in what I firmly believe is a vocation. Now this is not the sort of thing you can cross-examine. I merely tell you that I humbly believe it is so. At the time of the Jew's reception [a Jewish gentleman was received into the Catholic Church at the Monastery] the longing and conviction greatly increased though in Lent and Easter it

had intensified somewhat. I told my confessor I wanted
to go to Jerusalem, having decided that here was not my
true vocation and told him so; he began thinking of
ways and means. I then told Father Gray [Dom Andrew
Gray] my other spiritual director (in whose charge as
doorkeeper I am), and he said, 'don't worry about
anything: I'm waiting for a sign – some falling star.'
Three days later he told me that I was going to Rome in
a sudden vacancy owing to a lady's withdrawal from a
local pilgrimage. The good Jew, about to go to Rome
himself, footed the bill, very generously.

I leave from Newhaven on 19th September, viz
Tuesday next. When the 5 days in Rome are over, I shall
not return. However, it's alright, they know this. I mean
to go on to Jerusalem as God disposes, and I go with the
blessings of my two spiritual directors. My passport is
briefed for Israel.

The last 7 months have been of tremendous value and
have taught me much. Father Gray has given me most
wonderful friendship and help. His kindness has known
no bounds. Parkminster will be an unblotted and happy
memory always.

I feel that telling you this may shock you somewhat,
but I ask your prayers and trust in faith that you will be
the friend you have ever been to me.

I do not expect slaps on the back or cries of 'of course
it's your vocation' nor yet their antitheses. I ask your
prayers though, and your trust of old.

I am so useless, and clueless and un-illustrious. That
makes me more truly confident in the power and guidance of the Holy Spirit. Blessed be the Lord to whom
and in whom nothing is impossible. And blessed be Our
Lady whose consecrated children we are.

I cannot think of two orders more wonderful than
yours and the Carthusians. Pray for the odd ones of
Christ the King who fit no order, but whom He leads
and uses nevertheless. We are both pilgrims seeking the
same native land; you and I.

Thus he left the Carthusians on 19 September 1950, and
headed for Rome.

His subsequent pilgrimage was so full of enchanting adventure and divine providence that I badgered him to write a pilgrim's diary. He eventually completed it at Louvain in the spring of 1952.

PART III

A PILGRIM'S DIARY – ROME TO JERUSALEM 1950

The things which written here you see
The Holy Ghost has told to me
A wind-blown reed – and that's a thing
To make a riddle for the King:
Quia quod stultum Mundi sit
Deus Deorum Eleg-It.

(J.R.B.)

CHAPTER 12

Rome

The diary was prefaced in this manner:

Histoire d'un Ane

To my friend who kept on at Miriam and me until she told me what to say.

The eight chapters which follow are taken from the diary.

Dom Andrew Gray, my Carthusian guardian angel, had given me before I left England the name of a Franciscan monk of his acquaintance, whose convent was at Jerusalem. Wandering one day in Rome, I came across a monk (Franciscan) of St Anthony's Church and Convent, and in talking with him I found that the very monk whose name Dom Andrew had given me was at the moment in Rome on pilgrimage. So I asked his whereabouts, and that evening went to see him. I was undecided whether to begin my journey by going south east to Brindizi, or south west to Naples. He advised Naples, thereby saving me the expedient of spinning a coin.

On the evening of Wednesday, September 27th, 1950, I said farewell to my fellow English pilgrims, bound as they were for home, and we set off on our respective journeys. But I did not leave Rome altogether till late that night, when I caught a 'bus to take me the first few miles out of Rome. Until shortly before my farewell to the pilgrims, I possessed in all the world about £5 (in lire) and I was very fortunate and well contented to have so much, for it was entirely due to the generosity of a friend in Sussex that I had had the means to come to Rome at all. But another

Sussex Christian, whom may God also reward – one of the pilgrims – called me aside while the party awaited their 'bus, and in his goodness insisted on giving me an envelope telling me not to look inside till he had gone, and saying that it was merely an exchange for a pair of khaki trousers which I had auctioned that afternoon at a little sale of his kind instigation, and for which he had already paid. I will say too, that there were several kind well-wishers who had raised my funds, from far less, to its £5 standing, out of the goodness of their hearts. When I did look inside the envelope, I found at least £10 worth – bless him. So I was an English 'Milord' with £15 capital!

Now a few words about the time in Rome. What a noble city, and what amazing variety of architecture! Ancient and modern, yet wondrously in harmony, columns of the Forum and the massive Colosseum being on friendly terms with buildings quite modern, even with that monstrous white wedding-cake near by, cooked up during the last century. (I forget the proper name, so I'll just call it Lulu the Luvvly!) How strange was this compatibility of the monuments raised over a period of 2,000 years and more. I missed the geese on the Capitoline Hill – (what unlikely ghosts geese would make!) but the slick limousines which coursed so harmlessly in the thoroughfares were twice as furious, and I don't know how many times as fast, as Ben Hur and his boys. No claxons were allowed to be sounded (mixed mercy for the stranger-pedestrian or scholar-gypsy) and everyone riding his neighbour off for all the world like Hurlingham or the Étoile. But Rome is glorious, and she beggars all description this vagabond may try to give of her beauty and grandeur. For, from the ashes of ancient Rome, Christendom's citadel rose up like a Phoenix, and there 'the chariots of God are twenty thousand, even thousands of angels, and the Lord is among them as in the holy place of Sinai ...'.

(Here I would remark that Sinai is a figure of Jerusalem in bondage, and that Jesus of Nazareth, the King of the Jews, is gathering His folk fast in Israel, and that 'every valley shall be exalted').

I saw the Holy Father [Pius XII] thrice, once in St Peter's amid a tremendous gathering of pilgrims, and a second time at Castel Gandolfo with a lesser though equally joyous gathering. The Sanctity of our Pope is evident in his whole bearing, and in a demeanour full of humility and gracious dignity. And what a linguist he is, and how great a gift that is for him in these times.

The vast splendour of St Peter's Basilica overwhelmed me, until I saw the East Window which thenceforth dominated the scene for me in its beautiful simplicity: the Dove, all gold in silver light, sweet symbol: 'Come, O Holy Ghost, fill the hearts of Thy faithful, and kindle in them the fire of Thy Love.'

And there was very much singing in the four great Basilicas; particularly I shall always remember the joyful voices of a huge pilgrimage from Venice. These Venetians walked from basilica to basilica (fortunately for the 'buses!) and sang as they went.

The Italians are amazing: to see their warm, childlike devotion is inspiring. Of the four great basilicas, I personally had a definite preference for St Paul's outside the walls. This glorious temple spoke to me of Jerusalem, Athens and Rome – all these in a timeless unity – a temple for a Golden Age, spacious, serene, and of beautiful symmetry. My spirit breathed more freely there than anywhere else in Rome, wonderful as all Rome was to me. Our pilgrimage (with its patient, unflagging priests who guided it) visited a great number of Churches, and I'm afraid now and again I sloped off for a while to recover from monumental indigestion. One lovely memory of Rome to me is that of a simple little procession of singing pilgrims in the Colosseum at night-time; there, among the massive ruins they placed candles and left them burning in memory of those greater lights, Christ's martyrs, who once passed thence to their Native Land.

But to return to the 'bus which took me the first few miles out of Rome. I alighted about 11.00 o'clock that night in a small town, and began walking. At first there was no luck for a hitch-hike, though there was a trickle of traffic towards Naples even then. Having got quite out of town, I saw a farmstead in a valley near the road (it was a moonlit night) and decided to try and sleep in an outhouse among hay, but a dog heard me, and gave his alarm, so back I went to the road again. Soon, after midnight, I hailed an enormous lorry, which stopped for me. The occupants were two very tough Italians, as kind as they were tough, and with them I went all through the night towards Naples. We stopped now and again to have cups of strong coffee at a road house, and for the drivers to change places – one slept while the other drove.

By first light of Thursday morning, we were in the hills nearing Naples. It was a magic time: we passed peasants with mules and donkeys, and loads of wood. The driver tooted furiously at all and sundry, saying often that anyone in or near Naples was 'no good'. Going through these hills in the still of early morning, I remembered Dehra Dun in Northern India, and the charcoal burner men with their heavy loads and straight backs, inclined forwards, plodding along looking at the ground (12th degree of humility at least!). And there was the wood-smoke in the air which strengthened my oriental reminiscences. I thought too of the saintly sadhu pilgrims by their little road-side fires in Hindustan – strangers to this world on their way to heaven – 'Jerusalem, Jerusalem! When shall I come to thee?' Never, if I don't get a move on with my story.

CHAPTER 13

Naples

At about 8.00 o'clock I thanked my friends and got down in Naples. I went straight to the first church I could find to hear Mass. It was a Franciscan church as I might have guessed it would be. After Mass, I enquired there about a cheap lodging, and followed directions which eventually brought me to an hotel which showed appropriate hostility to a vagabond demanding such cheap lodging as I required. So I gave up the idea of lodging in Naples itself (St Francis' wisdom working for me again, no doubt).

The next thing I did was to book a passage, deck class, on the very next ship in Israel's direction. The damage was £7.10.0 as far as Piraeus, which was as far as I thought it was wise to pay for, having ideas of a land route lorry-hop thence to Israel. But there was a week to wait for the ship's sailing (4th October – St Francis' Day). So I walked out of Naples towards Vesuvius hoping for a very, very cheap existence in the more country places – hoping to find a barn or cave or some such to inhabit rent free for the week! It was a few hours' walk, but I travelled light. My luggage was contained in a 'senhora's' black shopping bag, purchased in Rome, and contained the following, roughly speaking:– 1 flute, shaving tackle and toothbrush, 2 spare shirts, some socks and handkerchiefs and a pair of pants, shoe polish, a Roman Missal, a black cloak given me by Fr Andrew, a little tin box containing letters and various things, and a polo sweater. I was wearing donated trousers, shirt and shoes, Carthusian socks, mine own jacket, and a miraculous medal (the gift of Charlie Coles). That's about the lot methinks! No. I had also in the tin some acorns from Sussex which I'd intended to plant in Rome, Athens, and Jerusalem, but they'd all got dried up. And two other things very precious I had – a small copy of the English Hymnal which Mother gave me, and a small copy of the Psalms, in the English Prayerbook version, from Dom Andrew. One other thing was treasured – a small picture of Da Vinci's 'Head of Christ' – yet again, a silver pendant (XV century Spanish) representing scenes in Our Lady's life – this last the gift of Mrs Walter Dunkeles, whose generosity enabled me to go to Rome, and later to return to Belgium. O blessed Lord, please reward them all!

I had an idea of going right up to the top of Vesuvius so as to spend the night 'on the edge of a volcano'! but the distance was more than I thought. During the afternoon, going through a little village, I was besieged by a motley of folk who wondered what was in my bag – in the end I parted with a pencil, my polo sweater, and some pictures from my Missal; and they parted with a bunch of grapes: 'sic transit gloria looney'.

Just before nightfall, I reached a small hostelry about two thirds of the way up the mountain. There I had a good meal of spaghetti and a bottle of wine called 'Lachrymae Christi' was set before me – 350 lire it cost as far as I can remember, and I didn't resist: it was a the best bottle of wine I'd ever drunk – nectar indeed. So there I sat outside the little hostel, looking down on the Bay of Naples and thousands of lights in a warm and tranquil evening....

It was a long walk down to and up from Resina, a country field outcrop of Naples where I went for Mass and Benediction each day, and where I fed. My staple diet had become excellent brown bread and grapes – good this was and very cheap. (Spaghetti was a luxurious item, for occasions only.) ...

On 4th October 1950 my ship S. Philip Grimian sailed out from Naples at about 8.00 o'clock in the evening. Deck class was jolly good, food and all. There were many Jews on board going to Haifa, three of whom I met again in

Israel – they arrived there a week before me as I shall show. No Mass the first morning – no priest on board. At mid-day, we arrived at Catagna in Sicily, and I went ashore for a few hours with a most friendly young English lawyer-to-be; he was on his way to stay with a friend in Athens. He was very knowledgeable about architecture, and we visited several churches, and lastly a huge monastery, once of the Benedictines but now used as town offices or some such. We went up the very high church tower and walked all round the roof-walks. It was glorious up there – St Bruno died in the Sicilian valley of Calabria long, long ago. That evening, back on the boat, I found to my joy a Franciscan priest, Fr Carmel. I asked him if I might serve his masses, and he agreed gladly ...

CHAPTER 14

Piraeus

We reached Piraeus on October 7th 1950 where the ship stayed for a few hours. Most of the passengers visited Athens and I also. I made straight for the Acropolis which, crowned by the Parthenon, rises like a pale ghost above the city – albeit a most beautiful ghost. I entered the Parthenon free of charge by climbing round the side of it. The view made me rather sad, for I'd always pictured Athens in a green, idyllic surrounding, rather like the Thames valley at Wargrave, Henley and Marlow. That's the worst of being a very minor poet with little idea of time and geography as they are. There stand great mountains round about, but they looked very bare. The city itself seemed most unprepossessing from where I surveyed it that morning. Where was Mars Hill of St Paul the Apostle? And where was the quiet wooded place near a river outside the walls where I'd always pictured Socrates praying 'O beloved Pan, and all ye other gods that haunt this place! Give me true beauty of the inward soul ...' That inspired prayer, which everyone should know, especially those who use lightly the words 'pagan', 'Christian', and 'heathen'. So I'd seen Greece, however briefly, and only Echo seemed to be left. Yet Grecian lineage may still be found in England among our temples, and, for those whose souls are wide awake, among our woods and meadows.

In the early afternoon of the same day (October 7th) we

sailed for Cyprus, and reached Limasol on Monday morning, October 9th. It had been a happy voyage. On two evenings I had been invited to join a party on the top deck aft – all Hebrews, who passed the time till turning in by singing national songs, ancient and modern. It was wonderful to hear, in the Mediterranean night under the stars, songs of David and songs of to-day, all in Hebrew and mostly in harmony, very well sung by both men and women – and all the time we were getting nearer to Israel ...

The friendliness and welcoming spirit of the Hebrew passengers I shall never forget. How full their hearts were, and how young, as they approached their native land. Among them were many going there for the first time, leaving all their old life and following their dreams to reality. Thanks be to God for the spirit of pilgrimage and the love of home. Faithfully followed, this leads all men through much hardship home to heaven, our true native land in the heart of God, the joy of all desiring, and 'faith shall vanish into sight'. We are all Hebrews, spiritually speaking – strangers and pilgrims 'in via'.

CHAPTER 15

Cyprus

The good Fr Carmel invited me to go ashore in his company and to come to the Franciscan convent in Limasol. This I did gladly. Fr Carmel's work was to be in Cyprus, and I had to procure a visa for Israel as soon as possible. As far as I can remember, all the money I had left was about 500 lire, which I changed at Limasol Customs for a very few Cyprus shillings. It was necessary to go to Nicosia, the capital, in order to procure the visa, so thither I went, having enjoyed the hospitality of the little Franciscan convent in Limasol where they very kindly gave me lunch. Fr Carmel also gave me a letter of introduction to the Franciscans of Nicosia, and a Cyprus pound. Bless him for all his kindness to me, I'll never cease to say, I hope.

The bus hurtled along inland like a flying bedstead (four-poster!) keeping the crown of the road and making much use of the horn (as is the custom in India). Arriving at six or so in the evening, I found my way bit by bit, being much and kindly assisted, to the Franciscans, who agreed to put me up till the visa was secured, because of Fr Carmel's letter. I visited the Israeli Consul the same evening (October 9th) and he sent off a telegram to my brother Philip in Tripoli, North Africa, to confirm my identity (certainly my appearance can't have been encouraging!). There followed a delay till Thursday, 12th, owing to time lag in communications. Meanwhile, Fr Carmel himself came to Nicosia, having received orders to take over the parish there in charge of Terra Santa. This was the second time his work was in Nicosia. Naturally I was delighted to see him again.

On Thursday at noon, complete with Fr Carmel's blessing, the remains of yet another pound from him, and the visa (which had cost about a pound owing to the cable sent) I took a bus for Famagusta, the most likely port for scrounging a passage to Israel. While in Nicosia, I had been to the aerodrome and tried to persuade the Yanks to fly me to Israel 'stowed away' but no success! I reached Famagusta on Thursday in the late afternoon, and walked straight to the docks to see what the form might be. I was directed to the Harbour Master, a kind-hearted Scotsman, who gave me a note to a Greek friend of his, an important official in the shipping and commercial concerns of Famagusta (to whom I still owe one Cyprus pound in case anyone madly rich reads this!). This good Greek, Mr Paparasilon, promised to find a passage free for me very soon, and in the meanwhile introduced me to a friend of his who owned a little hotel, and gave me the money for a night's lodging – a good Samaritan indeed.

Cyprus amazed me. Everyone seemed to own an enormous car, or if he didn't, to afford an enormous taxi. The young men were visions of sartorial perfection – the young ladies dreams in a perpetual mannequin parade from morn till eve! The country-side is dry-looking outside the areas near towns, with straggling flocks here and there. It is hilly and rugged and there are considerable mountain ranges. Even so, the land appears to abound in all sorts of fruit ...

In both Nicosia and Famagusta there are great Crusader-built churches turned into mosques: I said a chaplet in one. My word, how the Crusaders built – for an eternity at least! I've seen their churches now in the French Pyrenees, in Cyprus, and in Israel ...

At Famagusta too I was fortunate in meeting an Austrian and his Hebrew wife, and also a British doctor with a great love of Israel. He was not a Catholic, but he gave me a pamphlet he'd written on the Jews and prophecies concerning this present time, which inspired me considerably. On Monday evening, October 16th, the Austrian and his wife who were so very good to me during my short time in Famagusta, saw me onto the ship, and gave me a parting gift of grapes and bully beef – may we meet merrily in Heaven. The 'San Antonio' was a little wooden cargo ship, with a sail as well as her engine. We did not cast off till the following morning, so I slept on board that night. I'll always remember Cyprus as a kind sunny land where no one hurries, and all are polite and helpful, even to one who must have looked like a beachcomber.

On Tuesday 17th October 1950, we left for Israel, and very soon I began to feel sea-sick. The ship's motor was that of a sea-going camel, so I thought. She was the size of the smallest of the Armada, maybe, and her shape was somewhat galleonesque. The Captain and crew were a jolly good lot, all Italians save for one Jew, and I think the latter pulled his companions' legs even more than they pulled his. So apart from digestive hazards, the voyage passed pleasantly enough.

CHAPTER 16

Israel – Nazareth

We reached Haifa on Wednesday morning, but had to be out till afternoon, during which I admired the port of Haifa and her modern buildings climbing all the way up Mount Carmel's long flank ...

The 'San Antonio' was my fourth Franciscan link: firstly was St Anthony's Church in Rome, where, as I have told, I was directed to the monk of Jerusalem who advised me to make for Naples. Secondly, I sailed from Naples on the Feast of St Francis; thirdly, I met Fr Carmel who boarded the same ship at Catagna the next morning; and fourthly the 'San Antonio'. How well John Bernadone was looking after John Bradburne. Deo Gratias.

Dusk was falling when I left the docks and began walking in the direction of Nazareth, which I wanted first to visit. I stopped to ascertain the route with a police sentry outside the barracks on the outskirts of Haifa. I told him I was hoping for a lift. He advised me to stay with him a little, and within five minutes he had kindly fixed me up with a large lorry which he'd stopped whose driver agreed to take me with him to Nazareth, his destination that evening. So very soon we were crossing the plain land and climbing steadily into the hill country around Nazareth. The driver was a member of a Kibbutz, and interesting to talk to. How wonderful it was to be driving through the twilight, up and up, beyond the fertile (and now well-cultivated) plains, to Nazareth, where the Word was made

Flesh, and spent nearly 30 years in His visible life on Earth, as hidden almost as He is now, in all the Churches which are in the world, in thousands and thousands of tabernacles.

I had arrived in Haifa with (once more!) two or three shillings – a fact which had caused some surprise to the shore officials. When we reached Nazareth it was dark but the sky was full of stars. We were stopped by the military police on the outskirts, for there were big military manoeuvres going on in Israel at the time. The driver, a Hungarian Jew as far as I can remember, asked where I would like to be put down. Since I had not the faintest notion of where I would spend the night, I asked him to dump me somewhere in the middle of Nazareth. He did so, and I thanked him and bade farewell, and started strolling up the main street.

Yes, this was the Orient again right enough – the dear old bazaar set-up which I love; but I was walking in NAZARETH, where the King of Kings so often walked, where He ran and played as a boy. It's all up hill and down dale, with a maze of narrow cobbled streets branching off to right and left; some climbing, others descending. Soon I had a small but very vociferous following of little Arab boys, more curious than hopeful I should say, considering my 'luggage' and un-moneyed appearance! I went on with no plan, and no worry at the lack of one, until I came to a happy orientally noisy place at a junction of three main roads or streets. In the centre of this thoroughfare was a well, founting at a tap set in a stone facing, where dozens of women and children were queueing with pots and buckets for water. Adjacent to the well was an open-air garden cafe, with an awning over it, where little groups of Arabs sat smoking and conversing contentedly. I crossed the thoroughfare to a tiny cafe on the other side, determined to get as square and oriental a meal as I could for the money I had. The proprietor was a most welcoming and affable chap who spoke quite good English (would that my French were as good!). I asked him for something to eat and some tea to drink, and we began to talk. Once again St Francis had led me it seemed, for I found that my new friend was an Italian, and a Franciscan Tertiary of the best kind (though perhaps not officially one). He had been some years in Palestine, and had been some time with the Franciscans – (he still wore a pair of very ancient Franciscan sandals!) but finding his calling was not wholly with the first order, he had left – in body, though not in spirit, and now kept this little shop in Nazareth. He was completely Franciscan towards me – God bless him. He showed great interest and asked me about my travels; he then flatly refused to let me pay anything, and invited me to breakfast the following morning. He told me where the Franciscan church was for Mass, and then insisted on taking me to the Edinburgh Missions Hospital (Protestant) to spend the night, saying that I would be sure of a welcome there. So off we went past the well, and uphill, through the Streets of Carpenters and a maze of alleys, twists and turns in a lovely October night, lit by moon and stars.

The well, Brother Amelio (his name) told me, is known as Mary's Well, because at that same source, acording to tradition, Our Lady used to come to draw water. Knowing this, the night became even more beautiful for me.

When we reached the Hospital almost at the summit of the high hill on the north side of Nazareth, there was a wonderful sight to see. Nazareth's multitude of lights below and around, and above, the myriad stars and a bright clear moon. This was Omar Khayam's 'bowl of nights' in its fullest beauty. We went in together, and soon the doctor came in to see us – a Scot he was and therefore generous, and he welcomed me to spend the night in his own house which was quite close by on the same long hilltop. There was still work to be done at the Hospital – it must have been between 9 and 10 o'clock so Brother Amelio took me to the house. There we bid one another good night, and I was received by the doctor's housekeeper, who showed me my room for the night ... The moonlight was radiant by this time, and all the dogs of Nazareth were barking their raucous serenade (or perhaps they sensed a vagabond!).

When I awoke the next morning after an excellent sleep, they were still barking, those that had any voice left – and all the Nazareth roosters were vying with one another, at heralding a new dawn. Soon I got up, and went down the hillside, which was all lined with Cypress trees in the still morning air. After ten minutes or so, I reached the Franciscan Church of he Annunciation. There I heard Mass and received the Lord within a few feet of a slab whereon was written 'HIC VERBUM CARO FACTUM EST'; the altar stood over and astride the stone. After Mass I walked up to Mary's Well and breakfasted with Brother Amelio – this was Thursday, October 19th. He advised me to get work temporarily in or near Nazareth – he even offered to take me into partnership in his cafe, such was his bounty and kindliness. Although I wanted to get to Jerusalem, I liked the idea of working hereabouts for a time, till the Lord should make the next step clear to me. So Amelio took me to see the Chief of Police at Nazareth Police Station – a very influential man. He was extremely pleasant and anxious to help me all he could, and asked what work I could do. I replied 'Forestry', not adding that any tree felled by me looked as if a beaver had been on the job. He then `phoned the keeper of a forest on the North East side of Nazareth, who was, however, out. Then he 'phoned a certain Fr Robert (Franciscan) to see if there might be any chance of employment with the Franciscans in their woods on Mount Tabor, where there is also a Convent and a very beautiful Church of the Transfiguration ...

Fr Robert said he'd ask his Superior what could be done. I'll never forget this good Jew – the Chief of Police in Nazareth. He was a soldier of considerable experience, let me say, having fought successively for the Turks, the British and his own people. Nazareth keeps him pretty busy, I should say, because it is over-populated, and most of its inhabitants are Arab (I think) both Christian and Mohammedan. Moreover, it is on the borders of the Lebanon and Israel terrains.

Though it seemed at first quite likely that I'd get employment on Mount Tabor, the project fell through completely on Friday afternoon, until which time I'd been blessed in the hospitality of the good doctor on the hilltop.

At about four o'clock on Friday afternoon, I went to say farewell to Brother Amelio. I don't think I possessed more than sixpence or so, and I unburdened my 'luggage' a bit on Brother Amelio, telling him that I had decided to become (perforce!) more completely Franciscan, and to continue my steps in the direction of Galilee and Tiberias, abandoning myself utterly to Divine Providence. Brother Amelio seemed very concerned however, and in his kindness insisted on giving me a Palestine pound for which I was most grateful, though (for once!) I accepted with much reluctance, because Brother Amelio was by no means a millionaire. (Happily I've been able to refund the money since). Then we said farewell, and leaving this true Franciscan friend, I walked eastward uphill out of Nazareth, feeling extraordinarily happy.

After only a few minutes a jeep overtook me, and stopped just ahead. It was my benefactor, the Chief of Police, who asked anxiously what had happened and where I was off to! I told him, and he took me on to the next Military Traffic-Control Post, where he told the sentry to fix me up with a lift as soon as possible and wished me good luck. After a few minutes, I was in a big lorry hurtling downhill on a road all hairpin bends, having asked the driver to put me down at Cana of Galilee, thinking the Lake and Tiberias must also be near at hand! The weather was fine and pretty hot, because the dry season was not ended, though there were clouds accumulating gradually.

CHAPTER 17

Cana

We soon reached Cana, and I got out and started walking once more. I did not stop at all in Cana, town of the first miracle, because I wanted to reach Tiberias that evening. In this I was quite clueless, because Tiberias and the Lake I longed to see were at least twenty miles on. But this was lower Galilee at any rate, and the very word is magic with all its blessed associations. I went on for a mile or two, and then asked a passing Arab where Tiberias was. He pointed vaguely with a gesture embracing latitude, and I expected to see the Lake on reaching the next rise on the road ...

Since then, I have often thought of those hours' trudging up and down, and I have connected it with the 'blasted heath' of King Lear. There was a strong feeling of exile and loneliness as it got darker, and still I wondered when I should see the Lake – over the next brow, or the next again. And the Lord, who had walked these very hills, did not seem nearly so close as He had seemed in English woods and meadows. For He, the King, is in exile there yet, from His own countrymen. Even so, He was very near me in that dusk – 'foxes have holes, and birds of the air have their nests ...'. Being Franciscan was becoming real!

I went along a stony ravine into the village. It was a ruin, and all deserted – laid waste by the warfare of 1948. Our Lady may have crossed these hills not far from where I had been walking, on her way to salute Saint Elizabeth in Ain Karem. But the hills were surely not so barren then, the whole land looked far different, for the Hebrews then were the same keen farmfolk as they are now showing themselves anew in Israel. Yet Our Lady's journey must have been a rough and tiring one. The Angels were in her path, made them the 'crooked straight and the rough places plain' for her, and her heart ran, for she was in love in the Lord God, and He whom the whole world could not contain, was contained in her. At least one Angel, my Guardian, was in my path too that evening, as I shall show.

A little beyond the village I heard many voices singing – not angels, but young Israelites, for it was the eve of Shabat, or Sabbath. But I still went on – they sounded too big a proposition for a beggar somehow – and I still thought that Tiberias could not be too far to reach in half an hour or so! Soon I was walking through a small settlement – a rough road with bungalows on either side, some under construction it seemed. I came up with a man in khaki shirt and shorts who was calling his little boy to come home. I asked him how far was Tiberias: he said it was a long, long way, and that there was no hope of a lift on the main road nearby because this was the Shabat (which begins on Friday 4.00 o'clock). I said I'd go on nevertheless, but he persuaded me to spend the night at his home – how very hospitable, and how spontaneous! And how lucky for me. So I went home with him and his little boy to their home nearby – it was by now almost dark. There I met his wife and very little daughter – about three I should think. They were very welcoming, and gave me an excellent supper, and, after chatting till about 9.30 or so, we all went to bed. I spent a very comfortable night on a couch. My hosts were from Tripoli in North Africa – Hebrews of course, but they had not been long in Israel. The next morning, it being a holiday for everyone, my host took me round the settlement after breakfast. He kept a small farm of poultry – (white Leghorns in excellent condition, many of them in aluminium 'spectacles' to prevent them from fighting!). He also kept a goat and pigeons, and he had an acre or two of land which he had cultivated himself, right from the drudgery of its stony age.

Not all the homes were new because this was one of the oldest settlements – Sedgera by name. About 50 years ago

I believed – maybe more or less – someone had come here from the Diaspora and had started work from scratch, rather like the first Boer settlers in South Africa. I began to understand that exceedingly hard work has been done and is now being done in the reclaiming of Israel. Stones, stones, and stones abounding! They have to be picked up one by one in their thousands, and dumped, before anything can be done with the land. Israel was fast becoming a skeleton, a desert, resulting from eighteen years and more of neglect. Harzl and his Zionists were heroes: how they must have said on seeing their native land 'Lord, can these bones live?' And they were helped by God, because they helped themselves so manfully. How they have worked, these Israelites returned! ...

My host also showed me the traces and scars of the recent warfare – the ruins and barbed wire remaining, also a minefield awaiting demolition. He was not there in that war, but he knew the history well. I say nothing against the Arab. May he too be greatly blessed, but his habits enrooted are those of a Nomad – (perhaps that's why Palestine agriculturally speaking became a nomad's land). The Arab is a moving herdsman, that is why he is quite happy to live in houses all dishevelled. H.V. Morton says that it always struck him, when seeing an Arab village, that there'd just been an air-raid! Arabs remember their tents, and ancient, restless, tribal days. Again I say, God bless them; may He grant a happy solution to the present difficulties and estrangements.

The recent war in Palestine (1948) was vile and terrible, like all wars. Somebody had to bear the brunt of Israel's returning home, somebody besides themselves and the Arabs. The British it was who bore it and 'carried the can', because, out of the long succession of Israel's diverse foreign rulers, it was the British who were there at the time. And so there was a war, a miserable war of carnage – Britishers, Hebrews, and Arabs, and outrages on all sides. But let us hope that the fighting is all over, for "the voice of the turtle is heard in our land' ...

The place from which I'd heard the singing on the previous evening was an Agricultural College for boys and girls from 14 to 20. Hither my host took me when we had looked over his immediate surroundings. As we arrived, we heard more singing, very full and whole-hearted – it was their service for the Sabbath, which was taking place in an upper room fitted out as a Synagogue. I was introduced to the Principal's wife who very kindly showed us round. It was an extremely well-organised establishment I thought, and everyone there looked in the best of spirits.

About 10.00 o'clock that morning I thanked and said good-bye to my good host and hostess, who had given food and shelter and the warmest hospitality spontaneously to a complete stranger, out of the kindness of their hearts ...

Walking along the main road towards Tiberias, I looked back at Sedgera, and behind it in the distance I saw Mount Tabor, crowned with trees and the Franciscan church and convent. There are two schools of thought about the Transfiguration, one that it was indeed where I now saw Mount Tabor, the other that it took place in the far more mountainous country upon Mount Hermon or thereabouts. And for my part I like the Hermon idea better. Soon I was to see Hermon afar off, from Tiberias. After fifteen minutes or so of walking, I had the good fortune to stop a big car, a taxi I think, whose owners or hirers kindly agreed to take me as far as Tiberias which was on their route ...

CHAPTER 18

Galilee

Before long our speedy chariot, having climbed steadily for some considerable distance, topped a crest – and I saw what I so longed to see; the Lake of Galilee, the sea of Jesus and his fishermen, spread out in a glorious expanse far below, sparkling and deep blue in the sunlight. And all about it rose the hills and mountains – a blessed sight.

My motoring benefactors continued on their way northwards, and I began on the road's long descent, and walked down towards Gennesareth and Tiberias. On the hill-side was a large immigration camp, with scores of tents and hundreds of inhabitants. Tiberias itself straggled down to the Lake's shores, where it concentrated in a biggish town, its white roof-tops and walls against the blue of the waters made the panorama still more lovely to me. Somewhere along the nearest slopes of those great, bare mountains on the east side of the Lake, the local folk had besought the Lord 'to depart out of their coasts'. With the sun and clear sky, and blue, blue waters, the barrenness of the mountains was grand and wonderful to see. Yet in David's time, and in that of Jesus, how much more beautiful they must have appeared with their forests of cedars and green slopes ...

After a very simple lunch in a cafe by the Lakeside, I walked south-wards along the road which runs very close to the water. I had watched a big, bespeckled kingfisher from the cafe, to the accompaniment of modern Israeli songs on a radio or gramophone with a mighty loud amplifier. Many people were sitting and chatting in groups round small tables by the Lakeside, for it was the Sabbath. Nevertheless, there was a great calm and air of peace. I hadn't seen a kingfisher like that since my India days. All the hills and waters were bright and clear in the sunshine, and it was hot for me, though not for Israel. The calm of Shabat is something quite unique and revealing – especially in Jerusalem, as I found later.

Walking along the road, parallel to the water's edge, I was utterly uncertain of what to do in the immediate future. Then I noticed some caves in the hill-face nearby on the west side of the road, and I thought 'Shall I live in one?' Why not begin being an apostolic beggar here? A priest of our pilgrimage, who had been very good to me, said to me in Rome, 'What are you going to do when you get to Israel? Live in a cave like St Jerome?' and I had replied 'Maybe'. So now, which should it be – stay here, or go on that day towards Jerusalem? Olivet had been my objective – it has been so ever since the summer of 1949, and still is. The Lord ascended to Heaven from Olivet, and I believe it is there that Israel will have knowledge of their King, not so long hence.

On the ship, between Naples and Cyprus, an English Jew, who had not been in Israel for some time, had said that he thought Olivet was in Israel's territory. But in Nazareth I had been told that Olivet was in the Old City, and therefore out of bounds to me, like Bethlehem and the Holy Sepulchre. So I spun a coin by the roadside – Galilee or Jerusalem? Jerusalem, said my oracle, and that was that.

At about 4.00 o'clock of that Sabbath afternoon, I took my last look at the Lord's Lake from the hilltop, whence I'd seen it first that morning. The skies were more clouded now, and there had been a shower in the afternoon, but all looked very beautiful and lay in a great calm. (There can be sudden violent tempests on Gennesareth, as we know from the Gospels). As the sun was near his setting I hailed a lorry which took me back as far as Nazareth. I wanted to reach Tel-aviv before it was too late and visit the kind man who had given me his card in the car that morning, in the hopes of a roof that night, but I was too optimistic. Nevertheless, I was greatly blessed because, by dint of four lifts in all, I reached Tel-aviv by about 11.30 p.m. having passed through Haifa. It was of course too late to visit my kind charioteer of the morning, so I walked out of Tel-aviv in the direction of Jerusalem. Much ground had been covered since sundown – the Lord had been very kind. It had rained heavily between Haifa and Tel-aviv, and the night was chilly.

Not long after midnight I was given a lift by a soldier in a military vehicle for a dozen miles or so as far as a place called Er Ramleh. There the driver put me down at a sentry post on the road, and turned into his camp for the night. As I've already mentioned, there were very big military manoeuvres going on all over Israel at that time. I stayed with the sentry for about half an hour, hoping vainly for yet another lift towards Jerusalem. Then he packed up and returned to the camp, and no other sentry came. It was cold, and after spending a short time seeking a shelter, I started off once more. I had not gone more than two or three hundred yards, thinking it 'a long way to Jerusalem' (thirty or forty miles, I'd say) when I espied near the roadside, behind a row of trees, a whole line of military lorries 'hulled down' for the night. At the same time it began to rain again. Well, I've slept in army lorries before very comfortably, thought I, and so, like the unconsidering looney that I was, I approached the nearest vehicle and found the cab empty; a polite cough from the neighbouring lorry encouraged me to speak to the driver thereof. He spoke quite passable English and was very charitable, telling me I might sleep in the empty cab, and plying me not only with a blanket but with food also; may God reward him – and I hope he didn't get into trouble on my account.

I'm afraid I overlooked the fast for Sunday Mass, in other words I ate what he'd given me. But very soon there was a commotion without (no trumpets however) and the sergeant of a duty-picket came to see what was going on – a tendency with sergeants everywhere as you know. By then it was pouring with rain. I was escorted to the Duty Officer, who questioned me more charmingly than narrowly. He was extremely cordial, and regretted that he could not give me tea there and then, for he'd served with the British in North Africa, and knew how partial we are to cups of 'char' at all times and in sundry places.

We then went off in his grey jeep through the teeming rain to find the Intelligence Officer, who was in bed, sensible fellow – the hour was roughly 2.00 a.m. He gave word from his bed that I was to be taken forthwith to the Civil Police Station, and off we went again. I'll never forget the friendliness and goodwill of these soldiers to such an infernal nuisance as I must have been to them that night in the middle of manoeuvres.

I only hoped that the next day would be uneventful enough for them to sleep it off. When I arrived at the large barracky Police Station, I was re-questioned very briefly and given a bed there for the night. So this was my first Sunday morning (3.00 a.m. or so) in Israel, and I was (very justly considering) under open arrest. At about 7.30 a.m. I was given something to eat, and then began the questioning good and proper. It was to continue, on and off, till midday ...

I think the Israeli Police were right to doubt me somewhat. I'd walked into the cab of a military lorry in the middle of the night during a highly security-ised week of manoeuvres. And I was an Englishman withal! They gave me some lunch, and then there was a wait until H.Q. at Jerusalem had phoned that I could be let loose. I had said that it was my desire to spend the rest of my days in Israel, and that I might join a kibbutz or work on a forest, but that I wasn't sure. This was the truth, for I know that if I crossed to Olivet I couldn't return to Israel, except via the Lebanon and Cyprus, again to get a new visa (or some such Heath-Robinson performance). Finally, however, at 4.00 p.m. or so, I departed, and soon was in an army truck going towards Jerusalem.

I'd deserved all the drawbacks and none of the kindness to me, and my plans were vaguer than ever. Before very long we were among the hills approaching Jerusalem, while the sun was setting in great majesty. I decided to go to Mount Zion when I reached Jerusalem, to hear the Benedictines sing Compline. This became my only plan, except for a half-decision to see the Consul next day, to find if there might be a loop-hole in the restrictions of passing between the Jewish and Arab parts of Jerusalem.

CHAPTER 19

Jerusalem

Soon after sunset, in the midst of Jerusalem, the last
soldier got out of the vehicle, and I did likewise, I alighted
quite near the Knesset, Israel's House of Parliament. Of
course I had no idea at that time where any particular
place was, and I very soon asked a lady the way to Mount
Zion. 'Zion?' she said – 'you are very near', and kindly
directed me to Saint Pierre, House of the Jerusalem
Community of Our Lady's Fathers of Sion. It was a misunderstanding, but I recognised the voice of Providence,
thanked the lady, and went thither. It was very nearby: It
was the nearest dwelling of Christ the King in the Blessed
Sacrament to the spot where I'd got out of the truck. The
doorkeeper of this house (which enjoys the special
patronage of Heaven's Doorkeeper) rang the bell for one
of the fathers to whom I stated my position very briefly. I
told him that I had no credentials on me except Fr
Carmel's letter of introduction to the Jerusalem Franciscans, but I asked him whether it would be possible to hear
Compline at the Benedictines of Mount Zion and then
return to St Pierre for a roof during the night. He told me
that Mount Zion's Compline was out of the question, since
the Abbey is now used as a frontier sentry-post overlooking the border line, and the monks themselves only use it
for very special occasions. He advised me, however,
because of my letter, to visit the Terra Santa College of the
Franciscans, and see what might happen. After that he

said, very kindly, if unsuccessful, I might return to St Pierre and he'd see if I could lodge a night there.

So off I went; the Terra Santa College was quite close by, and there I asked for the Fr Superior. He came, and I handed him the letter of Fr Carmel, telling him I was an Israel-loving pilgrim possessing two shillings or so. He too was most kind, but explained that the Terra Santa College was now used as an Israeli Institution and the best thing for me, he said, in view of my desire for Israel, would be to return to St Pierre. He very generously gave a Palestine pound and wished me Godspeed. Then I went back to St Pierre, who welcomed me in the persons of the good fathers, and I was given good supper and a bed for the night. It was Sunday night, 22nd of October 1950. Next Sunday would be the feast of Christ the King, and I had told my sister Audrey in London that I believed I'd get to Jerusalem for that feast – the Feast on which I had been received into the Church of God at Buckfast, three years before. 'Non nobis, Domine, non nobis, sed nomini tuo da gloriam.' The King had led me to Jerusalem, and cared for me in everything all the way: Blessed be He and 'Amen', for He taught me to "take no thought for the morrow". And the Holy Spirit had answered most wonderfully the first prayer I ever wrote to Him:

> Joy of the living and loving,
> Fire-spirit fusing all tongues,
> Swiftness of Mercury's wing-borne steps,
> Light from Our Father in Heaven,
> Shine on the paths of Thy journeying one!

The next morning after breakfast, I asked where the Consul's office was, for they had told me at St Pierre that it was only on Mondays that the British Consul came into Israel's part of Jerusalem. It was arranged that the Door-keeper (a good Jew who speaks about seven languages, and renders great service to St Pierre thus) was going in that direction and would show me the way. I was sitting near a statue of the Virgin and Child in front of the build-ings, waiting with my 'luggage' to depart, when one of the fathers (by origin a Syrian Jew of Aleppo) came out to me.

He said, 'I hear you are interested in the conversion of Israel. If this is so, why not stay with us for the time being, for I think we can employ you here; your position in Jerusalem otherwise is a difficult one.' Again I thought I recognised the voice of Providence, and although I longed to set foot on Olivet, and in the Old City of Our Lord, I found myself agreeing gladly with the good Father's kind suggestion. So he saw Père de Condé, the Superior at St Pierre, and the thing was done. But for this, I think I'd have crossed to Olivet that day.

As you know, I stayed at St Pierre for the next seven weeks. My days were spent very peacefully in doing odd jobs about the Ratisbonne property: collecting olives, pumping water, sweeping and picking stones out of the garden. Later on, when the decision had been made for me to go to their Novitiate in Louvain, I also did some Latin and French. May God reward Père de Condé and the Fathers and Brothers, for all their welcome and kindness to me.

Now a very few inadequate words about Jerusalem. Israel's Jerusalem is a new city; walking in its wide streets full of traffic, one does not seem to be in the Orient at all. Modern shops, European dress, very clean thoroughfares and streets all combine to give this impression. I love bazaars and most of their odours, but these were not to be found it seemed.

As for languages; now there are dwelling in Jerusalem Jews, many of them devout men, from every nation under heaven. The atmosphere in Jerusalem today is one of tremendous activity, materially speaking – spiritually speaking the nearest word I can find for description is 'awareness'. The city is intensely alive and pretty wide awake. As far as I could make out, speeches in the Knesset (parliament) are amplified so that they can easily be heard in the surrounding thoroughfares.

Jerusalem is full of the sound of children's voices all day long, or so it seemed to me. There are many schools in the city, and in the play-times shouts of happiness abound.

The calm of the Sabbath which begins when a hooter is sounded at 4.00 o'clock each Friday afternoon, holds a supernatural charm – magic almost. And from 4.00 o'clock until Saturday is over, the calm remains well nigh inviolate all thro' Israel. In every Kibbutz and settlement, and throughout the land. It cannot be measured by speaking of sound or silence, one may only say that there is a great and indescribable calm. Christ the King is gathering His people to Israel and to Jerusalem out of every nation where they have been in exile.

From the extensive roof terrace of St Pierre one has a magnificent view: hills on every side – as the Psalmist says 'the hills stand about Jerusalem, even so standeth the Lord round about His people, from this time forth for evermore.' One saw Olivet and Mount Scopus quite close by, perhaps a mile or so, and all the mighty wall of the mountains of Moab in the distance, as bare as the hills of India's North West Frontier, barer maybe. Olivet was almost bare too, except for the olives of Gethsemane and the gardens of the Benedictines and Greeks thereon. Behind to westward lay Ain Karem, and south-westward Bethlehem, both towns hidden by hillcrests. The view northwards was hidden by buildings – but when Père Marie-Alphonse Ratisbonne had built St Pierre, it had been the only big building in the neighbourhood surrounded then by more spacious grounds, and the panorama had been yet more wonderful. In the middle distance were the walls of the Old City, and the buildings of Mount Zion Abbey and Notre Dame de France were prominent, so too was the great green dome of an Orthodox Church higher up in the new city. I used to say my chaplet each day walking to and fro on this roof, so the view is fixed for ever in my memory. Though bare, it was full of grandeur; I shall never forget the glory of the sunrise over Moab as seen from the roof of St Pierre.

On Sunday afternoons I used to go for walks with Brother Laurent, a young Italian brother with whom I spent a good deal of time in the garden of St Pierre during the week. We went twice to the Israel boundary southwest of Jerusalem, a few miles out, and from there we looked over a valley to Bethlehem, that little town so blessed. On two or three Sundays we walked to Ain Karem, about four miles due west of Jerusalem. This was my favourite walk, for St John Baptist (who is my holy patron) was born there.

Ain Karem is a large village rather than a small town. It has an enchanted atmosphere about it and deep peace. All the hillsides and valleys are well-cultivated there, and there are acres and acres of olive plantations. Both the Churches we visited are Franciscan, that of the Nativity of St John, and that of the Visitation; the latter is now renewed greatly, and most beautiful murals are being painted on the walls inside the Church by an Italian artist. Yes, Ain Karem has an air altogether supernatural, and the spirit of the Lord's Herald seems now to move powerfully there, especially in the hush of twilight.

Père Marie Ratisbonne, our co-founder, who was converted in Rome by Our Lady directly, built a house on a hill of Ain Karem for the Sisters of Our Lady of Zion. And there he spent his last days, and died in the midst of that peace. We visited his tomb and prayed there. Ain Karem is all a garden and an olive grove, a garden and a grove enclosed by hills. It is my most treasured memory of Israel – I would add that Bethlehem was out of our reach, being in Arab territory. O may the time come soon for the lifting of barriers; may the time soon come when the children of Israel may delight in Bethlehem where their King Jesus, the Son of God was born – Bethlehem – Nazareth – Jerusalem: those words are heavenly words. But as you know, I was disappointed in the realities, because I had been regardless in my imagination of the devastation separating our time from the time of Jesus. All that was green and wooded, all that was freshened by streams, all that was pastoral – such were Jerusalem, Nazareth and Bethlehem in the mind's eye; an idyll for the shepherds and the angels at all times. Even a setting for 'Dominus regit me' (Ps 22). But the Hebrews are in Israel, so perhaps before very long the dreams of Christians the world over concerning the Holy Land will come true ...

Very near the gate of St Pierre (Ratisbonne House) stands a large modern synagogue, whence on the Sabbath one hears the shofar (Hebrew trumpet) sounding; there are a number of other synagogues all over Jerusalem. Nowadays, one is told, there is a lack of conformity in the Jewish religion – high, broad, middle, liberal and what not. The Old Covenant is losing its grip, but the Lord of the New Covenant is ready to gain His grip in Judah when God the Father wills it, 'To be a light to lighten the Gentiles' – that is at hand.

There is among the Jews in Israel now, an oriental Hebrew people called the Yemenites, whose history is remarkable. This people dwelt among the Arabs in the district of Yemen far away to the south of Israel, for about 1,900 years. Although living in Arab country they preserved for all that time purity of race and religion, and an ardent longing to return to Israel. When, two or three years ago or so, the State of Israel came into being, the Yemenites one and all were flown from their place of exile to their own, longed-for Israel. Something very wonderful was then made known by them to their rescuers: they said with joy that a prophecy which had kept them in hope through the time of exile had come true. This prophecy was that the Lord would bring them back to Israel 'on the wings of an eagle'. I saw many of these Yemenite Jews in Jerusalem: perhaps they are, in build and features, more like the country Jews of Our Lord's time than anyone else. They are farming folk, very simple in the best sense ('of such is the Kingdom of Heaven') and are deeply religious and patriotic. Among them one may see faces of great nobility and beauty. They are essentially oriental. The Old Covenant by itself is dead; joined with the New it is fulfilled by the New as Christians know. Now these Yemenites are said to be great lovers of their religion, and I believe that the Lord, who is Love, has a very special part for them to play, pure and simple as they are. They are a lowly folk, these children from Yemen, and their hearts are right: such were the countrymen of Galilee whom Jesus made His Disciples. Mark them well.

Now I must draw this account to a close, an account for which, before starting, I asked Our Blessed Lady to guide my pen, and so I believe she has; it is as accurate as my memory can manage.

It is not for me, the last among the sons of Ratisbonne, to try and sing a song of St Pierre. But I would like to bless Père de Condé and his community with all my heart for all they did for me. Père de Condé introduced me to many Jews and took me to the houses of his friends. Because of him I heard Mendelssohn's 'St Paul' sung in an evening gathering of German-Jews – none of them Christians.

Père de Condé is an aristocrat, and like all true aristocrats he moves freely among every kind of people and society, making happy those with whom he meets. Whether it was a pen-repairer at a street booth, or the Chief Rabbi – he was always welcoming and therefore welcome. For him and all at St Pierre, and for everyone, mentioned or not mentioned in these pages, who helped me in my journey, I pray 'Deign, O Lord, to reward with eternal life all those who have done us good.'

I saw the Old City's roofs from the terrace of Notre Dame de France: the domes of the Holy Sepulchre, and of the great Mosque on the site of the temple which was destroyed so long ago. I heard the singing of Jerusalem's folk during the Feast of Lights (Hannuka) which commemorates the gallant Maccabees – the New City then was full of singing till midnight. And on the wireless I heard a Jewish choral society sing Handel's oratorio 'Judas Maccabeus' in Hebrew! Music and musicians abound in Israel, where royal David made melody to the Lord.

On the 13th December 1950, I sped in a taxi, across the cultivated plains with their orange groves, through Tel-aviv to Haifa. That night I stayed on Mount Carmel with the Carmelite Fathers, who were very hospitable.

Next morning a Father took me up onto their flat roof, whence I saw a most magnificent panorama; the hills of the Lebanon with Mount Hermon highest of them all, the multitude of Haifa's buildings running all along the slopes of Carmel and down to the Mediterranean shore, and the bay itself with its ships on the sunlit waters. Here on Mount Carmel, Elijah and his monks had dwelt, praising the God of Israel, Him who is the God of Love and the Son of Mary.

Later that morning, the 14th December, Père de Condé in his kindness arrived to see me off. The ship did not leave Haifa till evening. The last we passengers saw of Israel was the far-off lights of Haifa showing from the shores and from all the way up to Carmel's summit, where they seemed to intermingle with the stars. And most prominent of all was the regular flash from the lighthouse which stands high up on Carmel, next to the monastery where I had slept the night before.

Nunc dimittis ...

I had not visited the tomb where Christ the King was laid and whence He rose: but every morning I had received Him in Holy Communion, in the midst of Jerusalem and in the midst of His people Israel. Therefore I lack nothing. Thanks be to God.

And now this scrawl is finished, and it is nearly 11.00 p.m. on the Feast of Corpus Christi 1952 LAUDA SION, SALVATOREM ...

Amen, Alleluia.

PART IV

A CONTINENTAL JOURNEY

Some think it may be well if they but dream
All their lives long of what they'll never get,
Whilst others follow, as it were, a stream
They know will find the sea although not yet.
                                        (J.R.B.)

CHAPTER 20

The House of Ratisbonne: Louvain 1950–1952

Before completing the diary of his pilgrimage from Rome to Jerusalem, he wrote from Jerusalem in October 1950 to say:

When I set off on this pilgrimage I believed firmly I'd find my vocation, but I thought it'd be something fantastic. The journey was fantastic here in its luck, though perhaps that ain't the 'mot juste'. I am being helped very firmly now by a most saintly priest, the Superior of this Home (there are other homes of the order) by name Père de Condé. He has a wizard sense of humour and rings absolutely true in all he says and does. I said to him I hadn't a vocation for the priesthood because I had not a great desire to celebrate Mass. He replied, 'So what' in a very excellent sort of a way, and reminded me that there was such a thing as the apostolic side of a priest's work. I have written to Fr Raphael (I hope he'll be lenient and forget June 1949) also to Father Andrew Gray – I know he'll speak well for me – for references, and Père de Condé has written to the novitiate (in Louvain) I think, or maybe it's the Superior General he's written to. There's something very similar to the Society in this order – and Alphonse Ratisbonne was a Jesuit for 10 years before his days with this order of which his brother was the principal founder.

I've seen a lot, Rome and Turin and Naples. Catajnia

(Sicily), Athens, Cyprus, Nazareth, Tiberias, and the Israeli part of Jerusalem, and, from a distance, Old Jerusalem and Bethlehem. But wonderful as it all is, the eye is not filled with seeing. The Lord knew I'd have to go here in fact, just to find my vocation, and to become doubly sure that the altar of God with its Tabernacle, throughout the world is Nazareth and Bethlehem, Galilee and Calvary. Emmanuel God is with us, and Our Lady makes it clearer and clearer, without whom is no Incarnate God and no Salvation. The Enemy has been knocking me about somewhat, especially this last week, so that I can't pray hardly (I mean spiritually, though my tummy's been out of order too!). But a supplication, however short and incoherent to Our Lady always wins the battle, in which I am so feeble.

The journey was amazing and people were wonderfully kind. The day before leaving Rome I possessed in the world about £5. The next day and thereafter my purse became a sort of widow's 'cruse' sometimes down to two shillings or less. Helpers of one kind and another seemed to be posted along the way, and to have got here for this Feast of the King, my third anniversary, is a joy indeed.

He then added a telling postscript:

P.S. My soul's a desert just now, and I had today a fearful go of black depression and doubt. But I am learning to recognise these attacks not as signs of failure but of victory and progress.

John's first letter from Louvain was written from the Novitiate of the Order of Our Lady of Mount Sion (House of Ratisbonne), Louvain, Belgium dated 28 December 1950. In it he says:

I arrived here last Friday morning. Here is the news; negotiatons were made, references received (Fr Raphael and Fr Gray were both more than generous), and it was arranged for me to leave for the novitiate in Louvain. I spent my last night in beloved Israel on Mount Carmel, with the Carmelite Fathers, on the site of the traditional place where Elijah said (sitting under a juniper tree) 'It is enough, Lord, take away my life, for I am no better than my Fathers.' A monk showed me all over the House in the morning, and showed me the glorious panorama of sea and hills from the roof, and I saw Hermon (almost always it has snow on the summit) rising above all the mountains, and I saw the Mediterranean blue and quite calm in the early Winter morning. And the monk drew my attention to the Cross in the refectory, which has no Christ-figure upon it; this is customary with the Carmelites ever since St John of the Cross said that it is we who should be on the Cross ourselves. (The Carmelite Fathers have a tradition that their order on that mountain goes back to the times of Elijah, when he and some monks dwelt there. That is a wonderful tradition). Then I left and embarked on a ship in which I was the only non-Jew among the passengers, we all watched the shores and Carmel, and the thousands of lights that go up the hillside and join the stars. Later, when Israel was gone or almost gone, I took out my rosary (the one Hugh gave me, which has a picture of Our Lady of Mt Carmel on its medallion junction) and I found that, for the first time, the Christ-figure was missing from the Cross. I remembered the Carmelite refectory afresh then and vividly. For Christians there is no such thing as chance because Christ is with them: He meant that figure to be lost. It wasn't in my pocket, and I did not find it after at all.

The voyage was pleasant and I made many happy acquaintances. The sea made us toss about a bit, because the ship was very small. I managed to keep my food down (just!) but I'm afraid some people suffered a lot. There was a tiny synagogue on board, where there was much prayer made by three rabbis – and others. I talked a bit with one of the rabbis – a dear old man who spoke fair English and knew the Whitechapel area well. During his meals he would burst into psalms (his psalms of obligation) from time to time, completely unselfconscious and at home in the presence of God. May he and all those passengers come to know that God is none other than Christ their King. Many of their prayers begin 'Blessed be Thou O Eternal, Lord and King of the Universe ...' A young Dutch Jew, who is going to Europe to study Psychology and after to return to Israel, taught me the Jewish national anthem and translated it into English for me.

I reached Louvain via Marseilles and Paris, last Thursday evening, and have been deeply joyful and at peace since that time. There are seven here in all, the Novice master – a Frenchman; two French novices, two Jewish novices (by race that is), one Jewish (ditto) Priest, ordained yesterday; one English postulant. This morning the newly ordained Priest celebrated his First Mass, and a Priest (from the home of Ratisbonne in Paris) assisted him, together with the novice-server: all three of Jewish extraction. Our Christmas has been very happy, and the holiday has culminated in this blessed day.

It was wonderful for me to read your letter of assurance on arrival – knowing that you too believe I have at last arrived at my vocation – and I am most certain of it too. All the odd pieces of my jig-saw are falling into place, I wonder whether I will see the full picture on earth; not that it matters – the present moment being a Sacrament full of God.

O how good Jesus is! I tell you though having seen all these places and wandered so far, I now come to the truth, (my vagabondage burned out) and that is the Blessed Sacrament, in Whom and for Whom and through Whom are all things. So here is the conclusion of the whole matter – Deus meus et omnia – who has taught me (what a wooden pupil!) not only to seek and see Him in all things, but at long last to see and find all things in Him. All beauty, poetry, love and desire, all strength and joy. O pray that for us both He may be more and more all in all, and our only rest, our only gladness.

I'm not fully a postulant yet but I'm here at last. Priesthood seven years on if it's God's will that I live as long. But oh to love His present, His now, I am learning bit by bit at last. This has been the sublimest, fullest Christmas I've ever known.

Louvain is a tranquil town, quite large, which contains a University and no less than 65 religious houses, of all sorts and races. It reminds me of Ely and Salisbury, Exeter and Wells – it has a sort of medieval air. Of course Belgium is a very Catholic country, and among the host of churches ancient and modern, there is precisely one that is non-Catholic: the exception which proves the rule. There is a large Benedictine Abbey, and a large Jesuit House of Studies. We go to the churches of both – to the Benedictine for High Mass and Vespers and to the Jesuits for Benediction: that is on Sundays and great Feasts. Our little chapel is in the house with the Blessed Sacrament, but we are too few to have High Masses or even sung Masses. The singing both at the Benedictines and the Jesuits all during Christmas was exquisite. We went to the Jesuits for Midnight Mass, and they sung lovely carols in polyphony. We have not got big grounds and fields all about as I expect you have, but have a fairish garden with a rather hazardous tennis-court. We have been having plenty of snow and freezing weather – quite a change from the East! We play tennis on the swept court for recreation after lunch sometimes, and to get warmed up and exercised,. I have been very blest in arriving for the Christmas break, and so having a chance of talking to and getting to know my fellows who are a grand little company. One has to speak French which is the 'lingo' of all our Ratisbonne houses, and I find the understanding of conversational talk very hard often, but bit by bit I progress. Normally of course our days are almost entirely without conversation. So Christ the King holds a little court here – three Jews, three Frenchmen and one Englishman. I'm only the jester buffoon and even my jests have to be mostly to Him alone because one is made somewhat solitary through not knowing much French. But I love solitude – too much, I fear. And thus, I am very happy, very certain that this is where I must be and stay.

These are days of grace when Our Lady is spoon-feeding me with her gentle consolation.

Pray the love of the Cross for me, because through love of that, one becomes closer and closer to Christ and brings others closer.

Forgive all this exulting, but I feel as if I'd come to port after a long stormy time at sea. Now my ship can be repaired and fitted well for more "voyaging". I speak only in a spiritual sense of course. My vagabondage is done, and I'm under orders as you are.

He wrote fairly regularly from Louvain in the year 1951, and in particular for my first vows. He seemed to be well-settled, complaining only of being a bit bound up, due to the change in diet. He was always unduly sensitive about anything which might 'bind me up'.

In one letter he remarked upon hearing a nightingale singing in a deserted garden of an empty convent next door. He said, 'Pretty good for a town I thought. It made me think of you and I listening to that nightingale at your home from the "Trappist Dorm" two years ago.'

Whilst at Louvain he received a letter from his father, The Reverend T.W. Bradburne, dated 10 July 1951. This letter was among his papers at the time of his abduction. It was always a source of joy to him.

John's unique vocation had caused a gap of misunderstanding between him and his father. It caused him unrest in spirit. This letter, and one later written when he was in Italy, came as healing balm.

An extract from this letter reads as follows:

I hardly know what to say or how to thank you for your generosity in thanking me for anything which I may have been the means under God, of doing for you. But alas from my side as I look back in my old age upon many things there are that I might have done for you and failed to do. And it may well be that in the white light of the Judgement day I shall be found owing a great deal more to you than you to me. So as between father and son we won't say too much about that. And do remember that whatever stresses and strains between us there may have been in the past – as were almost inevitably bound to arise in this our present state of imperfection – there cannot now or ever be any question of mutual forgiveness.

Any shadow of that across our lives shall, please God, be banished for ever. Otherwise dear lad we could not approach our respective altars which would mean the outer darkness for one or other of us. So rest assured on that point son John. And if there is any debt of gratitude supposed or real that you feel you would like to discharge towards me as your father in the flesh, I'll tell you how to do it as I hope you will. Give me a real front seat in your prayers. And for your guidance I'll tell you what to concentrate upon.

The first thing I need and want before I go home and am no more seen is a good and true repentance towards God. As you may find in years to come if you ever have to deal with penitents, the greatest difficulty lies in the dismal power of self-deception inherent in our fallen Human Nature which is one of the direst results of the fall into Sin. A kind of spiritual blindness which afflicts so many of us.

So much of our so-called repentance – mine anyway, has not been repentance of the Godly sort at all, but only wounded pride which has had its fall, and rising from the ditch is rubbing its bruises. It is sometimes spoken of as 'being or feeling sorry for oneself'. Wounded self respect which may give one a very bad pain indeed. That is the sorrow of the world which worketh death. Its proper name is remorse which springs really from a love of self, but not in so many cases I'm afraid from the genuine love of God. What you say about the unities among Christians is I believe perfectly true. The differences of course are enormous and humanly speaking insuperable. Only God the Holy Spirit can resolve them in His own time and in ways we know not of as yet. However we must hang on to St Paul's words at the very end of his Epistle to the Ephesians – the great Epistle about the Church as the mystical Body of Christ. 'Grace be with all them who love our Lord Jesus Christ in sincerity.'

So again as I may be a memory before we meet again, for your guidance in any prayer or Offering of the Mass you may be kind enough to make for me, I would just add this. In matters of the Faith I think I can honestly say that in mind and will, I wholeheartedly accept and believe every word of the three Creeds. That is what unites us. So God bless you and ora pro me.

I am thrilled and almost envious to hear that you are living in an atmosphere of Ecclesiastical Latin which is the Holy Tongue. And French – the more languages the better. And what about a bit of Hebrew? But there I must frankly confess that this last stumped me completely, when once at Cambridge I tried to tackle it.

But I refresh my small stock of Latin continually by taking special note of the Latin headings of the Psalms as I say my Office Morning and Evening – which still survive from the Vulgate in our Prayer Book.

CHAPTER 21

On The Move – South

Just after a year and a half at Louvain he wrote about his impending departure on 16 July 1952, the Feast of Our Lady of Mount Carmel:

All being well, I leave here on Wednesday 16 July, as a vagabond of God, moving towards the Old City of Jerusalem – when I shall reach Jerusalem I have no idea; that is in the hands of God entirely. This decision was made a week ago, with a cool head. You will recall that almost exactly three years ago I 'quit' a Prep-school on account of being in love – a seeming 'catastrophe', an outrage and a cowardly escapade with no excuses: yet it was the means of reaching the Charterhouse and Dom Andrew Gray, Jerusalem and this Congregation of Our Lady of Zion. During these last, *essential* 18 months here in Louvain, many stones have 'rattled' against my 'bathi' (hurricane lamp), and only by the grace of God have I stayed. The stones were all trials allowed by the Lord. My Superior and Brothers have shown me great charity and generosity throughout. For my Superior (Novice-Master) especially I have a deep admiration and everlasting gratitude – he is one of the best men I have known, and absolutely right of heart and very generous. If I had left because of constipation, or social difficulties, or any of the other 'stones' – none of which were the fault of any man save myself – then I could be charged with running away yet once again. But it is not so. I am following a clear and irresistible call of God my King to be His tramp and set my steps towards Jerusalem.

'Qui s'excuse, s'accuse', so I will insist and explain no further, except to quote the far too generous letter the Superior-General has written me for the Mother-Superior of the 'Ecce Homo' in Jerusalem. This'll tax your French!

Ma Révérende Mère,
Je me permets de recommander à vôtre bienveillant accueil le porteur de ce billet. John Bradburne est un converti du protestantisme qui aspire à une vie chrétienne parfaite. Divers essais l'ont amené à conclure qui'il n'est pas fait pour la vie religieuse sédentaire: il se sent porté plutôt à imiter les examples d'un Saint Benoît Labre ou d'un Père de Foucauld. C'est pour marcher dans cette voie que, de son plein gré, il a quitté notre maison de formation de Louvain, où il a passé une année, et où il n'a laissé que de bons souvenirs.

H. Colson: Superieur General

(My Reverend Mother,
I permit myself to recommend to your gracious welcome the bearer of this letter. John Bradburne is a convert from Protestantism who aspires to the life of a perfect Christian.

Different attempts have led him to the conclusion that he is not suited to the sedentary religious life; rather he feels himself drawn to imitate the example of a Saint Benedict (Joseph) Labre or a Pére de Foucauld.

It is in order to follow this way, of his own free will, that he has left our House in Louvain where he has spent a year and where he has left only happy memories.

H. Colson: Superior General

This is too generous, and let me hasten to say that I do not presume to class myself with either of the great saints mentioned, and that I imitate no-one: but oh may I imitate Christ the King of Israel! His young ass I am, loosed because He, who has need of nothing, has need of me who am nothing. He alone can use me, and in an extraordinary way which He calls me to walk in.

The past 18 months have been spiritually essential for me, and highly profitable – therefore I was guided hither from Jerusalem. Thanks be to the All-Merciful God, and to Our Blessed Lady who has intervened so much, especially lately and done great things for me. Through love of her I trust one day to attain purity of heart. Hugh [his godfather] will perhaps be furious, bless him. You, maybe, will say 'There, crashing off again without giving us time to stop him!' If you write to me please address your letter to c/o British Consulate, Rome, if within the next month. If later, to the British Consulate, Jerusalem (Trans-Jordan), where I shall reach if and when God wills.

So it was that he left Louvain with a note of true wisdom and inner discernment by his Superior General H. Colson. John indeed was to prove to be something of a St Benedict Labre and a Père de Foucauld – he was to become a pilgrim, and a hermit of God's design.

Why St Benedict Joseph Labre?

Benedict Joseph Labre came from a well-to-do family who lived in Artors in the North of France in the mid-eighteenth century. They were farmers and merchants. Benedict was sent to stay with his priest uncle, the Curé of Erin. There he learnt about service of the poor and about the Cistercian Monastery of La Trappe whose monks became known as 'Trappists'. The Curé of Erin died of the plague and so Benedict went to stay with another priest uncle who lived a very austere life. This uncle recommended the Carthusian Order rather than the Trappists – they were more solitary and perhaps at the time less severe. Benedict, therefore, with his parents' permission, set out for the Carthusian Abbey of Val-Ste-Aldegonde. It was full. He tried the Charterhouse at Neuville and, though refused entrance at first, was accepted later when he was a little older. He entered but soon discovered that he was not called to the Carthusian life. How about the Trappists? He tried one monastery and was refused – he was too frail. He tried another at Septfonts and was accepted. He was clothed in the white habit of the Cistercians and given the name of Brother Urban, but once again God made it clear that the Trappist life was not for him. His health broke down and he was obliged to leave.

He decided to go to Rome. 'There are many monasteries in Italy', he wrote to his parents. He always travelled on foot and his journeys were never void of purpose. He sought always the will of God moved by an inner desire.

In those days there were many genuine pilgrims, good folk who went to pay homage at this shrine or that. Benedict decided to go and pay homage at the tomb of the Apostles in Rome. Thus began his final vocation. He, in great poverty and silence, went from shrine to shrine all over Western Europe, praying as he travelled, living out and begging his food. He carried a New Testament, the Breviary, and a prayer book. Soon his pilgrim's tunic became ragged and his beard grew long – worse for a fastidious young man, he became infested with lice. He went to Rome and right across to Montserrat in Spain. He visited Assisi and there entered the Third Order of St Francis. He loved the great Abbey of Einsiedeln in the mountains of Switzerland with its shrine to Our Lady. Above all he loved Loreto and visited its shrine every year. On his journeys he not only suffered from the cold and wet but often had to endure ill treatment, severe beatings from brigands and even prison as a suspect. All the time he was alone with God, seldom speaking but always showing a great love and tenderness to the sick and poor. Finally unable to walk any distance he found a shelter under the arches of the Colosseum in Rome. It was Good Friday: he collapsed on the steps of the Church of Santa Maria dei Monti and died later that same day – worn out. The people all declared that the Saint was dead. They noticed his likeness to St Francis.

John's Superior in Louvain had detected some likeness in John to St Benedict Labre – the pilgrim, the solitary, member of the Third Order of St Francis, great lover of poverty and the poor. John, too, had tried the Carthusians and later the Benedictines. Their way was not to be his way.

What of Père de Foucauld?

One can trace a similar pattern. Born of a distinguished and devout family in Strasbourg in the mid-nineteenth century, he started life in the army as a lieutenant in a cavalry regiment – an unwholesome life for him. He then undertook an expeditionary work in North Africa through Morocco, a dangerous venture but he loved Africa – especially the desert. The saintly Abbé Huvelin brought him back to the practice of his faith which led him upon a pilgrimage to the Holy Land. This accomplished, he felt much drawn to a life of prayer and solitude. He entered the Trappist Monastery of Notre-Dame-des-Neiges but left in search of increased poverty and austerity. Thus he lived as a servant of the Poor Clares at Nazareth and Jerusalem until the year 1900. The year after he returned to France and was ordained priest. Within a few months he was back in Africa, in Algeria, where he established a hermitage near the oasis of Beni Abbes. He moved later to the more remote mountains of Ahaggar settling in a hermitage near the oasis of Tamanrasset. There he learnt the language of the Tuaregs, ministering to the poor in their need. He was killed as a martyr in a complex war situation. Publication of his writings led to the founding of the Little Brothers of Jesus (1933) and the Little Sisters of Jesus (1936). The writings of Carlo Carretto of the Little Brothers of Jesus have become world-renowned revealing the spirit of their founder's life.

John's Superior (Père Colson) in the House of Ratisbonne again detected something of a Père de Foucauld in John: noble family, army background, conversion, the call to solitude and poverty, pilgrimage to the Holy Land, the search for God within a monastic framework. He could not, at that time, have foreseen the unfolding of John's life – a hermitage in Africa amid the poor, and death like Père de Foucauld.

On leaving Louvain John completed his letter to me by saying:

Please always consider me as a Monk, a monk of Our Lady and a vagabond of God. Saint Francis Bernadone (Francis of Assisi) is my spiritual master – but no imitation. Let us imitate the KING, so shall we be true originals. O pray, pray that I may follow Him well and fulfil my odd role in this short Earthly Play and sojourn.

His faith was like that of those great men to whom St Paul refers in Hebrews 11: those 'who recognised that they were only strangers and nomads on earth. People who make it quite plain that they are in search of their real homeland ... in fact, they were longing for a better homeland, their heavenly homeland.'

CHAPTER 22

The Pilgrim's Way

I went through France when all her corn
Was cut and stood in golden sheaves;
I slept in barns, forestalled the dawn
Ere swallows left their mellow eaves;
Oddly or not I even slept
In ditches for God's paupers kept.

(J.R.B.)

He left Louvain on foot: his destination Jerusalem via
Rome. What of the journey? He tells us a little:

I've never once gone hungry all this picnic, and God and
man have befriended me continually – blessed be God
for this, blessed be He that I have no athletic feats for
desert fatherdom to my credit, because I am a vessel of
His mercy, His astounding mercy. Pettiness, fits and
fury, intense egoism and selfishness, impatience and
intemperance in my appetite for food – these are my
distinguished roll of honour: but nevertheless, in spite
of all my frailty the Lord and His Lady are with me
always.

Considering that he ate very little, and only what he
begged – bread, grapes, a little wine maybe, his intemperance would put the most abstemious to shame.

The Lord never allowed John to have a very high
opinion of himself! Yet what John relates of himself here is

what St Paul 'in via' felt about himself as well: '... it is not the good my spirit prefers, but the evil my will disapproves, that I find myself doing.... Pitiable creature that I am, who is to set me free from a nature thus doomed to death? Nothing else than the grace of God, through Jesus Christ our Lord' (St Paul Rom. 7). Yes, it is a long haul to sanctity, but John kept up the steady climb.

He reached Italy. 'Italy would shake you,' he wrote. 'Thank heaven the Faith in England's loveliest land is on the battle ground: here one sees much that is good and joyous, but also much that speaks only of Laodicea.'

Rome and Naples did not open the way for him to return to the Holy Land and Jerusalem. He was at a dead end. He crossed to Bari. Perhaps a boat there would take him to Greece or Cyprus and so on to Haifa? Not so, but he wrote a lovely poem about the Cathedral Church there. He decided to walk back to Naples in the hopes of getting work on a boat to Israel. Again he drew a blank so he walked up into the foothills of the Apennines at the back of Naples, arriving in a little mountain village called Palma, in Campania. He called on the parish priest who very kindly took him in, offering him the organ loft as his dwelling. He used the fixed organ stool as a table kneeling to write letters thereon. He said, 'I slept in the organ loft and it was nice if one did wake up in the night, to play the organ alone in the Church.'

Father Francis, my Confessor, Spiritual Guide and Employer all in one, is wonderfully good to me. Here he has a parish which is no easy task – please God I am of use to him. Pray for his work and his parish please. He is a dear, charitable person.

It has been a fantastic $2\frac{1}{2}$ months, and believe me, I've just blundered along in a most unpraiseworthy way. More and more we learn to rely upon entirely, to love only – the life of grace, with utter contempt of our own strength.

Every evening I watch the sunset sky flanking Vesuvius – Vesuvius is due west, Apennines on the other three sides of us. On the East side our village or little town climbs up towards the foothills; on the other three sides, between us and hills, is a wide green plain.

All this I meditate over on the Campanile (Bell Tower) for an hour every evening, saying the 'De Beata' Vespers and the glorious mysteries of the Rosary – all distractions, but by God's grace much of the distraction is Heavenwards in nature.

Devon, Somerset, Dehra Dun, Campania – all these – how exquisite all these, but only beckoning us on: we know we have here no lasting habitation, yet we know too that all Earth's loveliness will be refound and multiplied. Our dearest views and loves possessed for ever and aye, in God our Home, our Native Land. Gloria Patri et Filio, et Spiritui Sancto.

Here I sweep and wash up and pray pretty distractedly and when I have a just occasion walk in the ways of Palma: always I am sure to be hailed and beckoned by sundry folk who like to have a laugh with or at (it doesn't matter which now by God's grace) an odd English looney-man. Sometimes, when nothing to do here, I spend an afternoon as dustman or cement-raiser with a pulley-rope, or somesuch. Dustman's my favourite – one of my oldest ambitions. And I tell them I'm the buffoon of Christ the King of the Hebrews, and the herald of His uniting reign.

The letter ended with a typical postscript:

P.S. Pray on for my sanctification because it would encourage so many souls if such a wreckage might come to canonisation, and I do so want to by-pass Purgatory!

He stayed on in Parrochia Mater Dei, Palma, from September 1952 until mid-1953, almost a year, saying:

I am deeply convinced, (and this half against my personal and poetic inclination) that for a time, maybe for a long time, maybe till the end, my role is here, nowhere else – and here no less than if it were in Israel.

Very much like Israel in the wilderness John was given by God to know that here or there was his place until the

'Cloud' moved him on. Thus, during the long pilgrimage of life, John felt 'at home' in his many ports of call until Providence moved him on.

An important event for John while at the Parrochia Mater Dei was something which he later described as a 'marriage' with Our Lady. In other words he took a private vow to her not to wed in this world, but to serve her and her Son as a celibate.

His father's death in May 1953 was the cause of his moving from Italy. He received a last treasured letter from his father at Christmas 1952. This, along with the one previously quoted, was among the very few letters found in his hut at Mutemwa after his death.

The letter, dated 20 December 1952, reads as follows:

It was a great joy for me to get your letter today and to know of your happiness and welfare with your feet safely set upon the way which in my old age I am coming to see more and more clearly is God's way for you, dear boy. Thank you so very much.

So in any of your thoughts of me or of yourself in relationship to me as your father, you must never think or feel that there is any need either to explain still less to apologise.

Who am I in any case to criticise the Ways of God for any of His children! God forbid that that should ever be allowed to add to my many sins.

Two days ago I came back from hospital. Pain in the hands of God can be a wonderful thing I found. It is one of God's ways of unclasping the fingers that otherwise might cling too closely to the world.

Of course one does not like to talk too much about these experiences – but you will understand, and I think I can say it to you without offence – but unless one's religion is a hollow sham and faith an empty boast, at such a time it is just a case of 'In Manus tua Domine' and letting go. Even leaving Mother standing in the road – absolutely alone. Well that is all I have to say about my rotten self.

What a lovely picture of Our Lady. It reminds me of a painting by the French artist Bouguereau.

I like to think of you in your organ loft. But I do hope you get your proper and sufficient share of sleep and rest – for we are not out of Brother Ass the body yet.

P.S. As a link between us henceforth I will say the Creed, the Lord's Prayer and the Hail Mary in the holy tongue.

So, in 1953, John left Parrochia Mater Dei, Palma, and headed for Devon in England to pay his last respects to his father.

PART V

ENGLAND REVISITED: 1953–1955

Farms and churches, meads and mills,
Charms one searches, daffodils
Which, for all my words are worth,
Grew not thus through random birth.
(J.R.B.)

CHAPTER 23

The Valley of the Otter

John returned home again to comfort his mother and to visit his father's grave in Ottery-St-Mary, Devon. It was nearly three years now since he had left for his extensive pilgrimage and sojourn in Italy. It was good to be back. He loved the Otter Valley and the hills that surround it. Buckfast and Hugh were not far away, Dartmoor too. A poem, 'By the Otter of Saint Mary', captures his mood:

> Psalm one might the otter whose song is a plain
> And tell of the bridges with ease:
> They never are crossed but gone under to gain
> Yet nearer and nearer the seas.
>
> The churches it passes, hard-by on the slopes
> Of Ottery, Tipton-Saint-John's
> And Newton the ford, which is poppled with hopes,
> And Otterton too, woo the swans.
>
> They say to the swans: Be ye still for a while
> And know that the smile of the meads
> And the beams of the sun are of God to enisle
> In eloquent silence the reeds.

There is a reference in the poem to a village known as Newton Poppleford. Two of John's closest friends, who will be mentioned later, have an oil painting of a West Country scene depicting an old stone bridge over a small river, with a village church and some cottages in the background. It is a fine painting and for many years they have tried to find out the location of the scene, writing to art galleries in Devon and other possible sources of information. They have lived now for many years in Zimbabwe and built themselves a house not far from a Mission where John stayed. One day he walked into their house and upon seeing the painting to the right of the entrance hall exclaimed, 'Why, that's Newton Poppleford!' That part of the hall is now known as 'John's corner'! Thus the beauty of Devon has found a niche in Africa. Below the picture on a shelf are some relics from John's hut in Mutemwa.

One cannot live on a view, as John often used to say, but he did try to establish a small hermitage in the vicinity of the Otter River, with a distant view of Dartmoor, but it was impractical – no raven fed him as with Elias.

What did he do then? Geoffrey Worrall wrote an article in the *Devon Express and Echo* just before Christmas in 1953, entitled 'The Piper in the Close'. It gives us some interesting news about John at that time:

Ottery St Mary Parish Church, which needs £10,000 for its Restoration Fund, has found a champion in a young man who plays a recorder on street corners in aid of the fund.

The young man, with his closely-cropped hair and cultured accent, talks with the evangelistic zeal of an early apostle, lives a frugal life in a hostel for people down on their luck, and calls himself "the Jester of Christ the King".

I first saw him at the end of Martin's Lane, Exeter, surrounded by an admiring group, including a number of children – a sort of modern Pied Piper.

From the wooden recorder, expertly played, dangled dozens of coloured ribbons. He wore a high-necked pullover, green tweed sports jacket, and corduroy trousers.

I listened as old English airs floated out over the Cathedral Close and then asked him what the coloured ribbons were in aid of. He gave me a friendly smile, and replied, 'Just to give the air of gaiety an Elizabethan jester ought to have; for we are Elizabethans, you know!'

When I asked him his name, he said 'Just call me the jester of Christ the King!'

He told me he was a poet whom nobody had yet recognised. ('They probably will do in another 60 years').

'Don't you have any permanent sort of occupation?' I asked.

His eyes twinkled as he replied, "Nothing is permanent in this life."

Surprised, I learned he is a Roman Catholic. 'But I love the church at Ottery, and it is so much in need of repair that I feel I must do something to help.'

'I long for the day when all Christians shall worship together, and for those in the Ottery area Ottery Church is obviously the right place.'

Mr. R. Illing, musical director of Rolle College, Exmouth, who also heard the music, praised the young man's efforts, and the piper accepted an invitation to play his recorder to the college students.

The Vicar of Ottery said he once gave the piper permission to go into the church when it was not in use and to play his recorder there. 'The acoustics in the church are excellent, and his music was delightful to hear. He is a perfectly genuine man, and I expect he wanted to come along and give me a few pounds for the Restoration Fund as a surprise.'

I believe he has been living the life of a hermit for some time in a little hut in an isolated spot, but is now helping to run a hostel for people who are down on their luck.

Another article by the *Empire News* reporter appeared at the same time entitled 'Mystery Hermit is a Jester to aid Church'. The article is similar to Geoffrey Worrall's, but it carried a photograph of John playing his recorder to an admiring audience of young. The article stated '... he has been living the life of a hermit for some time in a little hut in an isolated part of East Devon, but now he is helping to run a hostel for down and outs.' I remember John telling me that he had lived in a wing of an old house when helping at the hostel. The house had been given to some nuns, I believe. It was badly haunted and John said that he was often wakened by 'noises off', particularly the noise of claws scraping on his door. He said that he lay there, rosary in hand, awaiting the dawn.

Looking back over John's spiritual pilgrimage to date one notices a good deal of unsettled search and moving on. The world of friends, relatives and acquaintances wondered what next? Where was it all leading to? The less kind (and less knowledgeable) hinted at a 'rolling stone', a "drifter". Some questioned as to why he wasn't in an Order. If he were in a monastery we could understand that, but what does he do? they queried! He doesn't seem to stay anywhere; always in and out of Religious Houses but he never seems to settle anywhere. Then there is all this nonsense about the Jews. Why can't he put his mind to a real religious vocation?

John made his own comment on 'doing nothing':

> Define precisely what is doing naught
> Sannyásis I encountered, Sadhus too
> Preoccupied with neither work nor sport
> And yet intent completely on The True:
> With eyes upon the ball of rolling home
> I sounded them and found my way to Rome.

Some of this drifted my way. I was in an Order dressed up in black and called a 'scholastic'. (They think up the most archaic nomenclature for unformed, unprofessed religious. In the beginning I was called 'Knight' – 'mate' would have been better). Moreover I had just finished my studies of philosphy in the universal tongue – so I was alright. John, close friend of God that he was, was all wrong. His 'way' was no way to many. I was upset by these allegations. I believe that I did recommend Prinknash Abbey to him. I had visited a Brother there who had been a novice with me in the Society. He crossed to the Benedictines and was very happy at Prinknash. He had been in a special force during the war and had been parachuted into Yugoslavia. A man of few words but great depths.

CHAPTER 24

Prinknash Abbey

I told John all I knew about Prinknash Abbey. In 1955 the Abbey had not yet been built but it had been started. The old Benedictine Abbey, Gloucester Abbey, was taken over at the time of the Reformation and became Anglican. Prinknash, I believe, had once been the summer residence of the Abbot. It became a Benedictine Abbey in an unusual circumstance.

A certain Anglican Benedictine Community under Abbot Aelred Carlyle settled on Caldy Island in 1906. In 1913, as a Community, they converted to Catholicism. They continued as Benedictines but their conversion occasioned a decline in their material resources. Caldy (now a Trappist Abbey) was sold and the Benedictines moved to Prinknash Park situated on the hills overlooking Gloucester. The Park and the house were given to them in 1928. Under Abbot Upson (1938–61) Prinknash flourished and founded priories at Farnborough and Pluscarden in Scotland, and the building of the new Abbey at Prinknash was started.

John was accepted as a postulant in Advent 1955. The monks were still in the old house since work on the new Abbey was only at the level of the foundations and crypt. As I remember the postulants slept in temporary hutted accommodation at the back of the house. It was rather crowded but imbued with a spirit of life and expansion. Vocations were coming in well.

His first letter from Prinknash, dated 18 December 1955, radiated content:

To wish you the happiest Christmas you've ever had – I know it will be so for me and therefore, wish you and all men the same.

Medieval Jerusalem is realised here – all the good zeal of the Anglican Revival intact, all its flummery axed and brought to nought. I am convinced there is no monastery to rival this one either in tradition – the tradition of English. Truth beautified in Benedictine Obedience. It is the prelude of a Monastic Golden Age – steeped, thank God, in simplicity.

We cannot live on views, either personal or geographical, but you and I have been given to enjoy the heart of Green England, in our respective parks of Heythrop and Prinknash – Oxfordshire and Gloucestershire.

I must lay off buffoonery, contenting myself merely with a girth fast growing to equality with that of Sir JOHN FALSTAFF. The surroundings suit him well – as for recorders and my darling Lady 'Greensleeves', well, we have both here: both pipes and Notre Dame.

I will be with you in Spirit throughout Liturgy. How bad I am at finding places in Books. How I love the sound of my own voice! 'Our' voice now though, and have been told by the Lord of Heaven, via Father Abbot, to sing more softly! Glory to God, it'll probably avert laryngitis as well as much pain to our fellow monks; as a matter of fact I was hoping for the salutary warning. So no more the roaring bull of Bashan, but rather the far off cuckoo, trusting to become cucu with the love of our Lord, whom alone we may each rightly call 'mine'.

Pray for a perpetual and preposterous postulant. I do not look forward to Clothing, nor to Profession, nor even to becoming Cellarer – but only to the present moment, to which may the Lord of Eternity bind us in His Love till evermore. For me, to be here with Our Lady is to be a monk. let come what will come, I ask no more.

They are wonderfully good to me here, and helpful and firm and wise.

The Lord always seemed to allow John to feel at home in any new abode. This is not the case with many. I know of a number who have entered 'wrong' Orders who have been quite unable to pray, everything was against the grain. No so for John – Carthusians, House of Ratisbonne, Prinknash, he was as happy as a sandboy until it was time to move on.

'Time to move on' came on a strange day – Good Friday 1956. I asked him why he did not wait until Easter dawn. He answered simply that the time came on Good Friday.

He wrote in a rather apologetic vein about his departure in a letter from Ottery-St-Mary dated 15 April 1956.

I am very sorry indeed for the trouble and dismay I have caused you, 'Qui s'excuse, s'accuse', so I shall not be wordy: I left not in a tempest, not impetuously, not in a brainstorm, but exactly as and when and how God wanted me to leave. For this please be patient and refer to the Last Judgement. The only reason why I again had a shot at being a cenobite was a certain letter you wrote me last Summer, for which letter may God reward you for I have profited and learnt much in an Advent, Christmas-tide and Lent at Prinknash: such kindness then was shown me for any apparent discourtesy in my way of departure.

The hermit bug and the Jewish bug I am proud to share with my Precursor Patron (St John the Baptist) in my most tiny degree. The hour of the fool's departure was just that in which his King was made a fool of by the Gentiles (Good Friday).

Further, I am by God's grace a monk till death. I do not refer to Ecclesiastical litigation or terminology but to the essential, original meaning of 'monachus' viz. 'a man who is alone with the One'. Meanwhile my affection and respect for Dom Andrew is in no way lessened, neither my gratitude to him.

Back at Ottery-St-Mary he wrote:

My 'monastery' is a loft above a stable in the outbuildings here. My rule (approved by Père Geza Vermes who is providentially detained near here through having had a sudden operation – he is a Père de Sion who knew me well at Louvain) is simply as follows:

Office   –   that of Our Lady (I am once more a Franciscan Tertiary),

Matins   –   when I wake up during the night,

Lauds   –   at first light,

Prime   –   at sunrise,

Mass daily and

Communion   soon after.

From 'Tierce' till 'None' with a break for Sext and lunch, I am fully occupied washing up and cutting wood and what not. 'None' at 3 p.m. From then on till 7 p.m. the time is with God and Our Lady. 7 p.m. wash up, then Compline, then bed. Board and lodging and Insurance stamp in exchange for my humble services. All found not idle, not a cadger, not a drone, but always a recluse of Christ the King, who does, (and in His mercy will, please God), deign to answer for my comedy of errors. His fool's fantastic fiasco. My cloister wall is the two hills on either flank of the Otter Vale. My vocation is the least of all vocations. Blessed be God in this.

Prinknash will not be worse off without me and I am better off for four blessed months of training there. Please note that my total postulancy and novice periods now amount to about $2\frac{1}{2}$ years – and I know beyond all doubt that my calling is a monk's calling though not cenobite, but unique. As for marriage, I wedded with the Fairy Queen in Campania three years ago – a fact she does not let me forget with impunity!

Thus he lived as the spirit directed him in his new 'monastery' – a loft above a stable in some outbuildings. A simple order of the day similar to that which he adopted in Campania, Italy; similar to that which he would adopt in Africa to the end.

He remained, henceforth, a layman, member of the Third Order of St Francis. He never again entered a religious Order, nor attempted the cenobitic life in a community. He emerged now more and more as the solitary, but his pilgrimage continued.

CHAPTER 25

An Elizabethan

It was sometime in the autumn of 1956 that I read an article in the London *Evening Star* about an 'Elizabethan' piper piping madrigals in the streets of London. So now it is London town which is graced with Elizabethan airs! the Otter vale left behind. In his own words John said, after leaving Prinknash Abbey, 'A little later I was a street musician in London for two months.' He slept the odd night on the embankment, I remember, but for the rest he stayed with friends. His friends were many and various. Geoff was an out and out communist who took a great liking to John. He admired his poetry and wrote to him on and off, even to Africa. John next took a job as a porter in St Mary Abbott's Hospital in London. There was a lot of night work and among other things wheeling the dead to the morgue. John was rather shocked by the callousness of some of the other porters. He prayed a good deal for those who died.

Around Christmas he moved to Burns Oates, the Catholic Bookshop which used to be very close to Westminster Cathedral in Ashley Place. He was a source of wonder and joy both to customers and staff! Burns Oates is no more, and John himself would not know the fine piazza which now graces the entrance to the Cathedral.

Of course Westminster Cathedral attracted him greatly, especially the choir. He lodged with Ferdinand and his merry men not far from the Cathedral, and spent long hours in the Cathedral at his devotions. He wanted to lend his voice to that choir but there was no vacancy. However, he left Burns Oates and became, as he put it, fifth sacristan at the Cathedral just to be close to the Lord and near to the choir. He was very happy there and on my very rare visits to London, it was a joy to see him about his tasks within the Cathedral.

He visited me at the 'old' Heythrop on one or two occasions and in particular for my Ordination on 31 July 1958.

We were all ordained together in those days in the chapel of our theologate at the 'old' Heythrop. It was rare for anyone to be ordained in his own home parish. In consequence, since our chapel was small and we were many, twenty or more I believe, we were restricted to ten guests each. Since my family was not large, John was foremost on my list. A photo of the Ordination luncheon (and two others) were found in his hut at Mutemwa after his death.

The next day he served my First Mass and we were then allowed five days 'home leave' – a rare privilege! My old home with the 'trappist dormitory' had been sold after my father's death, but some kind friends lent us their house overlooking my home valley. The weather was glorious and the views excellent. We went into Taunton each day for Mass at St George's Church. Monsignor Iles, the parish priest, had been at my Ordination and knew us both down the years. John served these Masses and we prayed together in a church which was full of so many memories.

The five days soon went by and we parted. He went to see his mother and I returned to the fold.

John continued as a sacristan at Westminster Cathedral until one day he bumped into Cardinal Godfrey in the sacristy. John himself said of this meeting, 'Cardinal Godfrey asked me if I would take care of his very old Elizabethan country house – Hare Street House in Hertfordshire. It was left for the use of the Cardinals of Westminster by Monsignor Hugh Benson."

He went on: 'I was there for two and a half years, 1959–1961, and during that time I was pretty strongly influenced by the spirit of Robert Hugh Benson – the author of *Come Rack, Come Rope, The Necromancers* and many other books. I used to sleep in the room in which he had worked.'

I also had a great admiration for Cardinal Godfrey. He was a very holy man. He was always 'on the mountain with God'. I remember John using a term which conveyed a spirit of inner understanding; he said that the Cardinal understood my 'madness and my love for solitude.'

John lived alone at Hare Street House since the Cardinal only came for rare visits. On those occasions he served the Cardinal's Mass acting as sacristan to the little chapel. A good sister or two accompanied the Cardinal on such visits to manage the kitchen and other domestic needs. According to John the Sister cook was a real 'Martha' but, he said, 'she didn't think me a "Mary" but a drone!'

Robert Hugh Benson died in 1914 and bequeathed the house to the Cardinal Archbishops of Westminster. Benson was the youngest son of E.W. Benson, Archbishop of Canterbury. His father sent him to Eton and Trinity, Cambridge. In 1894 Robert Hugh was ordained a Minister in the Anglican Church. After some time on parish work he joined the Community of the Resurrection at Mirfield but was not professed. In 1903 he was received into the Roman Catholic Church and re-ordained in 1904 as a priest of the Church of Rome. He resided at Hare Street, his home, from 1908 until his death in 1914. He wrote *The Necromancers* while at Hare Street.

Fr Bernard Basset SJ wrote me a few lines about Hare Street House as he remembers it:

Hare Street House lies outside the village of Bunting-ford, Hertfordshire, not all that far from St Edmund's Ware. Robert Hugh Benson owned it, he may have built it; he probably added the small chapel where he is buried. Benson was a curious man and I recall well that he fitted his house with various trap doors and mysteries. You pressed a panel over his bed and a secret cupboard opened in which he put a copy of the *Daily Mail* for August 4th 1914. Benson dropped dead in Salford very soon afterwards in about October 1914. He left Hare Street House to the Archbishops of Westminster as a private country home. I was taken there first as a small boy in about 1922 when Cardinal Bourne was in residence. It was a moderate sized country villa with a few acres of garden.

Fr Basset goes on to say that Mark Fawdry, one-time editor of the *Catholic Times* who died recently, rented Hare Street House from Cardinal Griffin for a time. Mark Fawdry met John at Southwell House when I was there on Fr Basset's staff in 1960.

Fr Basset mentions: 'One indistinct memory tells me that I went on a pilgrimage to Hare Street to Benson's tomb – in the aisle, I think, before the altar (of Hare Street House Chapel). It was quite moving because I read that Teilhard de Chardin had done the same directly after World War I. Teilhard had read Benson's "Lord of the World" in the trenches; he admired it enormously and may have developed his theories from that weird but wonderful book.'

Teilhard de Chardin, like John, had had a hard war in World War I as a stretcher bearer. He was decorated for bravery. He wrote in 1918, 'and above all, I shall tell those who suffer and mourn that the most direct way of using our lives is to allow God, when it pleases him so to do, to grow within us, and, through death, to replace us by Himself'. This was very much in keeping with John's thought.

I am not sure if John read *Lord of the World*, he probably did. He spoke much of *The Necromancers* and of Benson's interest in the spirit world and the after life. References to this book crept into John's poetry in later life.

John was blissfully happy at Hare Street House. He was alone in an Elizabethan setting living in Robert Hugh Benson's study, complete with harmonium. Then there was the chapel, also with harmonium but, more important, with the Blessed Sacrament reserved. It was ideal; he was a solitary caretaker with enough of this world's material goods to cover his needs. There was an old gardener, Fred, I believe, to chat to if he wanted local news. However, John was of the opinion that Fred, too, thought he was a drone! There was another friend who evidently thought more highly of him – a tame pigeon named Francesca.

John stuck to his approved 'rule' which he had adopted after leaving Prinknash based on the Little Office of Our Lady with sung matins upon waking in the night, lauds at first light followed by prime, and the other hours spaced out during the day ending with compline sung in the chapel at night. He preferred to sing this office in Latin and at Carthusian pace. He would at times play the hymn tunes in accompaniment on the harmonium. The rest of the day would be given to odd jobs, meditative reading, writing when the muse was upon him, rosary, song and 'Om'-type prayer.

He was at Hare Street House for two and a half years or more. John gained permission for me to stay a night there with him before I left for Africa and the Missions. I travelled down from Southwell House, London, by bus. It was 21 December 1960 and John met me off the bus. He took me to the house and, since there was a spare bed in his room – Robert Hugh Benson's study – this was to be my abode too. John was a superb guide and we saw around the house, the garden and the chapel. In the chapel John went straight to the harmonium to assist me in a short prayer! We then went back to the house to prepare the evening meal. I remember it so well – beans, fried egg, and honey in a bowl, followed by cheese and wine. John was the cook, and he believed in a monastic simplicity – a bowl and a spoon and mug. Excellent! And not too much washing up! We went to the chapel for sung compline and when eventually I got into bed I was entertained to a lullaby on the harmonium in his bedroom – 'Greensleeves' and Johann Sebastian Bach.

John was 'at home' in such a delightful place. Elizabethan chimneys, oak panelling and oak doors blended with his Renaissance character. The spirit of Robert Hugh Benson too, convert from Anglicanism like himself, writer and seeker of the mysteries of God and the universe all fitted so well. He could have stayed there for ever and anon, but this was not to be.

I returned to London to the business of packing for Africa and the unknown. Christmas was only a few days off and then a New Year – 1961. The ship, the *Capetown Castle*, was due to sail from Southampton on 12 January

1961. John got leave of absence from Hare Street and came up to London to spend a final night with me at Southwell House.

The ship sailed at 4 p.m. with sirens sounding and martial music from the dock. John stood waving on the quay until we were out into Southampton Water. I never dreamt that I would see him in Africa, but to Africa he came.

PART VI

AFRICA

*If Lord I should a leper be
Let it make leap
Into eternity.*
(J.R.B.)

CHAPTER 26

Africa 1962: Arrival

The Cardinals varied very much in their use of Hare Street House. At about this time it was decided that it should be used as a type of spiritual renewal centre for diocesan clergy after their first five years on parish work. Fr Basset told me that the candidates were to be known in the Archdiocese as "The Jugged Hares".

Since they were to spend some months at Hare Street House, structural alterations and renovation were necessary to accommodate the priests. Thus builders descended upon the house not long after my departure. There is nothing worse in a religious house than builders' noise, dust and general upheaval. It upsets the whole rhythm of an ordered life and, of course, is not a recommended prop for prayer. For John there was the added burden of people and further questioning about his mode of life. In addition he was ultra protective about the old Elizabethan fittings in the house – oak panelling and the like. I remember him writing to say that the builders were insensitive as to what should be removed and what was fit to stay. Any rate John wrote in verse great laments about it all to the Cardinal. He fasted and reverted to almost total silence. Finally, he left.

As I remember he went to his godmother first and then to his sister-in-law to help her with market gardening. In the meantime he wrote to me and asked if there was not some cave in Africa to which he could retire.

It was then the era of lay mission helpers, peace corps, and what-have-you. Missionaries soon learnt that a helper could be a hindrance if he had no skill or he was not practical in some manner. John was not much of a driver, not very practical, and there were no caretaker jobs going at the time. So what was I to suggest?

He was a devout member of the Third Order of St Francis and so I approached the Superior of the Franciscans in Zimbabwe, Fr Boniface Gaynor OFM. He said that he would be most welcome at Mount-St-Mary's Mission, Wedza. Archbishop Francis Markall SJ was next approached and a lay mission helper contract was drawn up. Moreover air fares for immigrating whites were subsidised at that time and so one got out for about £65 provided one intended to stay. John intended to do that all right. The stage was set.

John booked his flight for the feast of the Transfiguration, 6 August 1962. He took off from Heathrow in rain but was soon "transfigured" above the clouds in glorious sunshine. The sun was to remain with him for a long while.

I met him at Salisbury airport, Zimbabwe, the next day. It was a good time to arrive since the Msasa trees were about to bloom to herald the summer. Moreover, Africa looks sunburnt at this time of year since there has been no rain since April. The nights were still cool but the days were hotting up with a lovely warming sun. Zimbabwe is a high plateau with Salisbury nearly 5,000 feet up, thus it is never too hot. In fact I have never been so cold as in Africa, since in winter (June, July) there is frost at night in Zimbabwe, but Mission buildings are built for heat, not for cold. The only heating, for the most part, is the sun.

John stayed in Salisbury for two or three nights to get his papers in order and to meet the Archbishop and others. On the afternoon of his arrival we went out to Chishawasha Mission so that he could get a glimpse of an old Mission. The pioneer missionaries arrived at Chishawasha in July 1892. Two Fathers and seven Brothers. They eventually established a Mission under the most adverse conditions. Fever was their number one enemy but in June 1896 they also had to contend with an armed attack upon the Mission during the Shona uprising. This was soon over and by 1899 eighty boys were attending school at Chishawasha. They became famous for their band and their music. The Brothers taught agriculture, carpentry and brick-making, as well as reading and writing. In 1901 the present church was begun and on completion in October 1902 it was considered one of the finest buildings in what was then known as Rhodesia. It is still very fine and of great historical interest to visitors. John is now buried close to this old church.

That afternoon we visited the church, greeted the Fathers and took tea with some "Blue" Sisters up at St Patrick's Cottage on the hill above the Mission. Little did John know that he would later caretake at this very cottage, with its lovely view but its remote and thereby dangerous situation.

The next day Archbishop Francis Markall took John with him on a visit to Monte Cassino Mission near Macheke, about 75 miles out of Salisbury. After Marandellas, 45 miles out, one moves into open undulating country interspersed with rock and mountain features. The last three miles to the Mission are lovely and unspoilt, with two small river crossings.

Monte Cassino Mission is set in a broad valley which has a backcloth of rugged hills. It was once a Trappist monastery founded in 1904. In 1909 the monks became Missionaries in the newly constituted Congregation of Missionaries of Marianhill. They remained at Monte Cassino until 1927 when the Jesuits took over the Mission at a time of a general re-arrangement of the whole Mission of Zimbabwe. The Marianhill Fathers went south to take over the Bulawayo and Wankie areas; the Jesuits came north.

John loved the church at Monte Cassino. The fact that it had once been a Trappist monastery gave added meaning to him. People often visit churches as though they were museums, not knowing quite where to start, what to look at, or where to go. Tourists often look quite lost following the herd, and staring at people on their knees at prayer. John entered a church primarily to visit the Blessed Sacrament and to greet the Lord. Thus he would first find the

Blessed Sacrament and pray a while there, then he would visit the Lady Chapel – and pray there too. He "took in" a church and was quick to sense if it was indeed a house of prayer. Did it lead one to God or was it simply a stone edifice, empty, forlorn?

After his greetings to the Lord he would perhaps notice the organ, certainly the various shrines, always followed up by more prayer at each shrine. If the "Box" (Confession) was in operation he would probably go and receive absolution. John would come out of a church refreshed in spirit, making his huge, deliberate sign of the cross after taking holy water. He would comment on the beauty of the church, and if there was none he would be glad to have visited the Blessed Sacrament. He was quite dismayed by the fall off of devotion to the Blessed Sacrament in latter years. He wrote a lament about it on the back of a picture postcard which showed the inside of an empty church. A church was a temple of the living presence of God for John, not just a hall for occasional prayer meetings.

At the time of John's visit with Archbishop Markall, Monte Cassino had an excellent secondary school for African girls run by the Precious Blood Sisters, a large African primary school, a farm and the fine old church. A Jesuit Father was the Superior of the Mission, assisted by Jesuit Brothers.

Note: Place names known in John's life are used in the text. Since Zimbabwe's Independence (1980) some place names have changed; e.g. Salisbury is now named Harare.

CHAPTER 27

Mount-St-Mary's Mission, Wedza

A certain Brother Leopold walked over 40 miles from Monte Cassino sometime between 1902 and 1914 to found Mount-St-Mary's Mission at Wedza. Brother Leopold, being a German, was interned during World War I and thus his early Mission at Wedza was abandoned in 1917. It was not until 1951 that Mount-St-Mary's Mission, Wedza, was resurrected by the late Fr Böchenhoff SJ. It flourished under this great warm-hearted missionary. Fr Böchenhoff had little money but a great love of the people. The people flocked to him as to a much-loved father.

After only a few days we were on the road to Mount-St-Mary's Mission, Wedza. This was to be John's first Mission. It had just been taken over by the Franciscan Fathers. Father Böchenhoff SJ moved to Monte Cassino where he died not long after.

The Mission is just under 100 miles south-east of Salisbury. One takes the main Umtali road for 45 miles as far as Marandellas and then south along a minor road which soon becomes a country dirt road. At this point Wedza Mountain comes into view in the distance amid a fine panorama. The road becomes progressively worse as one heads into the Wedza Tribal Trust Land as it was then called. Finally Rusunzwe, the rock feature behind the Mission, is seen with Wedza Mountain over to the right. A few miles out of the Mission there is a village and school at Dendenyore. Ox-drawn carts stand sleepily outside open-fronted stalls. Children and chickens scatter as the truck approaches. The road then climbs up to the Mission where it passes over a cattle-grid at the entrance, leaving the hospital on the left. The Mission Fathers' house is in the middle of the main school area close to the Rusunzwe rock.

There is a fine long view over the plains to the north. Behind to the south is a mountainous terrain with deep wooded ravines; the home of baboons and the occasional leopard. It is splendid walking country with its rock features, startling mountain vistas, wild life, and the rusts and golds of the African bush. Brightness at dawn, heat haze in the day, with a stillness at sunset. Above all a vast sky at night, crystal clear in the moonlight.

The newly arrived missionary is astounded at the courtesy of the Shona people – the long greetings and the respect for elders. The villages, too, provide surprise in their orderliness and spaciousness. After big European cities with their herdlike conditions for their poor, the African village, by contrast, gives an air of spacious ease. There is a hut for the parents, another for boys, and one for the girls. Then there is the large "kitchen" hut where all are made welcome. The huts are made from poles and mud with a grass thatched roof. Most villages have a variety of chickens, cattle, an ox for the cart, maybe a goat or two, and the inevitable village dogs gone to skin and bone, which bring home to the visitor the scarcity of food. Most important of all are the cattle. Cattle, however lean or poor in condition, mean wealth. A young man will pay "lobola" (bride price) with so many head of cattle.

The staple diet of the people is maize from which is made a thick porridge. To this is added a little "relish" in the form of a hard-come-by vegetable of one kind or another. Meat is a rare luxury since, with the advent of the White Man, game is scarce and confined to game reserves. The success of the maize crop depends on the amount and spacing of the rains during the summer rainy season from November to March, and the control of pests. This causes headaches since a poor rainy season means hunger. Even in good seasons there is malnutrition from such a low-protein diet. Scientific agricultural methods are a top priority along with schemes for irrigation and nutrition.

The Wedza people near the Mission scratch out fields between the mountains and rock features and plant their maize soon after the first rain falls. Among the many hazards are the baboons at dawn and dusk. One often saw a big male baboon peering down upon the Mission from the top of the rock feature at the back of the missionaries' residence.

The villages have a host of children who run barefoot by jungle paths to school at the Mission each day, oblivious of danger from forest cobra and the variety of other snakes which inhabit that area. Some travel seven miles or more with little food in their stomachs but a great zeal to learn. They return in the early evening by the same forest paths to their villages for the first and only real meal of the day.

A central Mission like Mount-St-Mary's had a number of satellite schools or out-schools as they were called, which came under its care and management. These schools were scattered far and wide, some up to 50 miles, from the parent Mission. One Father was the schools' manager in those days. He had to visit and inspect all the schools, collect school fees, pay teachers, provide books, footballs and all that is required in the running of a bush primary school. John was to help in all of this. In addition, a monthly Mass was said at all of these schools to which the people came from the surrounding villages within a radius of five miles or more.Baptisms, marriages, funerals, all had to be attended to, along with sickness, disease, and all the problems of the people. A big undertaking involving day and night travel by Landrover or on foot, fording swollen rivers in the rains and climbing up to mountain villages to anoint an old man or woman lying close to the wood fire in a village hut.

In Europe the gap between the natural and the super-natural is enormous. The technological age has surrounded people with a materialism that enslaves them, body and spirit, to this world. The next life is remote if it exists at all, while death is anathema. The Mashona are a very religious people. For them there is but a thin dividing-line between this world and the next, between the natural and supernatural. In their thinking there is little or no secondary causality – things don't come about by chance. If one is run over by a bus, the spirit world has caused it in some manner or another and they will ask the witch-doctor for an explanation. The Mashona are monotheists; Mwari is the supreme spirit or God. Then there is a world of spirits in which the ancestral spirits ("Vadzimu") exercise the most influence over the people. The Vadzimu will protect their families if they are honoured by the family in a fitting customary manner. Thus the people will offer sacrifices of food and beer to the Vadzimu. Villagers consult their family spirits through a medium. They consult them about all affairs of village life – rain, harvest, sickness, birth and death. There are good and bad spirits. It is the task of the witch-doctor ("N'anga") to diagnose the type of spirit which may have possessed a person or which may be the cause of some ill fortune. The N'anga is also a herbalist doctor. He may attribute a disease to the work of a bad spirit, at the same time he will give selected herbs as part of the treatment. Some N'angas are very good herbalists.

The early missionary tended to put all of this belief and practice into the category of a pagan cult to be eradicated. Now, after a deeper study, missionaries direct their teaching to the christianising of local belief – inculturation. The liturgy is also adapted to Shona custom with regard to Church music, modes of prayer and the like. The harmonium and the Westminster hymnal have been replaced by the drum, hosho, mbira and lovely Shona harmony.

It was into this world that John came in 1962. He had been in India and Burma but had no experience of Africa. John was conservative in his beliefs, a traditionalist in the best sense and always an Englishman. A great friend of his, Mrs Kit Law, describes him as a Renaissance Englishman. How then would he adapt to Africa and the Shona way of life?

An early ballade of his gives a glimpse of his first reflections. It is entitled "A Ballade of a Gladsome people".

Mashona folk would pass the time of day
From when they meet you till the morrow comes;

Their manners are unhurried as the sway
Of nodding maize-cobs and of throbbing drums;
They sit not huddled over muddled sums
Prognosticating useless future care,
Their "Take no thought" sports more than Christendom's;
Their homes are huts, not castles in the air.

They are amazed at men that won't be gay
(Gray moods have many men of Christendom's);
Simply and gracefully their dames array
(In trouser-fashion not, that passion numbs);
They paint not nails of fingers, toes or thumbs;
Clad they are shapely and as shapely bare,
To sucklings' cries they are not deafs and dumbs;
Their homes are huts, not castles in the air.

Starlight by night, brightness of sun by day,
Tomorrow is tomorrow and it comes
Not brooding on the present moment gay
Until, with all the fright of Christendom's
Straying from Christ by paralysing sums
Steeped in anxiety. Vanity-Fair
Calls them to fret ... yet gently throb the drums:
Their homes are huts, not castles in the air.

Envoy
Prince, be a mellow headman, let your drums
Utter the glee of hutland free of care
Till comment from the deep in Christ thus comes:
Their homes are huts, not castles in the air.

He was given a great welcome by the Franciscan Fathers
(Friars Minor) at Mount-St-Mary's. The Father Superior,
Boniface Gaynor OFM, had paid his air fare and looked
forward to his coming. At the Mission there were two
other Franciscans and at the hospital two or three "Blue"
Sisters (Little Company of Mary). All were Irish.

Perhaps John's first problem was the missionaries? Bush
missionaries can be terribly practical and, like Martha,
busied about many things from dawn to dusk. Lay Mission
helpers, VSOs, and others were welcome at first but the
bush missionary soon realised that many had no practical
talents. The missionary looked for handymen, drivers,

typists, bookkeepers, schools managers. If these talents were absent, then, the lay Mission helper could be an odd man out.

Moreover with the advent of the Landrover or Mission truck the missionary was vulnerable for duties – sick calls, funerals, Masses, up to 60 miles or more from the Mission station. One missionary, I remember, had 30 Mass centres or parishes to look after. He could visit one parish per day per month; thus he was on the road all the time. The early missionary had to walk. The pace of life was slower and he could spend more time with fewer people. He could also find time to pray. I remember Fr Böchenhoff complaining that there was no time for prayer – yet his whole life was prayer in the service of the people. He simply wore himself out.

John had become accustomed to solitude and much prayer. Moreover, he was not very practical and certainly no handyman. He drove very badly and was unable to type when he arrived. People, too, were a problem to him in any number. The Mission door receives knocks from anxious callers day and night.

The Irish Franciscans were, for the most part, intrigued by this strange English poet. His comments on life and his general conversation kept them highly amused. They did not find him practical and so for the most part he just kept them company on their long journeys into the bush, doing odd bits and pieces of jobs that came his way. He could be maddening, as when he filled up a diesel Landrover with petrol!

John had, in a sense, come to Africa to look for a cave in which to dwell in solitude. Thus this new rush of Mission life, with endless people and endless chatter, caused him more than a small measure of suffering. He loved the African scene and adored the heat. The clear night sky delighted him and above all the eagles and birds. He envied the people for their pace of life but was saddened by their poverty and suffering. In a way he was frustrated that he could not do more for them. He found that they regarded him as the big white man which he abhorred. He wanted to be like them in their poverty, unnoticed.

John Bradburne after receiving his commission as an Officer in England 1941. He then sailed for India to join the 9th Gurkha Rifles.

John Bradburne and FR John Dove at Silveira House Mission Centre, Chishawasha, Zimbabawe, Christmas 1964

John Bradburne, caretaker at Lord Acton's old home M'bebi, Mazowe, 1964. He called the cat M'bebi.

'Baba' John with his basket of medicines for the lepers,
1970

A thatched kitchen hut and a leper hut.

Leper huts at Mutemwa

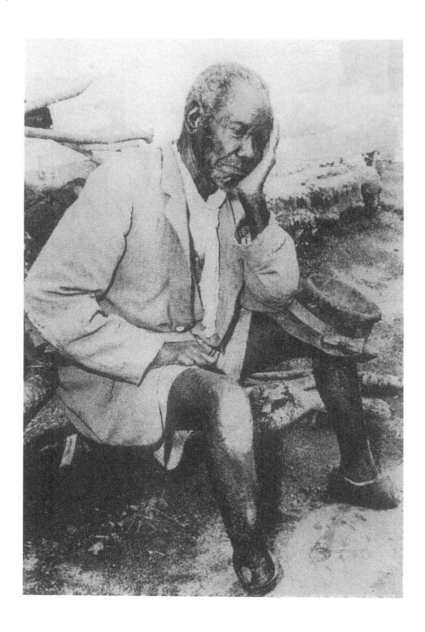

John with 'Amai' Jeromia; the lepers were his family

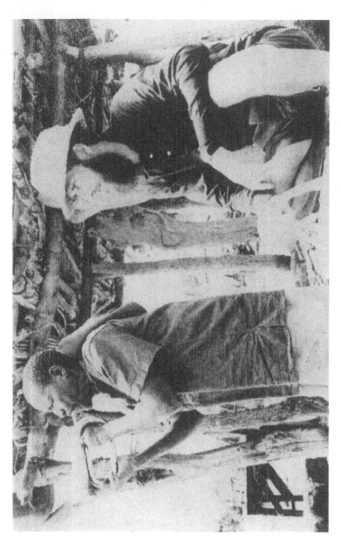

Joshua blowing the bugle to announce that John was coming with the medical basket.

John with a group of lepers' children

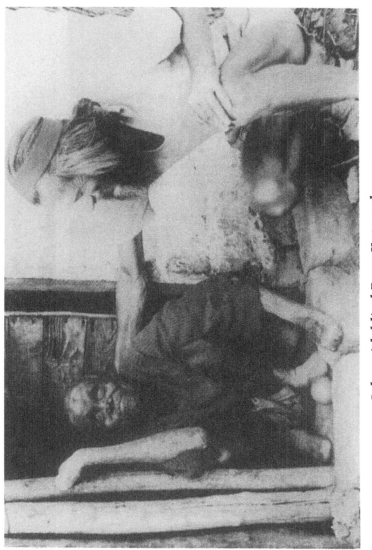

John with blind Peter Katsandanga.

Mutemwa chapel.

FR John Dove listening to John playing the harmonium in the 'rondavel' chapel.

John with FR John Dove outside his tin hut, 'Piper's Vale.'

John with the muse upon him.

Dr Luisa Guidotti's funeral, 10th July 1979.

Lepers at John Bradburne's grave in Chishawasha Mission Cemetery, October 1979.

Fr Desmond O'Malley OFM remembers him saying on arrival that he had three wishes:

First to serve and live with lepers;
the second, to die a martyr;
the third, to be buried in the Franciscan habit.

At that time he knew of no lepers and the country was at peace. It took 17 years for the fulfilment of those desires but the Lord granted him all three in the end.

Chivhu (Enkeldoorn)

John's stay at Mount-St-Mary's Mission, Wedza, was short-lived. After two months he was moved to Enkeldoorn to help Fr Sean Gildea OFM, who became a very close friend of John until death parted them. It was Fr Sean who awarded John the Franciscan habit, and in this habit John was eventually buried.

Enkeldoorn is a 'dorp' 85 miles south of Salisbury on the main road to Fort Victoria, the Zimbabwe ruins, and Beitbridge into South Africa. Enkeldoorn, as the name suggests, is a predominant Afrikaans-speaking area. A large percentage of Rhodesian farmers in those days were Afrikaaners. They were hard-working folk but they brought with them their apartheid mentality from South Africa. John's early poem 'Burdens' reflects his thinking about this problem which haunts this lovely Southern hemisphere.

John's abode was to be a small suburban house rented as the parish and Mission residence. Fr Sean, John, and Samson, the cook, shared this small house, while a middle-aged African lady lived in a small one-roomed servant's quarter at the back. This lady, Chizuva, was a somewhat eccentric character who, like Melchisedeck, seemed to appear from a mysterious past into an unknown future. She lived for the present which offered her free board and lodging. One could not help but notice her regal bearing. She evidently thought that John was someone out of the ordinary, too, giving him an odd bottle of beer – which he did not care for – much to the amusement of Fr Sean.

Even though this one-priest Mission was within a country 'dorp' it nevertheless had its fair share of out-stations and schools to care for and to visit. It was essential that John should be able to drive and drive alone to some of these out-stations, John had driven in war days and could have had his military driver's licence converted into a civilian licence at the time of demobilisation in 1945. Driving, however, seemed a remote possibility to him, and he preferred 'shank's mare' with the odd lift by a kindly motorist, to mastery of the art of driving. Undaunted, Fr Sean booked him for a test with the local police. John passed.

According to Fr Sean, John made friends with a variety of people in Enkeldoorn. One was Henry, the owner of the hotel. Sean relates one event at the hotel: 'The hotel was the centre of life in Enkeldoorn. Henry and his wife invited John and me to supper on one occasion and we had a wonderful night. John regaled us with stories ending the evening with an impersonation of the parson in an East Anglian Church telling the parable of the good Samaritan in the local dialect.' Sean goes on to say: 'John's freedom, his good humour and welcome acceptance of everybody made him a reconciler. He didn't need to know the local language. An odd word thrown in with his good-humoured laughter got the message across.'

John, in his unfailing generosity to the poor did, however, get taken 'for a ride' on occasion, as Sean recounts:

In November 1962, John went to Badza School which is about 20 miles from Enkeldoorn. He delivered the books and set out for home. He got to a turn-off about 9 miles from Enkeldoorn. There he was stopped by a number of women who wanted a lift. The trouble was that they were going in the opposite direction, through what was then known as 'Wiltshire Estates' to a town called Sadza. 'Was it far?' 'No.' 'All right, get in and I will take you there.' This was about 5.00 p.m. and John set out with his car load. It was a small Ford Prefect. The road through Wiltshire was very bad and twice the car had to be lifted out of large pools of water. It was raining heavily.

When he had gone about 20 miles, John came to a road junction. Some of the women wanted to go to Zvamatobje – to the left towards the Sabi River, others to a township in the opposite direction, called Sadza. I forget how they solved that problem, but John found himself at Sadza Township exhausted, frustrated about the 'short-long' journey late at night and the rain falling ... and nowhere to stay!

An African store-keeper gave him a camp bed and John slept under the various articles of clothing and kitchen utensils which were hung from the low rafters of the ceiling. The rats had a real celebration that night.

Meanwhile, I was very worried about John's whereabouts. We discovered that he had left Sadza, but where he went to after that no one knew. I did not know which direction to take to look for him.

Early the following morning John arrived back full of life and of the saga of his experiences on the road. Many a time afterwards he regaled us with this story. It was just like John to trust people without question and I suppose that the women told him the truth when they were on the way; in his generosity and gallantry he helped.

I remember visiting John on a couple of occasions when he was at Enkeldoorn. I stayed the night and was highly entertained by both John and Sean not to forget the quiet composure of Samson, who probably thought that we were all quite mad. Chizuva was not missing anything in the background. Sean remarks:

It was great to listen to John recalling his travels in Italy, the Holy Land or his days in London. In all these anecdotes people had the primary place and John always seemed to discover and recall the best. One felt his great tolerance, his non-judgemental assessment of people. His sadness at sadness in the lives of others. All these stories and anecdotes were told with great wit, vivacity and joyous humour. But in all of this John was a very keen judge of character.

Later when we met it was always an occasion of great rejoicing. John's freedom inspired me. His flair for the unusual, his going round in circles but always coming back to the centre, as Chesterton used to say. He was so like what I think St Francis was like. He had his foibles and his limitations, but if he had not he would not have been human. I regarded him as a friend of mine and when we met we shared at a deep level.

John's happy stay at Enkeldoorn ended in mid-1963 when Fr Sean was posted to another Mission. John was moved into deep bush east of Enkeldoorn to a new Mission in the Narira Tribal Trust Land, beside the Mwerahari River not far from the big Anglican Mission at Daramombe.

CHAPTER 29

St Antony of Padua Mission, Gandachibvuva

The Mission is situated at a place named Gandachibvuva about two miles from the primary school at Goveri. The word 'Gandachibvuva' is semi-onomatopoeic – 'bvuva' gives the idea of the surge and boom of the waters of the Mwerahari River over a fall and rapids. 'Ganda' really means 'skin'. The legend is that a chief when crossing was swept away by the rapids and they only found his coat made of skins. The Mwerahari in the rains becomes a fierce torrent at this point. It flows on down to the Sabi River, the haunt of crocodile and hippo. Sister Christiana remembers a big crocodile coming right up to the Mission. One lived in the pool near the Mission pumphouse. There are baboons in plenty. John used to love to watch them cross the river near the rapids carrying their young clutched to their breast. It is real wild country with the added interest of the river.

Gandachibvuva, a strong place-name for a hard terrain, became the turning point in John's missionary career. Up to now he had tried to be the lay Mission helper – a practical help, a 'go here, go there' assistant. This, however, led him up a dark alley.

At 'Ganda' Mission, as it was called Fr Paschal Slevin OFM was the Superior. John loved Paschal and deemed him a real Franciscan. There was also another assistant priest and two fine girls who worked in the kitchen. One, Annunciata, became a Sister later on; the other, Caroline (pronounced Caloline since the Shona have difficulty with 'r's) married and has a fine family. The Mission was only beginning in 1963. It was still small, with a Mission house and a kitchen, plus a chapel with a sacristy and small clinic.

John at first lived in the Fathers' house, offering his help where he could. Things did not go so well in the practical sphere. There was an incident with the Mission truck and an incident at the clinic. These were minor matters but John pondered about his value as a 'Martha'. He was greatly attracted to solitude and felt that his contribution to the Mission should lie in solitary prayer. His decision was helped on by a growing incompatibility with the assistant priest. Human relations are often a mystery and are not simply solved by being a religious. John felt it best if he moved from the Mission house. Fr Paschal, a man of great kindness and discernment, endorsed the decision, especially when he witnessed John's delight at finding a hermitage! About 200 yards from the Mission house stood a rock feature overlooking the river, with a water tank on its summit. The tank was supported by a very small brick shed. This had a door and a window. It was empty – what could be better! The window had no glass but this proved to be a great asset at a later stage when a visiting swallow wished to find a place in which to build her nest – a rare joy for John.

I visited him on about three occasions at his hermitage. It was a tiny place just wide enough for him to make a bed. I remember the bed: a piece of asbestos roof sheeting mounted on bricks, with blankets on top. His table was a tea chest and his chair a wooden box. He had put up some pictures from old calendars on the walls plus a few of his poems. He was in bliss. Moreover, there was a fine view and a wide sky at nights. We sat and watched the stars appear in the night sky one evening. He knew most of them; they were his friends who spoke to him of God.

On the hill there dwelt with John two cocks and about 20 hens. He called himself in Shona a 'fudza huku' (hen herdsman). The two girls at the Mission kitchen entrusted this little flock to his care. The flock soon had names and the two cocks were called the Earl of Ganda and the Duke

of Chibvuva! The cocks were wont to fight over their wives
and the supremacy of their kingdom. The Earl was a big,
bustling cock – fine to behold. The Duke was lean and
could out-manoeuvre the portly Earl. John wrote about
their antics in verse. They and the swallow along with
other birds and the baboons became his companions at
Ganda. What of people?

Rural peasants are courteous people for the most part.
For them, John was part of the Mission and they gave him
the respect meted out to missionaries. They were puzzled,
however, to see a white man living in such poverty. The
ideals of St Francis were still foreign to them.

One young man visited him every evening for a whole
month to converse about God and prayer. John was
surprised at his interest and regularity. The magic spell
broke, however, when at the end of the month the young
man asked John to lend him £20. John answered that he
must surely observe that he had no money when living in
such a poor hermitage. The young African replied, 'You
are a white man and so you must have money.'

Very gradually John began to experience the miscon-
ception which Christ experienced. In the beginning it was
more incomprehension than rejection: later he would
experience rejection.

Sister Mary Paschal LCBL, who was one of the two girls
at the time, remembers John with great affection. He
wanted to live like us, she said, and to eat our food. Sister
Paschal (Annunciata) showed him how to make sadza
porridge and cabbage which he took but once a day. He
refused meat or eggs. He took nothing more than this one
meal with tea and sugar.

Annunciata says that John used to help with the flowers
in the Chapel. This always ended with a sung prayer to
God which John had composed. We sang it in harmony,
she said, and the words in Shona were:

> Mari handina
> Mwari ndinoda
> Naye ndinofara.

Literally this means:

I have no money
But I love God
In Him I rejoice.

Annunciata remembers one occasion in particular. John used to visit the chapel last thing at night. The girls often came for night prayers too. One night a snake came in by the door near the altar. The snake had moved to the sacristy door which it could pass under. John struck it and held it with the candlestick when it was half under the door. Fr Paschal Slevin heard the commotion and ran into the sacristy from the other side to see the snake, head first half through and under the door on that side. He finished it off with a stick. Quite a big snake causing quite a bit of stir! Both John and Fr Slevin were both fearless about snakes.

Annunciata says that John volunteered to collect firewood for the stove which heated the kitchen and bath water. He also used to clean the Fathers' shoes unbeknown to them. A white man never did this type of work. John did it with joy to the astonishment of the girls. They loved him dearly.

Fr Paschal Slevin wrote very beautifully about John at Gandachibvuva:

John was a tower of strength at Gandachibvuva. What else could a man of prayer be? The new Mission was blessed with his presence. He refused to stay with us at the Mission and took up residence on the hill, making the little shed which supported the water tank his residence. This accommodation he gladly shared with the hens.

Once a week John joined us down at the Mission house for a meal. His own cooking of sadza and vegetable supplied his modest requirements of food for the rest of the time. What an example in Poverty. What a joy emanated from his person. John was close to His Lord. Three times a day John rang the bell, calling the Mission and the surrounding area to prayer. At six, twelve and six his voice was raised in praise of Him who gave us Mary as our Mother. Frequently, apart from these times, the strains of John's voice could be heard raised to the Father in prayer. How secure we felt in the knowledge that 'the hermit' entertained Love itself on the hill. Our work must be blessed.

Each morning John prepared the altar for the celebration of the Holy Sacrifice and he served. Frequently during the day John could be seen in the presence of the Blessed Sacrament. There he used to sing God's praises. I vividly remember erecting the Stations of the Cross in the Church with John present. We would have to have something special. John agreed and suggested we sing the 'Stabat Mater' which we did. I remember him saying it was a privilege for him to be at such a ceremony. In later days I frequently saw him walking the Way of the Cross.

He had many happy moments on the hill above Gandachibvuva. Possibly the one most treasured by John was the day the swallow decided to build in John's 'palace'. It finished the building, hatched and reared its young and with the landlord praised the creator.

John wrote of Fr Pascal in a poem titled: 'To a Franciscan'.

> I know a Priest and he knows me but such
> Requirements now are made upon his time
> And I adhere to solitude so much
> That barely have we met ere sounds the chime
> For his departing: not in many words
> Consists our bond in one who preached to birds.

In fact, John's departure from Gandachibvuva was not long in coming. The year 1963 was near to an end, new horizons were opening. The swallow had migrated, and it was time, too, for John to move along his pilgrim's way.

CHAPTER 30

M'Bebi Mazoe

Lord and Lady Acton lived at M'bebi, a farm in the Mazoe Valley some 30 miles north of Salisbury. It was an old house to which they had added a long corridor of bedrooms. The end room had a fine view of the Iron Mask, a large rock feature in the range across the valley with some caves which John frequented. In the garden there were some lovely trees and a pool. Below stood the small church which the Actons had built. The church was traditional in style, built in red brick with a fine stained-glass window behind the main altar. Further down beyond the church there was a small farm school with a playing field. Children from M'bebi and neighbouring farms came to the school and to the church. Lady Acton took a great interest in this little school.

M'bebi had welcomed a variety of guests, including Monsignor Ronald Knox and Evelyn Waugh. Lord and Lady Acton, however, decided to move in 1963 nearer to Salisbury. They sold the farm but very generously gave the church and the house to the Jesuit Fathers.

Fr Terence Corrigan was the Jesuit Mission Superior at the time and he invited John to caretake at M'bebi pending the move of the Novitiate to M'bebi in late 1964. John came in from Gandachibvuva in January 1964 and took up residence in M'bebi as its caretaker. The Acton's farm manager, Freddie von Nidda, was still there winding up the farm. Freddie and John hit it off at once. John soon got to know the family including Freddie's younger brother Roland who became a Jesuit a year or so later. Their parents, the Baron and Baroness, visited John regularly down the years.

M'bebi was very different from Gandachibvuva. The Mazoe Valley was lush with European farms and the famous citrus estates. It was not an African tribal area and so only African farm workers resided on their employer's farms. Many of these workers were migrants from Malawi and some from Mozambique. In general, wages for farm workers were abysmally low and hours of work long, and so the Shona preferred subsistence-living in their kraals to labouring on European farms. The Actons were very good to their labour-force. They provided a school for their children and gave them spiritual care into the bargain.

The house at M'bebi was very different, too, from John's solitude upon the hill at Ganda. Here he had a room and a bed in an all-but-empty European farm house. Moreover he liked the church and the view across the valley. In addition, he was his own master – he was alone.

In the beginning I used to visit him with Fr Corrigan. We always took a picnic meal since John ate nothing. We had some hilarious evenings with John and Freddie playing progressive table-tennis and generally relaxing.

Later I visited John at weekends, saying Mass for the farm workers and the children in the church. John was the sacristan and there were two owls on the rafters above the high altar, to his delight. The priest saying Mass was in danger of being 'bombed' from on high! John would allow no one to disturb the owls.

John also had a cat, an 'angelical' cat, black and white – good for racial harmony. The cat was born in an Acton cupboard and was very aristocratic. She followed John everywhere and was excellent with snakes.

In June we began some weekend courses at M'bebi for African youth and civic leaders. On one occasion the Apostolic Delegate paid us a visit. Margaret Horne, my cousin, helped to organise the domestic affairs. For the Delegate we arranged a tea party. John was given instructions as to how to make the tea and warm the pot. He had also decided to spray the pantry with insecticide as a precaution. When the cake arrived it had a decided taste of this spray! The Apostolic Delegate, Archbishop McGeough, did not seem to notice this nor the cracked crockery. He was a kindly American and, with Archbishop Markall, enjoyed John's company. He was subsequently posted to Dublin as Papal Nuncio.

John made some good friends when at M'bebi. Alistair Guthrie came out to advise about a multitude of hot water geysers which were dotted around the house. He became a great friend of John's and later played a significant role in the drama at the leper camp. John became godfather to Alistair's youngest boy, Craig.

Another good friend who met John at M'bebi was Heather Benoy, now a curriculum research innovator in the Department of Education and Culture and something of a musician. It was Heather who took John to Mutemwa to spy out the land before he finally settled there.

Heather wrote of that early meeting in 1964:

> I really got to know John at M'bebi. To begin with there was very little verbal communication between us because at this time he was withdrawn and silent. However, for myself, I lived, breathed and thought nothing but music and was in the habit of composing sung Masses, putting the psalms to music and had also composed one or two folkish songs.
>
> Our mutual love of music was the beginning of a long friendship spanning some 16–17 years. Soon I was visiting M'bebi often bringing my guitar. John would produce his 'pipe' which was a large recorder. He played it beautifully and I always marvelled that he could get such sweet and true sounds out of an instrument which I had always considered slightly sharp or flat and dull.
>
> At this time John also composed music and we would exchange new compositions. Sometimes singing or playing together but more often listening to each other's music. He was particularly fond of a Kyrie and two psalms which I had put to music – 'Have mercy on me Lord' and 'O Lord, you search me and you know me'. But I suppose the one he liked best was a folk song

which I composed for R.L. Stevenson's poem 'Sing me a song of the lad that's gone'. He always remembered it and would play it years later.

Heather continues

The composition of music or the writing of poetry or any such ultimate, creative work inevitably exposes and makes vulnerable the composer or writer. It reveals the beliefs, sorrows, hopes, fear and joys – and in many ways the secrets of the soul. To reveal oneself in this way requires love, trust and compassion. I make this point because in later years when our discussions became highly complex, I could never avoid an issue or skirt round a truth with John. He had the most wide ranging perception of all facets of thought and feeling, and an uncanny way of saddling me with the truth – sometimes hard for me to accept. Thus we had some fierce disagreements over the years. At M'bebi though, we would take long walks and talk about God and Our Lady – long walking meditations. Being a new convert to the church of Rome I was anxious to share these prayerful times with John.

M'bebi was so close to Salisbury that gradually one or two seekers and even distressed folk found their way out to John.

In December 1964 a strange event took place. It was decided that the Jesuit Novitiate should move from Silveira House to M'bebi. Strange, because in many ways, Silveira House, built as a Novitiate, was so much more suitable. However, M'Bebi had the little farm school where the novices could teach religion and there were more trees giving shade, along with the pool for a cool swim. It was said to be less bleak.

Thus, on 14 December 1964, John and I loaded a few things from M'bebi on to a two-ton truck belonging to a mutual friend, Fr von Kerssenbrock, and set forth for Silveira House. The few things included John's cat, now named 'M'bebi', but not the two owls! We arrived in the early evening to find the place stripped bare with long grass up to the windows. The last pantechnicon was about to leave. The African driver was not sure of the way. John volunteered to go with him to M'bebi, returning early the next day. The Silveira House era was thus begun.

CHAPTER 31

Silveira House 1964–1969

Silveira House is named after Fr Goncalo da Silveira SJ, the first Jesuit missionary to enter Zimbabwe. John was very curious about the name 'Silveira' and was delighted to learn about it from Fr W.F. Rea's brief history, *Missionary Endeavour in Southern Rhodesia*.

Fr Goncalo da Silveira, a 'saintly Portuguese Jesuit', was the first missionary to Zimbabwe and to Southern Africa. He was killed in present-day Zimbabwe while on Mission in 1561 and Silveira House is named after him. Situated on the southern heights overlooking the Chishawasha Valley, it has a splendid view to the north and John used to boast that he could see Mutemwa rock as far away as Mutoko which is 80 miles by road. Its situation could not be bettered – a mere 12 miles from Salisbury, the capital city, to the west yet right in the country on the famous Chishawasha Mission lands.

With a view second to none and a vast expanse of sky, John was in paradise. Moreover, the wooded slopes to the north-west are covered with Msasa trees, a joy to behold in the African spring. There are birds in plenty and eagles too, with a smattering of game – buck and even a cheetah. One can hear the cry of the jackal at night, but baboons are rare since Chishawasha is surrounded by European farms. A family of plovers always takes up residence in the autumn, seeing the winter through on our short grass to the front.

Then there are the swallows which John loved. They come at the beginning of the summer rains in November and stay until April and the dry winter: big fellows with a graceful air of freedom who migrate to far away climes. We have our share of snakes – forest cobra, two pythons, and a host of smaller fry.

Silveira House had two watch dogs when we came – alsatians named Huru (the big) and Simba (the strong). They were brothers but Huru always bullied Simba. John took them for long walks and Simba, in particular, took up his abode near John's room.

The house had only been built in 1958 just six years before we took up residence. Fr Wallace, the first inhabitant and Novice Master, had planted a good number of trees so the bundu had begun to become a garden. We never found it bleak and never understood how the Novitiate could have left such a beautiful place – their loss our gain.

John wrote about his new abode:

> Now, if I will consider well the things
> Which go to make the wonder of the land,
> Mapped as Mashona habitation, wings
> Of eagle I shall need to see them spanned;
> Expanding, from this eyrie where I dwell
> Four thousand feet above the even sea
> Which Eastward lies three hundred miles, I'd tell
> What Pan has scanned since here he planned with glee;
> River, and valleys, granite ranges, vastness
> Of Tawny glory's barelypeopled weald,
> The bulbul's wooded waste, the leopard's fastness,
> The hutted village and the mealie-field:
> As to the Piper, like a hornbill He
> Goes whimsically, blows from tree to tree.

The night equals the day with its vast display of stars, crystal clear in an equally vast sky. In the Southern hemisphere the mountains on the moon are so arrayed as to give the impression of a Madonna and child. John loved this sight and wrote in great admiration of the moonlit night:

Mashonaland by moonlight is my joy,
When sitting sleepily athwart the track
And pangolin goes forth with armoured back
And moths and blithe cicadas make their ploy;
While it is moonlight at the brightest full
Charmed is the valley and the granite hill
And tracks retain some warmth of day where still
Ruminate heifers on their mate the bull;
As I go down from where I spend the days
To where I spend the night in moonlight I
Discern no man face but Madonna, high,
Holding her Child thereon beyond the haze:
Only in this Mashonaland I've seen
So great a boon upon the Moon, my Queen!

He often wandered out at night or in the early dawn. This beautiful 'nocturne' captures the joy of his inner soul:

Between the midnight cockcrow and the cry
Of chanticleer at dawn, I rose and went
Out of my dwelling to inspect the sky,
Under its wonder walked on pleasure bent:
Orion's belt hung high and every star
Stood bright in declaration of its being,
Out to the North upon the hills afar
There glowed a forest-fire, fair to the seeing;
Pleasure it was to pause between the pines
That stirred to praises in the early breeze,
They stood like psalms appointed in their lines,
They sighed like reminiscence of the seas:
Isled as in awe while starlight held its sway
The land lay locked in longing for the day.

At Silveira there was need for a secretary and so John learned to type. In consequence the poetry began to flow in an unequalled measure!

We were together now in this beautiful Mission. We really had not lived under the same roof for any length of time since the war, yet our friendship never waned. We respected our different calls in the service of God – John more to a solitary, contemplative life, and I as Jesuit to a life of 'in actione contemplativus'! John's routine centred round the sung office of Our Lady, rising early and retiring

late. I often heard him singing in his room – Terce, Sext,
None, Vespers. He loved the psalms and wrote:

> The Psalms are as a series of explosions
> That still go off as oft as they are sung,
> They take small count of weather, wind, erosions,
> Simply remark them with a joyful tongue
> And go on praising God, on the account
> Of all Creation, bidding it to mount!

He always said that he did nothing but he did so much. He
was sacristan, ostiarius (doorkeeper), guest master, atten-
dant to bell, and keeper of the watch dogs Huru and
Simba, to say nothing of M'bebi the cat. Every door was
securely fastened at night, every light turned off, and every
dripping tap tight closed – water is precious in Africa. I
was out a good deal in those early days; he was always
there to guard and protect.

After only two days we were joined by Fr Peter, an
African Jesuit priest who hailed from Uganda – a missionary to what was then Rhodesia. John did not join us for
meals, he collected some food, very little, from the kitchen
and carried it back to his cell followed by M'bebi the cat
with Simba in the wings. He often came to evening recreation which was a great boon to me. Otherwise he kept
much to himself, his cell and his long walks into the
bundu. In solitude he wrestled with his turbulent nature,
bringing himself to heel under God's love.

John was not perfect – who is? He could be intolerant
and resented it much if one intruded when the muse was
upon him. He was in a sense the proud Englishman who
did not suffer fools gladly. He felt it much if others
thought him a fool even though he wished to be God's
fool. There was much in him reflected in that lovely hymn
to the Holy Spirit – cleanse what is soiled, heal what is
wounded, bend what is obstinate in us. Give warmth to
our chilled hearts, straighten what is crooked. His deep
humility knew all of this. He wrestled with God, wrestled
with himself, longed to be healed. He was the first to smite
his breast after any difference of opinion or misunderstanding. He was very sensitive to any hurt he may have

given to another – quick to make amends. Saints and martyrs are for the most part very ordinary folk who struggled their way to God against themselves, the world, and the flesh – to say little of the devil. John had much to put up with at Silveira House and elsewhere. His sensitive, passionate nature reacted to increasing activity, increasing numbers of people, a lessening of solitude.

In June 1965 Brother John Conway SJ, who was later killed at St Paul's M'sami along with six other religious, persuaded John to spend some days with him in deep bush in the Muramba district. John loved Brother Conway. He went to this very wild outpost. One day he walked too far and crossed the Mazoe River. A little dog followed him and proceeded to sniff at the mouth of a den. A roar came from within and John and the dog fled back over the river to safety. No one crossed the Mazoe river unarmed at that point.

CHAPTER 32

People and Visitors

In July 1965 or so Chris turned up. He was not long out of Ampleforth with very few 'O' levels. He was unqualified and lacking in self-confidence but very likeable. The young Chris fought with the old or older John. Chris did not really understand what John was about. John put up with Chris. A crisis ensued. Chris decided to go to the Congo as a mercenary to earn enough money to train as a pilot. Every ruse was used to prevent him; all to no avail. John was upset as we all were. Much prayer went up for Chris's safety. He came back large as life with quite a haul of money. He is now a pilot.

Later in the year Jim appeared. A number of people like Chris or Wolfgang just came to Silveira in those days – to lend a hand and to sort themselves out. In the meantime Silveira was slowly emerging as a centre for leadership training and development. There were courses and there were people. It was not quite such a paradise for John.

Jim was very practical – just what the mission needed. John knew this too but was sad that he could not match his abilities. Jim had just finished law at the Sorbonne in Paris. He wanted a break before going into practice. He was a handyman; he could fix things and he had an eye for a bargain. He soon knew all the car breakers and junk dealers in town. He got to work on repairs and made two fine benches for the chapel. He was able to lecture as well at the Civics or Industrial Relations courses. Jim did the shopping, the driving, the maintenance. He was a godsend. John withdrew more into solitude. 'I'm a drone,' he used to say.

One day Jim jumped up on to the rock in front of the house to look straight into the eyes of a hooded cobra. He yelled to John for help. John came out with his recorder. Jim called him a silly fellow. 'This is the real thing, you so-and-so,' John replied. 'That is exactly why I am bringing my recorder!' Fortunately the cobra went into a hole.

Jim and John were really great friends: each appreciated the worth of the other but John felt useless in such a powerful, practical presence. He decided to move out of the mission buildings into the hen house. He built a lean-to shack next to the hen house with bits of roof sheeting, bricks and wire. In the daytime he put his typewriter upon a box amid the hens and typed away merrily. The hens did not expect anything of him except possibly some food, which he gave them but slowly they lost all their feathers. He was surrounded by naked hens! Heather came out with an expert. He could not diagnose any hen disease. Finally, he asked John what he fed them on. John told him that he gave them layers' pellets. 'Let's have a look.' They went to the storeroom. They were layers' pellets sure enough, but the sacks had got mixed up with compound D fertilizer! The expert separated the fertilizer from the chicken food and new feathers started to appear.

Jim's six months were up. Heather motored him away north to Malawi. He hitched on up through Tanzania to Kenya, caught a cargo boat to India and came back to the Holy Land via the North-West Frontier. On a bench in Tel-Aviv he wrote a strong letter to my Superior saying that I needed a practical guy at the Mission as well as a sadhu! Nevertheless I valued John more than all and managed to persuade him to come back from the hen house to the Mission buildings where we found him a little end room with a door opening on to the glorious north front view. John was at peace, at any rate for a while. It was when living with the hens in 1966 that he met Kit and Arthur Law. They describe their first meeting in the following terms:

It all began with the bees. They lived in a hive in our garden and, one evening, as our neighbour was getting a lettuce for supper, they decided to go wild and sting her (with no serious effects, fortunately!). However, as a result the bees had to go.

My husband, Arthur, was always a keen walker and on one of his rambles in the bush, he had noticed a mission quite near us – Silveira House. We decided that here might be a haven for an unruly swarm and the following morning, we arrived there – rang the bell and the door was opened by John who made us most welcome. When we explained our presence, his enthusiasm was very encouraging. The Father Superior was not available at that moment but John was sure that he would approve. In fact, as far as John was concerned, the one thing that was essential to the well-being of Silveira House was a swarm of bees in residence. Fortunately when Father Dove arrived, he agreed with John and thus began a friendship, which has become ever deeper through the years. At that time, John was living in what was known as the second Hen House. Now that may seem very strange, unless you really know John. There are always many visitors at Silveira House and courses taking place and so, if you are the sort of person who likes to play a recorder at any hour of the day or night, or if you want time to compose poetry and think, this more unconventional accommodation can be very suitable.

John had a generous creative spirit, which he shared with all his friends. His love of God embraced all that was beautiful in God's creation – music, art, literature and nature itself. To go for a walk with John was revelation. Through his eyes one appreciated the wild life of the veld, trees, flowers and for him the song of a bird and the flight of an eagle were the crowning joys of the day.

What happy times were spent together at Silveira House and in our own home. He had a special affection for a Ciaconna by Pachelbel, which he would ask to hear on almost every occasion, singing the base line of the variations with great gusto. Music was a vital part of John and he expressed himself in music and poetry as naturally as he breathed. His thoughts flowed into poetry and his letters were poems. In fact, one felt that he was all spirit and that his closeness to God was manifest in all he said or did.

Heather used to visit John at Silveira where she noted the emergence of the serious poet: 'It was at Silveira House that I started to understand just how seriously John took his poetry.' She took him by surprise one day when he was in the middle of a line: he leapt up and swore! 'We didn't speak to each other for at least three weeks,' Heather remarked. Nevertheless she came back and notes: 'We had many good walks. John could be quite brilliantly witty – hilariously funny. Our mutual sense of humour sustained me through some torrid years. I always sought John out if I was unhappy – he was the best person to be with.'

She goes on to say: 'During these years he became more sociable and often visited my family. They all loved him, particularly my grandmother. She grew to think of him as the son she'd never had and they used to write to each other. He filled the time he spent with her spiritually comforting her one moment and making her laugh and laugh – the next. I was always delighted to hear them laughing together and to see her face light up when John came to visit her on the farm.'

It was about this time that Fr Peter, our African Jesuit, decided to hold a fête at the Mabvuku African parish. He co-opted the help of no less a personage than Lady Acton. Lady Acton attracted a clientele of young intellectuals, tough and willing to stand up against the (R.F.) Rhodesia Front. Lady Acton detested the R.F. She decided to use their talents for the fête. Mabvuku parish had never seen the like. The youth in particular were enthralled. They made money and caused the Rhodesia Front town superintendent's hair to stand on end! All of this put these young men in touch with John since they used to come to Silveira to discuss arrangements for the fête. One of them is now Fr Peter Sanders OP. The others have married and scattered. They all took to John and visited him whenever they could.

In September of 1966 we had a huge bush fire. Grass stands at 7 feet and higher in the bush and becomes as dry as matchwood in the winter season. Small boys are wont to put a light to this grass with a view to chasing out game. Normally the Chief orders the burning of the bush veld about three weeks before the rains are due.

A bush fire is a terrifying sight. Flames leap up to 20 feet as a sea of fire moves swiftly in the wind. If there are enough people one can burn ahead of the fire, but in a wind this can get out of hand so easily too. At this time we had no helpers. Only dear old semi-blind Francis worked in the garden. John fought the fire like one possessed but it came right to the windows of the Mission. We lost 800 small trees: John walked around sadly counting the loss. He loved trees. In subsequent years with more help we have managed to burn fire breaks in early June.

On his long walks with the dogs John once descended to the old Mission below. The path leads down through woods and drops steeply in places over rock features across a little mountain stream. The dogs love this. At the bottom it flattens out and one passes the cemetery on the right and then on to the old church. The first person he met was old Fr Esser, well over 80 and since gone to his rest. He took John aside and told him not to look up at the bell tower since there were women up there and seemingly they were up to no good. John saw no one but consoled the old priest. The next man he met was an old African who had been in the Shona rebellion in 1896. He raised his walking stick, took aim and pretended to shoot John dead. He 'shot' everyone in like manner! On the way home the dogs suddenly stopped, hackles raised in fear. John noticed a grave. It was 'lion' Stephen's grave. He had been killed on the way back from the Mission to Salisbury in the 1896 uprising. That was quite a walk for John!

CHAPTER 33

An Eagle's Eyrie

One day, as John walked down the path to Chishawasha, he came across an eagle's eyrie. He wrote of this discovery which occurred on the Feast of St Thérèse of Lisieux – 3 October.

Upon the Feast of Little Sainte Thérèse
At maybe four o'clock of afternoon,
Leaving the track which cattle take to graze
On higher pastures from the vale, a loon
Together with his dogs took rest awhile
Nor dreamed that there nest eagle-pair in style.

But suddenly, as if by chance, he saw
Settle upon the summit of a tree
A single eagle seen not there before
By him, by whim, by fancy or by me:
The tree was leafless, rooted into rock,
A lofty sentry-post for taking stock.

No trick of fancy, though since morning Mass
The fellow had been meditating on
Some words therein that wheeled and would not pass
Proper of Sainte Thérèse, ablaze it sings
How bore her up the Lord on eagle-wings!

There was the eagle, poised upon the tree,
There perched the bird like silent bard elect,
There was the pointer to the Liturgy ...
Nested the rested eagle? I'd detect:
It wanted three days only till I'd find
An eyrie that was fork attuned, assigned.

He noted that the communion antiphon for the Feast of

St Thérèse read as follows:

> He led her about and taught her, and He kept her as the
> apple of His eye. As an eagle He has spread His wings
> and hath taken her, and carried her on His shoulders.
> The Lord alone was her leader (Deut. 32. 10–12).

This discovery remained with him long. He visited the site
as often as he could. At the end of the month on the Feast
of Christ the King, he wrote again of his eagles:

> Upon this Feast of Christ the King I've found
> These eagles have accustomed grown to me,
> Resenting not that I frequent their ground
> Of nesting, yet, was aught more wild and free?
> Their flight is swift and soft and silent, they
> Soar through the azure sky towards the sun,
> Often I watch them wheel, thrice softly aye
> Their lighting is upon the eyrie won;
> Beautiful is their woodland court, as King
> And Queen of all the sylvan part they bide,
> Never went aught more silently awing,
> Their courtiers are weaver-birds besides:
> Their jester is a blackcapped oriole
> Surely as I am Christ's and Mary's fool.

The poem is long, containing a diary of eagle events
throughout that hot October month. He notes that this
pair are harrier-eagles, grey in colour. He called the male
'Tierce' and the female 'Thérèse'. He believes that the
eaglet was hatched on the Feast of St Luke (18 October).

His fascination for eagles sprang from his pondering of
Holy Scripture. St John the Evangelist's crest is an eagle,
symbolising his high flying in the realms of the love of
God. The Shona believe that the bateleur eagle is a
messenger of God. All of this gave John a great longing to
have an eagle close at hand. He prayed for this and his
prayer was answered in a strange manner.

One day quite by chance he bumped into a man of some
artistic fame. He possessed a bateleur eagle. It had grown
up under his care since it was found as a little eaglet in
Botswana, I believe. He was very devoted to the eagle. This

good man was looking for a suitable home for his eagle while he went abroad. He was very particular about the type of home and after his meeting with John came out to inspect Silveira House. The north front view captivated him and he thought it would be an excellent place for his eagle. The spot chosen for the perch was the veranda of our sitting-room. John was thrilled: this was an answer to prayer.

Strict instructions were given about diet, exercise and handling. Finally, a large chest arrived with air holes at each side. The eagle was to be sent by air to meet his master when the latter had arrived in Malta by yacht from England!

The eagle arrived and was sat upon its perch. It was tethered by a long line (100 yards or more) of fishing tackle which enabled it to fly out to the rock in the near foreground. The line was weighted to prevent a too sudden jerk at the end of flight.

John was in bliss with his new care. Food had to be found; no less a delicacy than vermin! Chishawasha schoolboys were bribed to hunt for mice and rats. The front veranda became quite white with eagle droppings plus the remains of the evening meal. John only noticed the beauty of the beast!

The presence of the eagle caused quite a stir for the locals. Elders would address it as 'sekuru' (uncle), a term of respect for a messenger of the spirits.

A wild bateleur eagle came to visit him (or her). There was an interesting scene in which the two eagles bowed to each other in a mutual exchange of affection. The poor captive eagle longed to go off with such a charming mate.

One morning there was a strong wind blowing before Mass. The eagle loved the wind and took to the wing at once. Alas, the line broke: he was free but trailing a length of line in his flight. John's distress was immense. Everyone was despatched everywhere to search for this lost friend. He was not to be found.

He wrote a lament to the owner but never received an answer, nor any further communication. No doubt the owner was deeply upset. He loved his eagle and John and I thought that he had a quaint look of the eagle in a distant way. Sometimes people reflect in some manner what they love. This is certainly true of the saints.

Three months later John himself found the eagle suspended from a tree by its trace. It was intact and at peace. It was given a royal burial and at the inquest it was noted that the loss was due to a faulty trace! The moral must surely be not to keep such fine birds of the air chained to this earth in captivity. They should be allowed to go wild and free, winging high in the heavens.

An interesting postscript to this chapter has recently emerged. A year and a half after John's death an Indian friend of his asked me to say a Mass for John's intentions. After the Mass I had a visitor. We went to the room with the lovely north front view. I suddenly noticed out of the window, two very large birds on the ground close to the little end-room which John had inhabited. They looked like cocks to me but on closer inspection we discovered that they were wild eagles. We were both astonished. One seldom sees a wild eagle on the ground and never close to buildings. The eagles looked as though they did not know why they were there. They stayed for about three-quarters of an hour, looking vaguely in our direction. A passer-by put them up. They have a seven-foot wing span and in two or three sweeps they were up on the thermals, and soon reached the cloud line.

When pondering about this, the Mass came to my mind. Did John send the eagles? Sister Bona and the other African staff were all convinced that he had done so to say thank you for the Mass. I wondered. There seemed no natural explanation. For the Shona people the eagle is the messenger of the gods.

Two days later I went to Mutemwa with Agnes and other friends of John including Judith Countess of Listowel. After a Mass at Mutemwa with the lepers we went to the site of John's death. We said a prayer there and on looking up saw a most beautiful bateleur eagle circling low close to us with the white under-feathers of its wings shining in the sun. He circled three times and then headed off in the direction of Mutemwa. I kept silent, but the others all said that John must be very pleased with our prayers.

CHAPTER 34

Special Branch

On the 1 January 1967 Brother Fitz arrived. Brother Francis Fitzsimmons was a Jesuit Brother. He had been sent by the Superior, prompted by Jim's letter from a bench in Tel-Aviv, and was a great boon to Silveira House. He was a most practical and capable person and a good religious into the bargain. John accepted him as such. There was no sense of challenge here.

John continued his life as sacristan, secretary when letters needed to be typed, doorkeeper, custodian of the watch dogs and guest master. Brother Fitz respected John's way of life and prayer. He was musical and set about in earnest to seek for a keyboard for John. John longed to play and to sing as he played. With the help of Kit and Arthur Law a keyboard was found – a harmonium. This was duly installed in the chapel and John was up to all hours of the night playing and singing to the Lord. Africans are very musical and harmonise beautifully. John got little groups of them to sing four-part Glorias in Shona and many other hymns and introits. He used to address the girls as Agnes "Contralto" or Maria "Soprano". The chapel rang with plainchant, Bach and John!

Silveira House gradually acquired a feel for those who were oppressed. Oppression can take many forms, some of them violent – denial of civic responsibility, non-recognition of dignity, racialism, discrimination, low wages, oppressive working conditions, police-state methods. We

never went out to look for these things; they just came in
the doors and windows. Our aim was gradually to put out
a hand of sympathy to all areas of oppression.

The workers came to us early on, asking us to help them
understand the Industrial Conciliation Act. Their wages
were about half the requirements of the poverty datum
line. We learnt this by simple sums on the blackboard and
by many requests for help with the rent, medical aid, food,
clothing and the like. We decided to help them as best we
could. This brought the special branch of the police to our
Mission. Were we engaging in subversive activity? Were we
planning a general strike? What were we about?

I was out when they came first and so they met John.
There were two plain-clothes detectives. John sat them
down and gave them a beer and proceeded to tell them all
about the bird life at and around Silveira. What goes on at
the Centre? they asked. Oh, Africans come here. What for?
They come on courses. Enough of that – John reverted to
trees, and bees and the story of the eagle. They were
bemused if not confused, yet even enchanted! John wrote
of this incident:

> Silveira House commands a height,
> Stands for the King of Kings:
> Shines no less bright for black than white,
> For Reds spreads not her wings.
> Since Reds are fed on dreads and dreams
> Of good to man from godless themes.
>
> Silveira, like a city bright
> Set on a hill that flings
> Forth graceful rays for black and white
> Whilst raceless lays she sings.

He backed all that we tried to do for these poor victims of
oppression with his prayers and his compassion. His real
love, though, was for the destitute poor. Some came our
way and John took them in as royal guests. They went
away with his blankets, with his clothes, with his all.

CHAPTER 35

The Ocean, Bees, and Tension

Zimbabwe is a land-locked terrain – a high plateau for the most part. We at Silveira were 5,200 feet above sea level. This caused an occasional longing for the sea. It came about that John was offered a trip down to the sea coast of Mozambique – to Beira. Surprisingly he accepted the offer, especially since he was to be alone in a little chalet right beside the sea. He enjoyed the sea and the wine immensely. He recounted with glee that he never had to buy food since, if one ordered wine enough, food was provided free!

On his return he was very sad to note that Arthur Law's bees did not do well at Silveira. There were not enough trees and flowering shrubs at the time. He tried putting them in the forest but the honey was stolen and the hive destroyed.

This gave John a great desire for more bees, especially to act as custodians of his solitude. They, too, serve the Lord. They provide wax for the Paschal candle and are mentioned in the Easter liturgy, to say nothing of the honey. He prayed for bees and put syrup out in a little hive which he placed under his table by the open door of his cell. A wild swarm came and accepted his invitation. From then on I visited John in fear and trembling. One keeps one's distance from wild African bees!

In the short period since his death, bees have played a strange role. The case of Judy Joe, a lovely coloured woman aged 26, is perhaps the most extraordinary. Judy contracted cancer of the stomach at a young age. Her life was in disorder. She had a child, a dear little boy aged three, but no marriage. Other things were in disarray, particularly with regard to religion. After painful investigation and treatment Judy was confined to a hospital bed. The hospital chaplain, Fr Riederer, did not make much headway until he introduced Judy to the life of John. After all, an African woman in Soweto claimed to have been cured of terminal cancer through John's intercession. Judy came back to the practice of her faith with astonishing zest, settled her marriage, and rose from her hospital bed, sick though she was, to seek out John's grave and his beloved lepers.

She came out to Chishawasha, visited the chapel at Silveira House, where John's harmonium still sits, and then went on down to the Chishawasha cemetery to where John's grave is to be found in the 'martyrs' row. She carefully selected a few pebbles from the grave mound.

She then went down to Mutemwa, a run of nearly 90 miles, with cancer pain as her constant companion. She fell in love with the lepers and began a frantic campaign to collect money and old clothes for them. In a very short time, from a comparatively poor community, she collected a great deal. She was now at home being looked after by a wonderful mother. I used to visit her and she gave me a little receipt book to sign as she handed over a wad of bank notes for the lepers. Poor Judy began to sink. 'Will John help me to reach the Kingdom?' she enquired. 'I am a worthless creature. Two cents Judy!' All the while she never adverted to her cancer pain, always saying that the lepers suffered far more. She died, to the sorrow of all, with grace and in peace. Her mother at once knelt before a picture of John saying that she wanted a sign that her Judy was safe in the Kingdom. After all, Judy had done much for John's lepers.

Judy's house is a small bungalow beside a busy industrial road: lorries, cars, trucks, noise – nothing to attract the lovers of flowers and honey shrubs. No sooner was the prayer over when in came a swarm of bees. The queen sat on Judy's bed, then moved into a deep bedside drawer where she and the swarm took up residence beside the pebbles from John's grave, a photo of Judy at his grave-side, and a picture of John himself. It was a big swarm, and the neighbours all came to behold this happening, wondering what sort of girl that Judy was. Her mother thanked John, convinced that Judy had completed her short life in the safety of the love of Christ. There was much talk of the incident and the local press had an article with the heading, 'Miracle in Arcadia?'

The bees proved a boon for John, who was receiving too many visitors for his liking. He sat in his room with bees swarming in and out. In fact he sat and typed at the table under which was the hive. His bare legs acted as a buffer for the bees prior to entering the hive.

Heather was a visitor who also had to keep her distance, as she describes:

> Later on at Silveira House John moved out of the hen house into a small room at the far end of the main build-ing. Here he continued to type his poetry which was growing immeasurably in volume. He also experimented with different styles. He did this surrounded by a buzzing swarm of wild bees – the beehive was beneath the table on which he typed. I did not go in as my nerve failed me when wild bees swarmed around my head. They didn't bother John at all – he liked them. I used to stand and talk to him just outside the door, or he would read a poem to me which I would listen to in comparative safety.

In a sense this marked the build-up of tension in John. Silveira House was slowly becoming an institution: there were people everywhere, and more and more of these sought out John, trying to make him become more socia-ble, to invite him out to dine, to meet the family. One day John vented his wrath upon me, tearing open his shirt and displaying a nervous rash upon his chest. 'This is what your so-and-so friends do to me!' They were not my friends really: they came out to 'sit at the feet' of John. The desert hermits suffered in like manner. John loved the tale about Abbot Moses: ·Abbot Moses lived in a hermitage in the desert. One day he was warned of an impending visit by an eminent lawyer. At once he up and fled to the marshes. On the way he came across a pilgrim group. They greeted him. It was the lawyer, who enquired the way to Abbot Moses's hermitage. The Abbot dissuaded the lawyer from proceeding further, stating that Abbot Moses was nothing but a fool and a heretic!

There was many a time that John took to the bush. The increasing tension was much aggravated by the events surrounding the Borrowdale Passion play. John was persuaded to play the part of Christ. He felt that he could not get out of it. The play was quite excellent with John as the Christ. Producer and friends never knew what it cost him to go through this ordeal. They would probably write about how he enjoyed it – how sociable he was. Back at Silveira I knew the truth.

At about this time he acquired a gramophone record – Couperin's 'Lamentations of Jeremiah'. He took this to his cell and played it until he knew it note by note, cadence by cadence. He sang it beautifully. It reflected his mood.

One day in the garden he said to me: 'Dear friend, I must take to the road, I am of no use here.' I knew what he meant: he longed for solitude. People did not really understand this. Some thought him lonely; others thought that he was coming out of his shell, becoming more sociable. The opposite was true. He wrote vehemently:

> Bereft of solitude my spirit stands
> At point of being murdered by its lack,
> My breathing bursts for freedom from the bands
> Of converse binds my being front and back;
> Being alone to me is company
> With love the Fount of life in all that lives,
> The Triune Lord accords in unity
> Of solitary God as good He gives;
> Consult the self-sufficiency of God
> And leap from out the chains constraining man
> To think him lord of every step he's trod, –
> Call the tune, Piper, and enwall to plan:
>   Heavenly Pan, loose me from earthly bonds
>   Of cloying pleasure whereat joy desponds.
> 'In medio ecclesiae remain
> Amidst your Mistress Miriam and reign.'

What could he do? One could not just take to the road in Africa like Europe: distances were too great and the people too poor to give shelter to a white stranger. He agreed to wait for a sign from heaven.

To me he was of immense value: his prayer, his advice as guru to disciple. Moreover, he was accomplishing much in a practical way. Recently he had agreed to sleep at nights at a lonely cottage a mile down the road. The cottage belonged to the Sisters of the Little Company of Mary – 'The Blues' as they were known, Irish nursing Sisters who ran the big St Anne's Hospital in Salisbury. The cottage was their rest house but they were seldom there. In consequence it had been broken into eleven times. John used to go down on foot by moonlight with his little cat M'bebi following him with her tail in the air. A dejected Simba, the alsation, was ordered firmly to stay behind to guard Silveira with his dreaded big brother Huru.

CHAPTER 36

The Death of Simba:
Time to Move on

Poor Simba, the alsatian dog, fell ill and then was given an overdose of cortisone into the bargain. He just disappeared one Sunday. Huru and John found him on the Monday morning in a glade amid the long grass, serene with the dew upon his coat – quite dead. John's poem 'The Passing of Simba' is not one to overlook:

> What *was* it to you who but mused on afar
> As I passed from a bond to a free?
> While I sighed to my God and the Morning Star,
> 'Je ne meurs pas, j'entre dans la vie'.

> So the odd dog died and the long long grass
> Sighed, 'Lay him away by the pine
> Where eagle lies buried while over her pass
> Her peers that her presence divine.'

> There lies like a lion at rest in the shade
> Of the pines as they sigh like the sea
> Old Simba the strong: there's a song in the glade,
> 'Je ne meurs pas, j'entre dans la vie'.

> That dog and that eagle were friends in their life
> And they share a penultimate plot:
> She had never a mate, he had never a wife,
> But their strife's at an end, is it not?

He was found in the hay, on his tail was the dew,
On his nose was the warmth of the morn;
His friends were the many, his enemies few,
He knew his penultimate dawn.

But a better he finds where the zephyrs are light
Over ground not for passing away:
The wind was a cold and a cold was the night
As he died ... but he's better today.

What *was* it to you who but mused on afar
As I passed from a bond to a free?
While I sighed to my God and the Morning Star,
'Je ne meurs pas, j'entre dans la vie'.

John was always very positive about death, whether it be
for eagle, dog or man. It was the gate to life, fulfilment
'For me life means Christ and death is the prize to be won'
(Paul). He longed for it in a strange manner. 'Roll on the
Kingdom,' he used to say.

People came and went. Fr Peter was posted to a rural
Mission station. He took so long to make a move that John
came to his rescue and packed his things for him. Fr Peter
left on the coal lorry for Mondoro – worse, it broke down.
Fr Martin Thomas waited up for him. Martin, a dear gentle
soul, full of old English courtesy, was gunned down later
at St Paul's, Musami, along with Brother Conway and the
others.

Fr Raymond Kapito, a local Jesuit Father, took Fr Peter's
place. Then Bernard arrived, a lay Mission helper, who
wanted to discern about religious life. He got on well with
John. Finally, dear Chris Shepherd-Smith, with his young
boyish looks and simple faith, came to give a hand with
the youth. Chris was not a priest at that time; he was
halfway through the long Jesuit training. John took to him
at once. No one dreamed that the young Chris would be
gunned down before John. Chris was indeed a 'lamb of
God' who went to the slaughter house at St Paul's,
Musami, after he was ordained. He died with two fellow
Jesuits, Fr Martin Thomas and Brother Conway, and four
Dominican Sisters who were all stationed at St Paul's
Mission at that time.

While at Silveira House, Chris became a favourite of Kit
and Arthur Law too. He loved chocolate cake and Kit used
to make the very best! John found Chris refreshing; he was
perhaps a little pious at that time but he knew how to put
first things first on the climb to God. Chris felt absolutely
at ease with John, who never questioned his piety or 'old
fashioned' devotions.

Time moved on while John prayed and waited for a sign.
He typed letters and typed minutes and typed his poetry.
On one set of minutes he got so confused with the
verbiage that he wrote '... here the unqualified typist
disqualifies himself: please give these minutes to a China-
man to complete!' He then broke into a lovely poem about
Mashonaland called 'Now that April's Here':

> The swifts are scarce and mainly have departed
> The swallows flown for summer to the North
> And yet, since clime and time and space were started,
> What country knew than this less winter wrath?
> The random flocks of speckled guinea-fowls
> Roam in the wildness, roost above the knolls
> In great and ancient trees; the eagle-owls
> Cry to the stars in solitude, all souls!
> The beaming noontide dances in a haze
> Of heat along the limits of our ground,
> The butterflies delight amidst a blaze
> Of such fair weather as is rarely found:
> Mashonaland, this most amazing clime
> Befits you for eternity in time!
>
> Mashonaland stands not too high for heat
> And not too low for comfort in its rays,
> Season 'twixt Easter and the Paraclete
> Heavenly most me thinks for beaming days;
> Out and afar her panorama rides
> Nobly towards those rosy bounds where dreams
> A-tiptoe touch infinity, she glides
> Lightly along strong crests of golden seams;
> A granite, rolling land, manned terrain, yet
> Not less caressing to our sense, aright
> Drawn by her beauty, than a lady met
> In every valley here, on each clear height:
> None other is Mashonaland to me,
> God, than Thy Mother's garment, flowing, free!

It was in April 1968 that my leave came up. I asked John whether he would consider taking an excursion trip to see his mother in England and then to the Holy Land to pray about his future? He agreed and we took off more or less at the same time.

We met in London at Claver House. Fr Paul Crane SJ knew John well from his trips to Africa and agreed to put us up. Paul had stayed with us on many occasions and it was amusing to hear him and John discuss the world situation. John never read newspapers and never listened to a news broadcast. Paul, on the other hand, was informed. But Paul has a generous heart and he took to the spiritual dimension in John at once.

At Claver House John found a trapdoor on to the roof. There he sang the 'Lamentations of Jeremiah' faultlessly over London's chimney pots. He came down to Henley-on-Thames with me to visit my old mother. The parish church is next door. It was joy to say Mass with John alone in that lovely church which has a magnificent reredos. The parish priest, Canon Toplass, and the parish have generously supported John and his lepers ever since.

John spent a while with his mother in Devon, visited Hugh, his godfather, in Tavistock, singing the 'Lamentations' on his front doorstep, and then departed by train from Victoria Station, London. I was there to bid him a fond farewell. I might not see him again. He would decide in Jerusalem what move to take – whether to return to Africa or seek a 'cave' in Israel.

His journey was not without adventure. Once again, I bullied him into committing it to paper.

PART VII

JERUSALEM REVISITED – THE 2ND DIARY

I know the Wailing Wall as none has known
That odd Westend of God since it was raised ...
(J.R.B.)

CHAPTER 37

In Via: The Continental Express

Near the end of May this year, 1968, on a Feast of the Jesuits called 'Our Lady of the Wayside', my niece and three priests – Fathers Greensward, Colombine and Panama – saw me off at the boat-train which left Victoria at half past three ... With Ostend reached by dark, I caught the train marked Milano. When I was in and all set and the train was soon to move off, two young men joined me. One was black and one with white, both were from America, the white from California and the black from Texas ...

We had each been a man of few words till at about noon the train reached the Swiss Alps. Then we rushed from side to side of our compartment and babbled in awe of the sights and the heights, which seemed not of this world. We did not want to miss or to let one another miss a least part of the glory as the train passed through; and we changed fast, as I have said, from side to side, from window to window. Our speech grew to being much, though mono-syllabic in the main. Our minds had gone up to a realm where hearts keep young, eyes get clear with gazing on the best which Love or Lord has made for us to see, through which He signs to us to climb fast to the Fount of all that is fair and pure. The Californian said at one point. 'The people here must all go to heaven!' That seemed to sum it up ...

If my mind serves me well, I reached Milan by four o'clock on Saturday, the last Saturday in May. It was just over twenty-four hours since I had left London. When I had changed trains I was bound for Venice and for a ship to Israel.

The wide province of Venice which the train passed through seemed to me like a noble chant sung by God on the plain of man's prosperity: as though He were singing all the time, 'And behold, it is very good'.

We did not near Venice till twilight, and by the time that I stood at the portals of the station it was dark. But what a delightful darkness! 'In such a night, in such a night, and in such a night as this ...'

To reach the ship for which I was booked meant boarding a motor-launch close to the station and going in it down the Grand Canal, towards the docks and the open sea. It was pleasant enough and, more than pleasant, it was idyllic and irenic and sublime. I envied not one in a gondola as we proceeded like a dream on the dark reflecting water, watching the myriad lights that shone from the streets on the banks and from the stately ranks of magnificent buildings. I saw the great dome of Saint Mark's as we went, and too soon we arrived at the docks. I passed through the Customs and embarked in the Greek ship which would sail on her way within the hour. No time had been lost, my memory of Venice is as fleeting as a dream, attended by the lights of Fairyland.

CHAPTER 38

Jerusalem and the Wailing Wall

John's first port of call was Corfu and then on to Piraeus
via the Corinth Canal. He went ashore and walked the
seven miles into Athens, wanting to get a distant view, but
a clear one, of the Acropolis, 'so that distance might
enchant the more what near I saw enchanting, those eighteen years ago'.

On seeing the Acropolis he sat for a while and was
moved to write, from memory, a quotation from Socrates:

O Beloved Pan
And all you other gods that haunt this place,
Give me true beauty of the inward soul,
And may the outward and inward man be at one;
May I reckon wisdom wealth
And here such a quantity of gold
As a temperate man
And he only
Can bear and carry;
Is there anything else?
I pray the same for thee, my friend,
For friends have all things in common.

Later, when on board ship again, he handed these few
lines to a fellow traveller who seemed to him to be in
search of an earthly paradise.

The ship reached Haifa and John decided to take a train
towards Jerusalem. He said that he sat in decided relief

amongst strangers 'whose new-found Hebrew I did not know. Relatively speaking alone at last I relaxed: O beata soltudo!'

In Tel-Aviv he set out for the main bus terminal only to be hailed en route by the very man to whom he had given Socrates' words of wisdom. The man thought that John, the 'guru', looked hopelessly lost in the thoroughfares of this world. He helped him with his suitcase and put him on the right bus for Jerusalem!

In Jerusalem John headed for the big youth hostel. 'There I sat', he said, 'on the steps, an odd-looking youth with a grizzled beard and greying hair waiting for the hostel to open.'

Once he had deposited his suitcase he made off in search of the Wailing Wall. It was his intention to pray there by singing the 'Lamentations of Jeremiah' and the Little Office of Our Lady, both in the Latin tongue. He desired to pray for the Jews, but he also wished to know – Whither Lord? To a cave in Israel, to the source of the Ganges, or back to Africa?

The sight of the wall moved him to write as follows:

What a vast, awe-inspiring place, the most hallowed space of the most amazing praiser in the world, to wit, Juda! The towering floodlit wall with its huge slabs of stone, hewn and set in the reign of David at David's desire, to stand in defiance of every successive vicissitude, bearing witness to an invincible endurance: the stupendous, patient wall, like the inscrutable face of the God of an unconfounded choice! There it had stood for nearly three thousand years; and there I had stood too, for at least five minutes, gazing astounded at the Wall and at the praising Jews that faced it at its foot. And I wondered to myself: dare I bray there tomorrow in Latin amongst so much solid Hebrew? Dare I stand there seven times and bray aloud?

I walked back fairly fast to the Hostel on Mount Hertzl, and slept on the matter till Saturday came ... I had decided that my debut at The Wall should not be until after First Vespers of the Feast of Pentecost. These I heard in due course at the principal conventual church of the Franciscans, the Guardians, under God Incarnate, of the Land by Him made Holy. Then I went down to The Wall, no longer named The Wailing but The Western, and the time may have been between four and five. I went to the kiosk at the entrance to the sacred area and took a Jewish praying-cap and set it, as do Jews, on the back of my head. The Wall at the time was not thickly thronged and any resolute singer might be then distinctly heard by man, let alone by God whose ears record our inmost thought. With my back to the pagan West I faced The Wall and the graceful East, and I did as Juda does and kissed The Wall, and as Juda does I clutched it from time to time. And I sang the Lamentations of Jeremiah to the exact strains of Couperin, top-blast: Eleph, Beth, Chimal, Daleth, He. When I had concluded with this first singing no one seemed the better and no one seemed the worse. The Western Wall had not shaken; an Eastern, a Southern and a Northern Wall to the whilom temple of Solomon had not arisen; angels invisible had not made to my singing an audible accompaniment upon harpsichord and viol da gamba, more fully to befit the Great Couperin's work. But a Rabbi of the Hasedim, with a beautiful countenance, who had stood to my left said, 'Won't you sing something in Hebrew? Here is a book.' I replied that I knew no Hebrew and then he smiled and said, 'God will love you for what you have sung, of that I am sure.'

By the sunset of the Day of Pentecost I had sung there Couperin's Lamentations of Jeremy seven times, and things had remained as they stood. There had been some indications of pleasure by Jews, and by one a strong objection. There had also been getting together of heads, and many a curious or suspicious look; but by twilight of Whitsun the game seemed to be over, so I closed an angel-guarded play at the Old Stone Wall, and gazed up at The Plough when the twilight went. It seemed that The Plough was for pointing beyond ...

The moral of such a rigmarole might be this: Christ the Perfect Jew who converted eleven disciples and established twelve apostles, all Jews, to convert the World, will alone convert his people Israel to Himself.

He will be their Glory, the Word-made-flesh. For this He will not know need of an agent, even of an ass that brays in Latin at a Wall towards Midsummer. 'Nothing succeeds like success' is a favourite maxim of the world, but nothing succeeds better to the throne of grace than absolute failure sustained with no trace of bitterness: and the best criterion of that is the fact of Calvary. Shalom! From there the sweet waters come, whereat 'the wild asses quench their thirst' (Psalm 104).

Here the diary ends. It dispelled any notion that John had that he was called to be a modern apostle for the conversion of Israel. it was clear to him that he must return to Africa – his vocation lay there.

He had already discovered that there was no chance to sail down the east coast of Africa to Mombasa and even to Beira. The Arab-Israeli war prevented such a venture. He thus decided to make for his brother Philip in Tripoli. He felt sure that Philip would find a way for his return to Zimbabwe. Alas, no overland route seemed feasible.

Philip eventually wrote to me. In consequence John was put on a flight to Rome by Philip. In Rome Fr Bernard Hall SJ took him in hand and put him safely upon a Mission charter flight heading for southern Africa. He finally put down in Salisbury and was soon home again in his little cell in Silveira House – but not for long.

PART VIII

RETURN TO AFRICA – THE THREE WISHES

I left Mashonaland for twenty weeks
And during five whole months my soul
asked why?

(J.R.B.)

CHAPTER 39

Mutemwa:
The First Wish

John was only back a few months when Mutemwa loomed up like a dark cloud. Mutemwa in Shona means 'you are cut off'. Here there was a leper settlement for about a hundred lepers. It had once been a huge leprosarium with more than a thousand lepers, but now with the wonder drug, Dapsone, most of these had returned to their villages while other live cases had been evacuated elsewhere. The remnants were either badly deformed or unable to return home for one reason or another.

Government social welfare had left this poor remnant in the care of an African Warden, an ex-policeman, and a few orderlies. They were given huts, scant rations, some clothing and blankets, Dapsone, but no love.

In Europe the Christian backcloth has pervaded for long enough to enable even post-Christian man to have some feelings of charity about his neighbour – call it humanism if you like. Within the traditional African tribe one helps one's extended family. Old people, for example, are cared for within the tribe. Lepers, as in biblical days, are feared, sometimes outcast, although the people like them to die at home. During the war of liberation a white patrol came across a cave in the mountains in which about a dozen lepers lived. Thus the African caretakers of Mutemwa had little or no time for the lepers. They did a job as a job: that was all.

Their plight was noticed by the wife of the local district magistrate. She began to seek a remedy.

Heather Benoy got to hear about Mutemwa and decided to visit the settlement with John. She wrote about this adventure as follows:

It was I who told John about the Leper Colony at Mutemwa. I cannot remember when I heard about it except that it sounded terrible. There was a plan to send the lepers back to their villages. This was unthinkable because many of them had been there for years and Mutemwa was their home; also, some came from Malawi and elsewhere.

Anyhow, John and I decided to visit the colony, which was about 87 miles from Salisbury, in March 1969. I think all who saw the colony at this time were deeply shocked by the conditions which existed. I for one was keen to leave. Imagine my shock when John announced that he wasn't coming back with me – he planned to stay. I was amazed and horrified and begged him to be reasonable. I pointed out all the reasons why he couldn't stay – what on earth would I tell Fr Dove – I've left John behind for good! I was close to tears and quite angry. Finally John agreed to come back to Silveira – only so that he could collect his meagre possessions and typewriter. I breathed a sigh of relief thinking that was that. However, on the way back he said: 'Damn you, Benoy, for taking me there; you know I've got to stay!' I thought he was being a little over-dramatic. How wrong I was. A while later John moved to Mutemwa and never left it again.

When he returned with Heather that evening he spoke of Mutemwa to me as a valley of dark depression. He wrote this verse soon after the visit:

In that I've always loved to be alone
I've treated human beings much as lepers,
For this poetic justice may atone
My way with God's, whose ways are always helpers;
I did not ever dream that I might go
And dwell amidst a flock of eighty such

Nor did I scheme towards it ever, No
The prospect looms not to my liking much;
Lepers warmly to treat as human beings
Is easy to the theorist afar,
Near to my heart from bondage be their freeings,
May it be flesh not stone, O Morning Star!
Miriam, shine, sweet Mistress, in thy name
Salvation wake, lepers make leap, unlame!

In the meantime the wife of the magistrate contacted Fr
Geoghegan of the Catholic Archdiocese. He in his turn
consulted the Jesuit Mission Superior, Fr Edward Ennis SJ.
Could anything be done? Fr Ennis looked around and
eventually contacted John. Would he go as Warden of the
Leper Settlement? John would go alright but he hated the
idea of being Warden which involved book-keeping and
administration; worse – to have orderlies under him; this
was the last straw. He went, and I watched him go, on 1
August 1969. Fr Ennis collected him and his few things
from Silveira House. I was so sad to lose him but glad for
the lepers. It was an answer to prayer and the fulfilment of
his first wish – to work with lepers.

I went down to Mutemwa a week later to see how he
was settling in. One goes north-east from Silveira to
Mutoko. The settlement is two miles beyond – 87 miles
from Silveira House. One passes through some fine rocky
country, crossing three major rivers – the Nyagui, the
Shavanhohwe near St Paul's, Musami, and the Nyadiri
close to where Pauline lives.

Finally, one reaches Mutoko, which is a dorp – a village.
It was a staging place, before sanctions and the war en
route to Blantyre, Malawi, and had a small hotel, two
garages and some stores. The hotel closed during the war.
There is still a post office. It is a centre for local farmers
and has an African bus terminus with beer hall, shops and
an African hotel. Beyond this one turns off on to a dust
road, leaving the little government hospital on one's right.
The dust road then drops down to the leper settlement,
flanked on the left by Mutemwa Mount and on the right by
Chigona Mount. In the distance one can see the Inyanga
Mountains.

The settlement consists of about 100 square huts built in lines. The huts are on the left of the road which has a fine avenue of Jacaranda trees. Mutoko is lower than Salisbury and everything is sandy and dry and hot.

John describes the descent to Mutemwa:

> As you come down, as adown you must
> On the winding road in its load of dust,
> A wide panorama and wild you scan
> Capriciously free from the hand of man,
> The landscape goats and delights to skip
> In the green that rhymes with summertime's grip
> Or, if in the waning of winter you come
> While spring is a-gaining, you'll sing or be dumb
> With wonder at seeing an avenue long
> Of blue jacarandas whose bloom is their song, –
> Stand strong in their century these.

At the far end of the camp there is a small one-roomed store which had been used as a butchery when the camp was large.

This was John's abode at the beginning. He soon settled in with his typewriter, a big basket of medicines, and some old calendar pictures on the walls. He had a bed and a mosquito net: not much else. He was already involved after only a week. One could see that he had found his journey's end. He summed up his task in a few lines:

> ... I made a point
> of visiting each house throughout this vale
> Compounding of deep woe and joy as deep,
> This little fold Mutemwa with its sheep,
> And since that morning I have daily tried
> To see each living one
> For whom God's Son has died.

Fr Ennis, the magistrate's wife, and a Rhodesian farmer formed a small committee named 'The Friends of Mutemwa'. Social welfare delegated the care of Mutemwa to them but continued to give an allowance of five Rhodesian dollars (about £3.50) per leper per month for food. Obviously more funds were needed and more medical help.

CHAPTER 40

'All Souls' and Early Days

Eleven miles from Mutemwa to the north there is a Catholic Mission named All Souls Mission. The present Archbishop, Patrick Chakaipa, was the Superior there at the time. In 1969 a little group of Italian medical lay missionaries came to All Souls to take over the running of the Mission hospital. They also agreed to take Mutemwa under their wing. Dr Marialena, Sister Caterine and Sister Maria began to visit Mutemwa regularly. Soon the leper settlement was lifted up by John and these good Sisters from squalor and neglect to care and love. The lepers became people and rejoiced in being children of God with the prospect of becoming 'That which has not yet been revealed'.

At the end of the year Dr Marialena was replaced by Dr Luisa Guidotti. John and Luisa were to work as a team. They were destined for great things and great suffering, even martyrdom, as events will show.

John was so happy in those early years. He soon knew every leper by name and their needs and their likes and dislikes. He became the eyes for the blind, ears for the deaf, fingers and feet for the maimed. He carried them, bathed them, fed them, kept long vigils with them in their sickness, buried them when they died. 'Gosh! It is good of them to have me,' he said, 'it is bad enough having leprosy without having John.' He wanted to identify himself with them, become the least amid them – yes, he even wanted to contract leprosy. 'I am a leper,' he said. We managed to get him to put such thoughts aside. We told him that he would be segregated to a white leprosarium if he contracted the disease. He took more care after that.

Fr David Gibbs, based at All Souls Mission 12 miles beyond Mutemwa, came to know John intimately. He gives us a pen sketch of John's day at Mutemwa:

John's day began in a sense at dusk with the chanting of the evening office in his hut. The night hours were his, unless there was a death or a very sick leper in the compound, to be spent in prayer and meditation and, 'when the Muse came', in writing poetry. In the early hours of the morning he would run a mile, 'just to keep fit', have a quick wash in the plastic basin outside his front door, and then set off for the compound to open the church in preparation for the morning communion service. A priest would visit Mutemwa each week for Mass and on the other days John would hold the morning service, reading from the Bible, reciting the morning prayers, administering the Blessed Sacrament and playing the organ.

The voices die away, the organ stops, the doors are opened and the lepers file out led by 'Baba' [father] John carrying a basket. As the lepers come out of the chapel, having just received the Body of Christ, they stop to chat to Baba John. Some just say 'hello', others ask for medicine for a headache, a cough, a cold, malaria, itching body or sore eyes. 'Baba' delves into his basket and produces a bottle, a tube, a few capsules, an ointment, a cream or just a few sweets for those who need cheering up. There is something for everybody. Spiritually fulfilled, materially helped, the lepers move off to their huts happy, cared for and at peace with God and with each other. Some walk, others crawl and still others are wheeled away in wheelchairs.

After the last leper has gone to his hut, 'Baba' John puts away his basket, closes the harmonium, shuts the church and makes his way slowly down the avenue towards his hut to have his breakfast.

John lived on bread, cheese, coffee, lactogen

[powdered milk], orange juice and the occasional egg, giving away most of what he was given to the lepers. 'After all,' he said, 'the lepers need these things more than I do.' He didn't believe in saving anything. The lepers were always needing something and John was always receiving just what they needed at the time they needed it, or else money would find its way to Mutemwa in time to buy what was wanted in the compound. 'Help', John was fond of saying, 'always comes from somebody.' He received clothing, food, medicines, and numerous other gifts which he used to make the lives of the lepers more bearable – snuff, pipes, sweets, sacks of nuts, powdered milk and fresh meat. All sorts of gifts came from all sorts of people – all were passed on to the lepers and all were used to help them.

Once breakfast was over, John went back to the compound for his 'rounds'. He visited every leper every day just to make sure that all was well. If anybody needed any help, John was there to give it. He would bath those who needed bathing, build fires, make beds, change dressings and give out whatever he had received or bought for his people. At the beginning of the 'round' his wheelbarrow was always full – full of sugar, tea, sweets, onions, vegetables, nuts, tomatoes, bread, meat – anything he had to give out. By the time he reached the chapel for the midday Angelus, the barrow was empty and each leper had been helped in some small way.

After a period of quiet in the presence of The Lord, the afternoon would be spent in much the same way – cutting firewood, cleaning out the cattle grid, collecting reeds for making hats, making tea or coffee for the sick or just popping in to chat and cheer up the people. Once or twice a week John would go up to the village to do the shopping for the lepers. For those really ill or dying, John would buy something special at the village – perhaps fresh oranges, an egg or two, an extra portion of milk or a pint of 'real' milk. On his return from the shopping he would visit his 'special' patients – those seriously ill at the time – and help them to get their fire lit, bed made, pipe filled, coffee boiled or whatever other small tasks needed to be done.

Sometimes he would simply crouch on his haunches and chatter away, trying to help and encourage.

At a death John was always present to give comfort to the dying and to all the lepers who were losing a dear friend. In a small community like Mutemwa a death affects everybody very deeply and John helped the lepers, even those who had no beliefs, to see that death was, in most cases, a blessed relief from many years of suffering and the opening of the door to joy, peace and happiness.

At about four o'clock the bell rang for the saying of the rosary and evening prayers in the church – held early so as not to coincide with the lepers' evening meal at five o'clock. After the last leper had left the church, John would lock up, pop in to see anybody who might need help to settle down for the night and then make his way down the avenue back to his hut to spend the night alone with his God, singing, praying, writing or just sitting quietly in the presence of his Maker.

In his early happiness he wrote some lovely poetry about Mutemwa and about the lepers too. One of his poems describes the leper community:

> This people, this exotic clan
> Of being less yet more than man
> As man is worn today:
> This is a people born to be
> Burnt upward to eternity!
>
> This strange ecstatic moody folk
> Of joy with sorrow merged
> Destined to shuffle off the yoke
> Of all the world has urged:
> This oddity, this Godward school
> Sublimely wise, whence, I'm its fool!

CHAPTER 41

Mutemwa Chapel and the 'Ark'

One thing was missing at Mutemwa – a decent chapel. There was an old derelict chapel which Archbishop Chichester had built years before when the camp was big. This was no longer suitable for Mass. Mass was said in a hall up beyond the camp. It was too far for the lepers to crawl. John discussed the possibility of a chapel with his friend Arthur Law, who drew a plan of a rondavel chapel with a thatched roof. John was delighted and took the plan to Fr Ennis. It was approved in 1970 and money came from kindly benefactors.

The opening of the chapel was a day never to be forgotten. A second harmonium had been found. John had taught the lepers plainchant and hymns, mostly ancient and not modern! They sang in Shona but John's evaluation of their singing is clearly recorded:

This Cohort, mixed, mercurial,
This battered, tattered throng
Goes halt towards its funeral,
Vaults to the Lord in song –

Song, and as harsh cacophony
You'd hardly ever find,
But hearts preceded harmony
And The Sacred doesn't mind!

> Martial, no threnody's the sound,
> It storms high heaven's gates
> Whence the sounded God who trod sits crowned
> And the King of Glory waits.

The chapel would only hold 50 so the invited guests were few. The lepers had to have priority.

A friend of John's, a French priest whom John called 'Pear Peachon', got wind of the opening. This good Father was way out beyond Mutoko at a brand new bush Mission. He prepared a little surprise for John and came in bringing with him on his lorry some 40 or more children equipped with drums, rattles and all that was modern in Shona music. They literally invaded the chapel and took over the choir, the music, the lot. Invited guests had to stay without. The Archbishop, undaunted, blessed and opened the chapel. The children went wild with song and dance, smashing John's treasured statue of St Joseph. The last straw was that they, poor children, were expecting lunch. John was furious, calling 'Pear Peachon' a gatecrasher and goodness knows what!

Later in the day he consulted holy writ. The passage that fell open before him concerned forgiveness. He at once smote his breast and wrote an apology in verse to 'Pear Peachon'! They were friends again!

John built a little Ark in his room – a pyramid of many colours, ribbons, pictures and holy ornaments. It was the dwelling place for his Bible – the Word of God. John's 'Ark' became quite famous. He had it until his dying day.

One day 'Pear Peachon' visited him and leant upon the Ark. John remonstrated with him. 'What's wrong – 'cest une idole,' retorted 'Pear Peachon'! John withheld his fury.

Not long after this John was persuaded to visit 'Pear Peachon'' at his Mission and to see his very modern church which he had built unbeknown to the Archbishop. On return to Mutemwa John remarked, 'It was good to get back to Israel out of Egypt.'

John was old-fashioned and intolerant in many ways and one could get a rise out of him, but he knew how to laugh at himself and always, unfailingly, was lavish in forgiveness.

John's dear friends Kit and Arthur Law remember those early days at Mutemwa, and wrote about them with much warmth:

John went to Mutemwa and, in doing so, experienced a fulfilment. He often used to say to us that he felt he had come 'home'. John's love of his fellow men extended far beyond the bounds of conventional charity. He loved as Jesus loved. To him, the lepers were his family. There was a deep personal relationship. They were Peter, Joshua, Hanzu to mention only a few. If he happened to be away from them for a short while, it troubled him. 'What if someone has taken ill and needs me?' he would say. He cared for them in the true sense of the word and they, in turn, gave him love and friendship. When we visited John at Mutemwa, we also visited his 'family' and were introduced to them all. One never came away from there without feeling spiritually refreshed. There was always something special to remember about our visits. The chapel was John's pride and joy. It was a warm homely place – really the heart of the village, sanctified by prayer. Music was provided by a harmonium, which John loved to play and Shona words were sung to well-known hymn tunes and even plainsong Gregorian chant. Whenever we were with John there was music. I remember one day when we were painting at the dam, with John sitting on a rock singing the office in Latin.

On two occasions, on our arrival, we were met by John in great distress – a sick leper had to be taken to the hospital at All Souls Mission immediately; so our car became an ambulance and off we went with the patient and handed him over to the late Dr Luisa, who soon had the sufferer in her capable hands and another life was saved. I shall never forget the day when we were taken with Brother Fitzsimmons SJ to see the Hamerkop's nest.

John was quite determined about this. It was a very hot day and the path took us through the bush, briar and mud at the edge of the river – our enthusiasm was waning a little by the time we reached the nest but John was so excited that we all agreed that the excursion was well worth while. Another day, it would be the fish eagle at the dam or the crystal pools at the top of the mountain, and off we would go! There was a beautiful jacaranda avenue leading into the village and a very vivid picture emerges of John coming to meet us carrying his basket of medicines after doing his 'rounds' morning and evening.

His home expressed his personality. The West Country calendar sent by his mother each year was a reminder of his affection for Devon, where he spent a good part of his youth. The Ark, which held pride of place was covered with symbols of his faith. He had a great love and admiration for the Jews. For him, too, the Ark represented Our Lady, for, as the Ark of the Covenant had held the scrolls of the Jewish faith, she had contained the Living Word, which was made flesh and dwelt among us. Every picture, every object in his dwelling had a special significance for him. This was obvious wherever he lived, whether it was in a room at Silveira, the old butchery at Mutemwa, a tent on the mountain or a tin shack. He transformed it into a place of welcome where, being with John, brought one closer to the spiritual things if life.

Poems to read, discussions, picnics under the mango tree – one could never leave Mutemwa easily. John loved to talk and there were so many things to talk about with him!

John was truly at home in Mutemwa. It reminded him of his first glimpse of true 'home' away back in India. These lines bring the past into the present:

> Faint is aroma here of cowdung dried
> And redolent of woodsmoke in this whole
> Magical region, legion here have died
> Long having suffered much, body and soul:
> Yet Fairly part is this, and linked for aye
> With Hindoostan's *contemplative* array.

CHAPTER 42

Pauline and Mass at Mutemwa

Pauline Hutchings, the wife of a Rhodesian farmer, came across John in a strange yet providential manner. She wanted to become a Catholic but did not know of any priest for miles around. She heard of me through a religious programme on the radio and she wrote to enquire what to do. On learning that her farm was not too far from Mutoko I concluded that John was the answer to her prayer. He could instruct her. The year was 1973. She wrote of her experience which led to a close friendship, and resulted in her taking the lepers under her motherly wing after John's death.

> From my home in the Mrewa/Mutoko district I can see Mutemwa mountain on the horizon. The leper settlement lies near the big mountain at the foot of a smaller mountain called Chigona. Fr John Dove SJ asked John if he would be prepared to instruct me in the Catholic Faith as there was no priest near by. Happily John agreed and my memorable instruction began on the running track which John had made on top of Chigona.

Chigona Mount became a favourite haunt for John. He wrote about his beloved 'Chigona':

> When every morn I walk through this enclosure
> Wherein our sheltered leper-folk abide

I look upon Chigona's bright composure
Backed by an azure sky where falcons glide:
And then meseems our village is a ship
Riding at anchor on the ocean's lips.

Pauline received all her instruction upon Chigona without book or paper – 'He fired my heart instead,' she wrote, ending with a little verse of her own.

Chigona, the enchanted mountain
Wove a spell around us
From which I hope we won't escape
For more than friendship bound us.

She goes on to recount:

Those were the early days, before John's confrontation with the Leprosy Association. After the weekly Mass we would go to John's little concrete box house, a disused butchery, perched against the side of Chigona. There we would breakfast on coffee and marmalade sandwiches – John's Wednesday treat. 'You make them in the nicest way, with more butter and marmalade than bread. That's the way I should make them myself!' he said ...
He hardly ever ate meat, but cheese, milk and eggs he welcomed. However, he would never keep a surplus for himself but gave it away, which tended to annoy his friends at times! Fresh oranges and orange juice he always appreciated but Lactogen was really what he survived on, although he had periodic qualms of conscience about himself drinking milk which babes might be in need of. John wanted to be thin. He said he could pray better on an empty stomach.

... thin
In body get and let your sin
Batten no more on fattened sides ...
Go lightly as a Cherubim ...

John was fascinated by the early Christian Stylites and their founder. St Simeon Stylites. Stylites were solitaries who lived on top of pillars. These pillars varied in height and the platforms, sometimes made more habitable by a small hut, were generally provided with a parapet against which the Stylite would lean for his scanty sleep. Food was supplied by disciples or admirers. Apart from prayer a Stylite would give instruction from his pillar to disciples and seekers below.

Pauline gives us her further impression of Mass at Mutemwa:

> Mass at Mutemwa was a unique experience: it was in Shona but the rubrics were as for English Masses. John played the harmonium – Gregorian hymns to which the lepers sang in Shona. He gave me a prayer book and I soon became one of the congregation. I cannot adequately explain the atmosphere and the graces of these Masses. Somehow, kneeling before the priest among all those physically wretched people, taking one's turn in the line-up for Confession at the side of the altar, with John 'ad libbing' on the harmonium, lifted one right away from the daily problems. John's whole bearing in that little church made one know that the King was in the tabernacle and could one but move the veil, one would see Him face to face. John knelt right down when he genuflected, something one felt drawn to imitate.

Heather's impressions of Mass at Mutemwa were of surprise:

> Imagine my amazement to hear Gregorian plainchant sung in Shona determinedly led by John simultaneously and strenuously playing a pedal organ. I must confess this serious and energetic liturgy had me often close to bursting with laughter. John didn't dare stop pedalling until all sound died.

She then observed:

> One of the things which happens in a leper colony is that the people all begin to look entirely normal. One ceases to notice that lips or noses or hands or feet are

missing. I used to feel a sense of surprise when visitors, who sometimes came with us, were so upset by what they saw. These people had charming dispositions and great humour. They unceasingly helped each other and were close – sharing each other's troubles and pains and laughter.

CHAPTER 43

Blind Peter

To say Mass at Mutemwa was a rare privilege. The little round 'rondavel' chapel was always full. Some lepers sat on the built-in seat round the wall, the rest sat or squatted on mats on the floor. The Mass started with Confession. I used to sit at the back of the altar and the lepers would crawl to my chair, the blind led by those with sight. Meanwhile John played loudly on the harmonium in case any should overhear the secrets of the soul. Perhaps I heard least and, in great humility, gave absolution to fortify them in their earthly plight.

At Communion time one did the rounds led by John. We climbed over or leant over the front rows in order to reach the back. The blind always sat in the same place against the wall. John tapped each under the chin with the communion plate when it was their turn. Mouths opened and shut with a loud 'Amen'. John's 'Domus Dei' recalls this memorable event:

> Four blind philosophers – Domenico,
> Peter, Thomas and Zachariah called,
> Sit as in senate roundly while I go
> Giving Communion where Christ is walled:
> May evermore these four adorers sit
> Where Gospel-Makers sing and merit it.

The blind ranked among John's special friends. There

were ten totally blind lepers in the camp at that time. John
notes this in a verse entitled 'The Vision of the Blind':

> All ye who see with eyes
> That earthly sights apprize.
> Give ear a little while to this my song:
> There are near where I dwell
> Ten lepers, blind as well,
> And, out of four score people in our throng
> Of motley lepers here,
> They shine with secret cheer,
> Their vision of our hidden God is strong.

Undoubtedly his favourite among the blind was Peter.
Peter has lost his nose as well as his sight. His face looks
for all the world a skeleton until he smiles: it is then transformed. He is deaf too and with no fingers or toes combats
the task of living out 'life' with a serenity amazing to
behold. John used to love to bath Peter and Peter enjoyed
his bath most of all. He was ticklish and bubbled with
mirth. On hearing of John's death Peter in his lament cried
out, 'Who is it that will bath me now?' John wrote of Peter:

> Empty of eyes, your face
> Is all a smile of grace,
> A sight that gives a brightness unallowed:
> Your soul it is that shows
> And outwardly it glows
> Declaring even blindness is enjoyed!

> I, when the night is deep,
> Survey the starry steep
> And strive to pierce its infinite beyond;
> But, Peter and the blind,
> More peaceful is your mind
> And you achieve what I have never conned:
> Your fellowship surveys
> What passes sight, – the rays
> Of hidden Light conduct you like a wand!

CHAPTER 44

Visits to John

It was fun to visit John in his solitary tin hut in the early days. He greeted one profusely on arrival and with a twinkle in his eye used to say:

Like a vodka?
Yes, I'd love one.
Haven't got any. Did you bring any brandy?
Yes.
Don't tell Stephano [a leper with a wooden leg].
No doubt he'll sniff it out. I'll give him some anyway.

He then brought out a mat and spread it under a mango tree. He had no table or chair at that time. I had brought a picnic basket. When one asked for water, he would produce an ancient watering can and pour out into cracked cups. He would talk and talk. After lunch we would climb Chigona. On top, in the rainy season, there was a natural pool. This was his bathroom. Sometimes I would stay till after supper, sitting out with him as the evening drew in, listening to him reading poetry and talking about the things of God. He would often ask for absolution on these monthly visits – sometimes on top of Chigona.

Heather often drove down with me in those early days and describes them vividly:

We used to look forward to these visits immensely, leaving early for the 87 mile drive and moving back into the setting sun through the magnificence of huge granite kopjies.

On these trips we always had a picnic lunch with

chicken, sometimes wine and other delicacies for John
to eat.

:John would eat very little, preferring only a glass of
wine. These days were filled with a mixture of merri-
ment and serious discussion about the lepers. We would
go through the camp greeting all of them, giving out
oranges, cigarettes, snuff, or new batteries for their
camp radios. The radios were usually strategically
placed under mango trees so that many could share the
pleasure of the music. John quickly picked up the local
dialect and went round the camp greeted by much
warmth and laughter.

People were greatly attracted to John and he was
never short of visitors. People would discuss him
endlessly, be it peasants round a fire or sceptics at at
smart dinner party. He remained a mystery to all save, I
think, Fr Dove, who understood the path that John had
chosen. I certainly never did until our last meeting one
month before he was killed. John had a great personal
charm which even drew a response of warmth from
hardened soldiers – victims of the terrible war. They
sought something from him – it might have been an
innate curiosity to glimpse the nature of an otherwise
remote Creator – it might have been his humour or
eccentricity or the personal interest which he showed in
everyone. More often than not when I would pitch up at
his dwelling in a distraught state I'd find myself forced
to laugh at myself after some time.

I sometimes thought him quite mad and lacking in
reason, especially when he lived in the hen house at
Silveira, giving names to all the hens, wearing a ribbon
in his hair – refusing to wear glasses because Moses
never had any – giving away all his clothes, food, gifts –
when he obviously needed them.

CHAPTER 45

Mutemwa: Christmas
and the New Year

People began to think about gifts for John and his lepers in late November, especially those who taught in schools. Sisters Julia and Trinitate collected old clothes in particular, while both Kit Law and Mary Scrase got their children at school to make cards and toys and to collect food parcels and all manner of good things. The Sisters at the Convent and at the hospital helped in all of this. The result was 90 hampers done up with coloured paper containing sweets, biscuits, snuff, candles, cigarettes, with toys for the children and orphans. It was my job to go round to collect all these gifts in the Mission truck. We stored them awaiting the great day.

I usually had two Masses at the Mission before I was able to leave for Mutemwa at about 9 a.m. We then set out hoping to arrive at Mutemwa at about 11 a.m. Christmas falls in the middle of the wet season and so one prayed for a dry day. When it rains it often rains in inches, not millimetres. One Christmas, early on, it was terribly wet. Frightening storms had poured down volumes of water, causing flooded rivers, mud, and felled trees. The new road to Mutoko was not completed. One went by the old strip road. Alas the ford over the Nyadire River was in full-flood – a veritable torrent. There was a queue of people and cars waiting for the waters to subside. Two Africans asked for a lift saying that they knew another route which would cross the river over a low bridge much further upstream. I decided to take them and allow them to guide us. We went miles through farms, bundu, and via tracks in the wilderness. I stopped at a remote farm, knocking on the door. A big burly European farm assistant, dressed in khaki shorts, shirt, and paper hat, opened the door. I saw plum pudding and wine on a rough table. Old traditions and customs find a home in far away foreign lands. He directed me on my way. It was already 2 p.m. We found the low bridge crossing over the Nyadire River and eventually reached Mutoko and Mutemwa at 4 p.m. instead of 11 a.m. John and the lepers had guessed our plight and were still hopeful about our arrival. The torrential rain had eased by now, although the canvas canopy of the truck had let in some water. Colours were running on the hamper boxes and some biscuit packets were sodden. Not to mind – the hampers were received with delight. I said the Mass of Christmas Day at about 5 p.m. while John at the harmonium regaled us with carols. After the Mass we did the rounds of the huts, acting as Father Christmas. The lepers were overjoyed. Stephano was on the look out for a tot of brandy. I whispered, 'Later.'

When all was done we retired to John's hut. There were a few special hampers for John including wine and brandy. He always ate at Christmas – cold chicken, cold plum pudding and about half a box of chocolates. We had a few drinks too. Stephano and friend were soon in sight hobbling shyly up to John's hut. They all got a stiff tot and anything else going. The war was not in those parts and so I could stay late. Sometimes John came back with me to Silveira on Christmas night and would stay until near the New Year. Heather adds a footnote about Christmas fare:

I remember well at Christmas. I was given an excellent bottle of South African wine. Feeling in a self-sacrificing mood, I decided to give it to John for Christmas. He thanked me for it with his usual enthusiasm and exuberance. I felt pleased. The next time we met I asked him how he had liked it. Again, with great enthusiasm he said it was marvellous. He and the lepers had had a great party. They ·had a drum of Chibuku beer [beer made from maize] – into which John had poured several gift bottles of brandy and my special rare wine. If we left a roast chicken or a new shirt, we knew very well that, as soon as John had waved us out of sight, he gave them all away to the lepers.

Father David Harold-Barry SJ joined the Mission staff at Silveira in September 1973. He had met John on only a few occasions but came to know him better than anybody in the years that followed. (David, in my absence, arranged the Requiem for John and preached the funeral oration).

I used to say the Christmas Mass at Mutemwa, but David always saw the New Year in with John and said the Mass for New Year's Day. David not only tells of this annual event but adds his own shrewd observations:

It became a tradition that I would go to Mutemwa on New Year's Eve to welcome in the New Year with brandy and a 'Te Deum'. On my first such visit, in 1973, it was Roger Riddell who drove me to the leper camp. We found John crouched in the hut of one of the few lepers who was not yet burnt out. John was reading from the Shona New Testament. As always, our visit was an interruption though he quickly turned it into a welcome. Afterwards we had some sort of supper but it was memorable only for the way in which John tried to dodge eating anything. We chatted for a while until an hour before midnight and then, inviting those lepers who were willing, he led us to the chapel and sang in the New Year with a variety of Gregorian, Tudor and Shona hymns and songs including the 'Te Deum'. Many are the Shona hymns that found themselves a medieval accompaniment; one in particular went well to 'Greensleeves'.

The next day started with a climb of Chigona at dawn, a run on his 'track' and a swim in his 'pool', both on the summit. Mass followed and I remember the reverence of the lepers and John, and also the bidding prayers whose source was deep in the lepers' hearts.

A round of the camp followed in which we greeted Peter, Joseph, Veronica, Hanzu and so many more. We had brought some bottles of brandy and wine for John – presents from Mount Pleasant Parish. These John proceeded to pour into the lepers' breakfast cocoa, protesting that he would become an alcoholic if they remained in his house, and anyway it would brighten the lepers' New Year. The latter was certainly true. The lepers, never steady on their feet (or what remained of them) at the best of times, were decidedly less steady and more jolly that New Year's morn.

With different variations, that was the start of each New Year. The initial lack of welcome, which was so fleeting, was characteristic. John hated and loved visitors. He hated his solitude being interrupted but he enjoyed the visits of friends.

John was drawn both ways, towards solitude and yet also to people and he was sensitive beyond what is common about others. Other people were 'colossal', 'rock-like'; 'serene', 'happy', 'like a queen', or 'handsome'., He himself was a 'clown', 'an idle fellow', 'a fraud', 'Master Shallow' and he would sign himself

> John Bee (drone) or
> John Bee (groan).

In such jesting there was a profound and constant struggle. He fought down any praise – and he did it vehemently. He did not trust himself with the knowledge of so much grace received from God. He seemed terrified of honour or pride and he struggled mightily not to take himself seriously.

John always kept himself both physically and mentally very active. He was a great one for going for runs. He never liked to stay still for very long and would be up and out, running or striding out as though he constantly wanted to give his spirit an airing. It always astonished me that he never looked tired, never yawned and never seemed to want to rest or retire to bed. No matter how late he went to bed, he would be up around three or four in the morning, making coffee, striding about, going for runs or playing the harmonium. And mentally too, though he read little, his mind was always active, mostly on the Old Testament and the New with sallies into Shakespeare.

David comments that as a writer one would have to have a fairly active mind to write some 6,000 pages of poetry. It could be light-hearted or serious. One evening, after a discussion about how the Bible came to be written, he expressed his feeling:

> With cacophonic dissonance Concordances avow
> That, since they didn't write THE BOOK, they are damned if
>   they see how
> Anyone could, as Moses did, write all the Pentateuch
> Which possibly was conjured up much later by Saint Luke!
> Being himself a Syndicate like Shakespeare and like Bach
> Saint Luke declares it was a fluke dug up in Regent's
>   Park.

John wrote profound poetry and nonsense poetry and, if he enjoyed a dig at the scholars, his main intent was to see reverence enthroned. He did not like the easy way in which the scriptures were handled this way and that by the new scholarship, though I am sure he recognised the basic validity of the modern approach to biblical studies.

Only two weeks before he was killed, John wrote to me to say: 'Perhaps I shall put a match to my nonsensical writings before the Portmanteau arrives.' (We were having a bookshelf made for all his writings). He had an ambivalent attitude towards his writings, often saying they were nonsense and that he would destroy them but also knowing that he had indeed written some good things. In 1975 he wrote to me: 'While you big men launch spiritual empires and keep them afloat, I churn out miles of stuff that never hits the highlights. But with this colossal co-operation of yours, Sr Angelina and 'Dom Tom', I might be able to publish say 50 out of 300 or more Ballades, Diogenes in a barrel while all the world slaves for the common good.'

David comments here on John's inward struggle:

In John's poetry there are glimpses of the man and his own struggle:

> God, and it comes upon me oft
> When times rave hard and crave I soft
> And while amidst the waves I wilt
> Thou pipest, piercest, to the hilt ...

There is a glimpse here of the Hound of Heaven and of
John of the Cross and Hopkins:

> thou mastering me ...
> with an anvil-ding
> and with fire in him forge thy will.

And again, on the lepers with echoes of John 10:

> My flock of eighty-three
> Whose names are known to me
> Know naught or little of mine inward way
> And surely little I
> Know of the agony
> Filling their pilgrimage until today,
> But Heaven help me now
> And hence to take the prow
> In orison and homeward lead their lay.

I have a little note which I made on November 4th,
1975, when I must have been rather struck by John
talking about his poetry. It reads: 'John says that in his
poetry he is telling people to use whatever their gift is –
even if it seems ever so little to us. Offer it to God, he
will purify it and make you whole.'

This leads me to try to focus on what particularly I saw
so special in John. In John I think there was the desire to
perfect the gifts God gives. And the greatness of John was
in his trust in God perfecting the gifts. We all have gifts
and the difficulty for most of us is to allow God to 'get at
us' that through the gifts he gives us we may grow to him.
Many of us find it so hard to free and trust ourselves. We
are on the watch, defensive of our gifts. We don't allow
them air and freedom. We don't trust them, ourselves or
God. John learnt to trust. This is so clear from his own
account of his journey to Jerusalem in 1950. It is also
clear from his life as I knew him in his last eight years.

CHAPTER 46

'Denizens of the Deep'

At Mutemwa, before John died he had written verses about every leper, and there were nearly 90 of them. He wrote about them all in an appreciation, 'Denizens of the Deep':

> They sit like sadhus by their walls,
> They crawl into the sun,
> They talk on what but now befalls,
> On what long since is done.
>
> They seem to cogitate for hours
> On what surpasses thought, –
> Their stunted limbs, their dwindled powers
> Revel in this resort;
>
> They crave the shining of the sun,
> Grumble like knaves when it is won,
> Complain of cold and cloud and rain
> And wish the warmness back again.
>
> They are a parody, burlesque,
> Upon the human race.

John studied the lepers' every action, wish or whim. He was sensitive to their least need.

A big fellow used to ring the Angelus 'bell' each day. This 'bell' was an old piece of railway line hung from a tree which gave out a reasonable note when struck with a piece of metal. Cogitating on this, John wrote a 'Lepers' Lepanto':

> Mime it I might and hobble lame across some stage
> Rigged up to tell some philanthropic audience
> What is true honour and true courage in our age,
> Heaven forbid that I shall ever get the chance!
> Dance me down, Fortune – saw I not this very morn
> Aristocratic spirits in their smitten frames
> Go nobly on with living?

It was at this time that Ann Lander met John. (It was Ann who asked Jill to put the three white flowers on John's coffin). She was invited to visit Mutemwa.

> I recall the moment of meeting with clarity. The day that we went to Mutemwa had a sense of event – that event was to be my meeting with John. A few of us had gone out to Mutemwa to see John and in my case to meet him for the first time. We arrived and were met by John with much generosity. His joy and exuberance were apparent as was his dedication to the people of the village. In his own inimitable way he shared himself and we were incorporated into the spirit of the place. It was during the lunch that we shared under a tree at the foot of Chigona that I became aware of the depth of John.

All the lepers were John's friends. His verses about them brought out their inner worth. It is hard to select from over 80 such character sketches, but one or two catch the eye.

Coletta, a widow, fingerless and without toes, was the sacristan. She also led the leper choir. She was among John's favourites, remaining loyal to him to the end. It was she who rallied the lepers to prayer in John's hour of need just before he was abducted.

> This lady is by nature like a queen
> And no infirmity can mar her poise,
> She is the dignity amidst our scene
> Filled with integrity, empty of noise.
> Through her I know what beauty truly means
> She bears Maria, wears the Queen of Queens.

Hanzu was a wizened little thing, gnome-like with a wry smile. She was one of the characters of Mutemwa, ageless as it seemed. Visitors always asked about Hanzu and loved to greet her to see her smile. She died while John was at Mutemwa and he buried her, glad in the way that one can be glad that such a one has gone to eternal rest. In a poet's dream he saw Hanzu:

> Hanzu I saw in stream of sunbeams bright
> That danced at width of window through her wall,
> Glorious morning there shed best its lights,
> On Hanzu concentrated more than all,
> She sat there nodding like a Godward gnome
> Sorting the maize-cobs on her happy floor,
> Wholly her form was warm – a smile at home
> With heaven upon earth till evermore;
> Of Eighty simple huts I visit daily
> This the bright sunlight crowned above the rest
> Or so it seemed to me as gleamed there gaily
> That quaintest of the saints, that Hanzu blest.

Each leper knows the frailty of the other. There is great concern when one is more sick, in more pain than most. They rally to each other's needs in a way that one seldom witnesses among the less handicapped citizens of this world. Veronica in particular sensed out the sufferer and went to his or her aid. She was always at the side of the dying.

John ever quick to note the inward man, wrote of Veronica's strength and compassion:

> Veronica indeed is like a veil
> Over the face of Christ, and in this valley
> Stands for the tears in fearless eyes that rally
> Over, over again, and tell their tale;
> Miraculously fails she seldom thus
> To triumph in the transience of sorrow
> And every time I say to her 'Good morrow'
> She makes some joke well-known to both of us;
> Somehow she walks on tips of wounded feet,
> Like to a toeless ballerina treads,
> Smiles with a guileless irony and weds
> Her woes to joy, from bitter goes to sweet:

On deepest need of any dying here
Compassionate Karugu hovers near.

Everyone who goes to Mutemwa visits blind Peter. He is
the leper of lepers in his deformity. Yet he gets on with the
business of living in a remarkable manner. John was ever
sensitive to his least needs. It amazed us all when Peter
decided that he wished to build a small hen house next to
his hut – a thing of sticks and dried grass and string. Peter
needed some help but less than one might imagine. Eventually it was made and a hen was found. All were
delighted, even the solitary hen.

Peter is blindman's buffer against woe,
Throughout the frailness of his stricken frame
There penetrates a state of God aglow
With grace, to holiness I trace its claim:
Beholding Peter, almost noseless, blind
And rather deaf, Our Father fast we find
And, having found Him, realise that this
Apparent wreckage is an heir to Bliss.

Under a tree in the middle of Mutemwa sits an old man
who, for all the world, reminds one of a biblical picture of
Moses. His names is Muchero, meaning 'fruit'. Muchero is
old and blind, but he sits making straw hats all day long.
He listens for the sound of step or friendly voice and then
proclaims his wares 'hat-y; one dollar.' John noted this old
man's peace:

Peace blossoms on that face
Which tells the wells of grace
Springing amidst his soul: Muchero weaves,
Makes hats the whole day long –
And on Muchero goes
Weaving away all woes
From cocoa-time at morning till the night.

CHAPTER 47

A Death at Mutemwa

The Last Days of Jocku Kimbini the Leper

He lay without a mattress or a bed,
Sick to the point of almost seeming dead;
To him the 'Tu es Petrus' text I read
And 'I will be a Roman now' he said:
All square, one month of labour more in pain
And Jocku, christened Joseph, went to reign.

(J.R.B.)

Deaths are fairly frequent in Mutemwa. Death can be a joy, a gateway into peace, a fulfilment, a love bond complete. But dying can be an agony, a thirst, a passion like unto Christ's dying.

John witnessed many deaths at Mutemwa and always kept vigil with the dying, reading to them from Holy Scripture by firelight inside their hut; comforting, consoling, praying, baptising the unbaptised. He was never alone. The more able lepers kept vigil with the dying too. This was no easy task for John in the cramped space of a leper hut, amid wood smoke and many human bodies with leprosy crowded together.

When Jocku Kimbini died it was in the last thrust of the rains. Rivers were full, underground streams were rejuvenated, and the heights were washed clean by thunder storms leaving behind rock pools brimming over. It was easier to dig the grave, but water presented a problem. John writes of the event in 'The Leper's Funeral':

> Wet granite glistened on the height
> But the sky was fairly blue
> That mingled with the grey and white
> Of a Sunday nearly new.
>
> Six feet of forty years of woe
> Which had been called Kimbini
> Lay in a blanket wrapped to go
> Down but for five feet, cleanly.
>
> We diggers stopped at barely five
> Feet, for the water ran
> Just below that: a spring alive
> To sing for a risen Man.
>
> Dwindling in weight, Kimbini lay
> Dying at yester noon
> Till there happed, at about that time of day,
> To baptise him this buffoon.

John was always at peace after seeing a leper safely 'home'. I never knew him to grieve over a death at Mutemwa. He spoke much of their high reward and of their new, glorious bodies. He often quoted Philippians 3.21: 'He will transfigure these wretched bodies of ours into copies of His glorious body. He will do that by the same power with which He can subdue the whole universe.'

The lepers themselves were not fretful about death, nor did they grieve unnecessarily over the passing of a friend. There was an inner, silent relief – it is finished, peace is restored.

One blind old man named Bofu with no legs below the knee and no forearms made his painful way from hut to toilet by propelling himself along the ground by his elbows as he slithered upon his seat. More often than not, his head was raised in expectancy, his face radiated with a smile. John asked him why he was so joyous. He replied simply that he had seen his friend, a leper who had died before him, bathed in light.

John and his lepers were one in their expectancy. St

Paul in Hebrews speaks of the faith of our great forefathers: 'All these died in faith, before receiving any of the things that had been promised, but they saw them in the far distance and welcomed them, recognising that they were only strangers and nomads on earth.'

CHAPTER 48

Silveira Interlude

John used to pay quarterly visits to Silveira House from Mutemwa. He would either come back with one of us after a visit or come in himself on the African bus, or 'flying bedstead' as he called it. He used to bring with him a load of stencils containing his more recent writings. The secretary of Silveira House, Sister Angelina, an African Sister, used to run off the stencils for him. There was always a good deal of leg pulling and laughter when John shyly asked Sister to do this. He used to ask me whether he should buy her a box of chocolates and I used to say that nothing less than a new duplicator would do.

On these visits John loved to go to a good film. I remember taking him on one occasion to see an excellent historical film. He loved it especially since it had some fine English scenery. On entering the cinema he said, 'I'll buy you a box of chocolates.' I replied that that would be fine. I knew he had no money. He then said, 'I've forgotten my cheque book. Could you lend me a dollar or two?' I did that. By this time people in the cinema foyer were beginning to stare as people do. The cinema was modern and at that time rather elite and white. He wore his habit, gym shoes with holes in them, no socks, and a red head band like tennis players. We took our seats. I could hear the rustle of chocolate papers during the first half of the film but took no notice since it was such a good show. The lights went up during the interval and I discovered a sea of chocolate papers all round our feet and into the aisle. People stared even harder. I told him that I just could not sit with him any more. He laughed, saying that he had not had such a good meal for a long time.

It was on one of his visits to Silveira that Ann Lander came out to see us both. Ann had a great spirit and easy converse with God. She also has the gift of healing which she attributes to a special grace of God received after her serious illness.

Sister Mary Hildeberta, one of our African Sisters, lost her voice some three or four years ago. The diagnosis was permanent damage to her vocal chords. She could whisper – that was all – but she was a good book-keeper, so did the accounts.

Thus I asked Ann to lay hands on Sister Hildeberta in our chapel. I requested John to go with Ann and to sit with them in the front bench. He was shy and told me to go. I pretended that I had a 'phone call. Sister Hildeberta sat between John and Ann. All three placed their hands upon the others. A prayer was said by John and Ann laid hands on Sr Hildeberta's head. All was quiet. I had crept into the back of the chapel. When it was over, John, Ann and I retired to the sitting room. Suddenly there was a commotion. Sister Hildeberta entered with a troop of girls singing loudly and surely in praise and thanksgiving to the Lord. She had her voice back. Ann knelt and we all knelt in thanksgiving. There are a good number of cures by faith healers in this day and age but, in this case, John said it was all Ann, whereas Ann said that it would not have come about without John.

John came in soon after the tragedy at St Paul's Mission, Musami, where seven missionaries died by the gun. We could see the big rock features close to Musami from the front of Silveira. John passed the turn-off on his way to and from Mutemwa. In fact, eight missionaries were lined up – four Dominican Sisters and four Jesuits. Fr Myerscough escaped with his life by falling as the first gun blazed. He was covered by the others' blood and left for dead.

This happened on Sunday night, 6 February 1977. Christopher Shepherd-Smith was coming in to Silveira that night but his motor bike failed him. John knew and

loved Chris. He admired his guileless charm. Chris had
been on the Mission staff at Silveira from 1968 to mid
1970. He was there when John left for Mutemwa in August
1969. Brother Conway and Martin Thomas had been
friends of mine from post-war novitiate days. Brother
Conway frequently visited John and myself. Martin came
in a few days before he died. John wrote an appreciation
of them all called 'Musemi ku Musami' (An enemy at
Musami):

> Last Sunday night they killed a man
> Who held the Piper's charm;
> Six others too they slew to plan
> Of the panic-Lord of harm.
>
> John Conway was the Jesuit
> Whom children loved to follow
> The saint's allure, the minstrel's wit,
> Gone, like a migrant swallow.
>
> And Father Martin too they shot
> And swiftly they despatched
> Christopher Shepherd-Smith ... sad plot
> That holds death's door unlatched.
>
> Four White-robed Sisters too were slain
> To stain with red the dust
> But Justice due comes on amain
> And Jesus meet they must.
>
> And are you ready now to go?
> Ready to go am I?
> We all are migrants, even so,
> But for these lost we sigh.
>
> John Conway gone, the shining friend
> Of every Shona child;
> The Land is weeping, end to end,
> Shall it be reconciled?
>
> Christopher Shepherd-Smith ... his smile
> Was like an angel's joy:
> All innocence, no hint of guile,
> An everlasting boy.

True Father Thomas, please to pray
With three on either hand
That we may follow in the way
Of The Captain of your band.

It was a terrible shock to us all, bringing the war to the door of every missionary. To make matters worse there was, and still is, a big question mark as to who was responsible.

PART IX

THE BEGINNING OF THE END

Like a deep vast plain
Where ten thousand watchfires are,
Was the sky last night
With its diadems afar.

(J.R.B.)

CHAPTER 49

Crisis

Everything went fine for nearly three years and then came the crisis. In the Lord's work crises are never quite what one expects. John, in a sense, was being groomed for martyrdom, which involved being asked to give his all and in the most painful, unexpected manner.

Fr Ennis, the Vice-Chairman of the 'Friends of Mutemwa', finished his term of office as Superior of the Jesuit Mission. He went on leave and handed over his job as Superior and that of Vice-Chairman of the 'Friends of Mutemwa' to his successor. His successor had a disagreement with the 'Friends of Mutemwa' Committee and resigned. Fr Ennis believes that the problem centred round an extension of the work undertaken by the 'Friends of Mutemwa' at a national level. The Committee, enlarged now, wanted to work for all lepers in Zimbabwe and to change their name to the 'Rhodesian Leprosy Association'. Fr Ennis says that he and his successor were against this since they had become involved as a specific commitment to the particular group of lepers at Mutemwa. On his return from leave, Fr Ennis's successor asked him to take over again on the Committee, but his place had been filled by someone else. Hence the new Committee was, in a sense, foreign to John and his ideals.

A key member of the enlarged Committee was a senior government doctor – a lady doctor. She appears tough and critical on the one hand, describing John in later years as a religious 'hippy' and 'perhaps a little mad with an innate fear of responsibility'; on the other hand she seemed to comprehend John's spiritual dimension and perhaps his vocation. However, she believes that lepers attract many religious people, often of unsuitable quality. John annoyed her by being against family planning and, apparently, by disapproving of old lepers being operated upon for cataract. There were other areas of minor disagreement. In many ways the doctor and John got on well together. There was mutual respect.

It is worth noting that Professor Michael Gelfand, top consultant doctor in Zimbabwe, had nothing but praise for John, and thought that he should have been awarded the Nobel Prize for his dedicated service to the lepers. He stressed that lepers are people who need constant help and John gave them just that, without personal or financial reward.

The main issue for the Committee, however, seems to have been over administration – keeping of books and the distribution of rations. This might well have been sorted out amicably had it not been for the introduction of an almost military attitude in the affairs of the Committee. Efficiency and regimentation coupled with bookkeeping came to mean more than individual people. There was even a note of antagonism towards the Church of Rome.

In April 1973 John was rudely sacked as Warden of the settlement by one of the Committee members. 'They claimed that I was careless with the rations and did not keep proper books,' John said in a newspaper interview two years later.

The settlement was to be run impersonally, like an institution. The lepers were even to have numbers round their necks. Severe economies on the already frugal rations were to be made. But John would have none of it. 'The lepers need me to stay and keep watch.' And with a great love and fortitude, keep watch he did.

What was the real crisis about?

John and his supporters felt that the rations per leper were wholly inadequate. They were receiving sadza, a bland porridge with little or no vitamin content, some sort of vegetable, mostly beans, twice a day, and also a mug of tea with a minimal ration of sugar and powdered milk. Meat or fish was a rare luxury. They possibly received a couple of oranges per month into the bargain.

It was argued that they should not receive a better diet than the local people otherwise there would be a queue to enter Mutemwa. John, as a lay missionary, had pledged himself to raise the people above their degrading level of subsistence.

John's quarrel was with one particular member of the RLA, who had instructed John to cut down the rations. This he utterly refused to do and, in fact, looked for ways and means of increasing them. John, who knew every leper by name, was deeply shocked when he heard that numbers were to be put around their necks – like cattle or concentration camp inmates. To him, each and every leper was a friend, a brother in Christ and a child of God. This impersonal, loveless approach cut him to the core of his being.

Then there was the issue of the account books. John was no bookkeeper and admits that he did not keep proper books, but he was not a thief nor did he sell the rations, nor did he take any for himself.

Nevertheless, in what appeared to be an off-the-cuff decision, the Committee member, with whom John had been dealing, sacked him and expelled him from the settlement. Two great friends, Alistair Guthrie and Peter Donnelly, pitched a tent for him on Mount Chigona which flanked the leper camp. Pauline wrote of this interlude:

> Later, after John's dismissal by the Leprosy Association, when he was living in Peter Donnelly's tent half way up Chigona, we started to climb the mountain again after breakfast. Sometimes John would take his recorder and we'd sit at the top viewing the world to the strains of 'Greensleeves'. Those were carefree days – in the desert, on the move. John's 'Ark of the Covenant', such an elaborate structure in his old house, was now stripped to the bare essentials, divested of unnecessary adornment. He had big 'throwing out' sessions and threatened to burn all his poetry. His spiritual renewal was infectious. We spent much time with Moses and the Jews those

Wednesdays – 'Religion is caught not taught,' quoted John.

That interlude in the tent was not unhappy. The lepers cleared a path up the mountain for him and visited regularly. Also he had tremendous support from many people, he knew his cause to be a worthy one, and we all imagined that John would soon be reinstated to Mutemwa. It was later that he really suffered, when it seemed nearly everyone had turned against him in his fight for the lepers' welfare.

I remember climbing up to the tent which was about two-thirds of the way up Mount Chigona – quite a climb. There was a lovely view but it all seemed very precarious. It is not possible to knock tent pegs into rock, so the tent was anchored with stones. One of those small whirlwinds, so common in the spring in Zimbabwe, would have been the end of it. John, however, was as cheerful as ever. We used to go up on top to see the view – a fine view across to the Inyanga Mountains. John could also see every hut in the leper colony. He could even observe the comings and goings. He stuck to the rules and went only to the chapel of which he was the caretaker. He would only go into the camp if a leper was very sick, and then at night.

It was the lepers who brought him off the mountain. They said that there was danger of a leopard up there. Thus they found him a disused hut across the way from the camp.

In the meantime, the Committee appointed an African Warden to take John's place, a big strong fellow who could drive and would be an efficient administrator. John liked him at first and co-operated in what way he could from a distance. Dr Luisa, Maria and Caterina were still coming. They had been joined by a young African girl, Elizabeth, who was a postulant. Elizabeth thought the world of John. An incident prompted the Italian Sisters to demand the dismissal of the new Warden. The Committee would not play. Consequently, the Italian Community, who, in addition to their good work had been supplementing the welfare of the lepers with donations of money and medicines from Italy, withdrew with great reluctance. It was a difficult and sad decision, leaving John alone in a tent on the mountain to watch and wait.

Lepers visited him in his tent bringing their tales of woe. Some grievances he referred to the new Warden, but as these multiplied and involved the Warden himself, John fell from favour, along with his informants. Gradually there was open confrontation – even enmity. In all of this the Warden had the ear of the Association.

By Easter of 1974 matters were coming to a head. The Leprosy Association sought legal means of evicting John from the vicinity. They approached the local District Commissioner and the police. The Chairman even came out to see me to enlist my help in a friendly removal of John. I declined to help in a matter which I judged to be morally wrong. The Chairman informed me that in the last resort they, the Leprosy Association, would confront government social welfare with the alternative of either evicting John or accepting the resignation of the Rhodesian Leprosy Association. Social welfare would not involve itself in such an issue. John, after all, as Archdiocesan custodian of the leper chapel, had the right to enter the precincts of the chapel.

It was stalemate.

Heather comments that at this time 'John didn't mellow into the picture saint' in this environment.

He retained his old fiery spirit, brilliant wit and carried on with zest a running verbal and written battle with several members of the Rhodesian Leprosy Association. This was exacerbated by the fact that, unlike lesser mortals who out of habit compromise on many things, it never entered John's head to do so. This could be awkward for the person trying to play a diplomatic role. He had no time for this at all – just came out with what he thought was right. John never feared doing what was right – and was only concerned with being right in terms of his great devotion to, and absorption with, the Word of God.

The lepers now had no John, no medical care and above all, no love. As a monthly visitor I noticed the decline in morale. Moreover, a very difficult situation emerged: pro-John and Luisa lepers were not in favour with the new Warden. This split the camp since many needed the little care available. Hence they could not afford to be friendly to John except at night. On my visits I said Mass and then, as a priest, visited some of the lepers in their huts. I noticed lepers who were very sick from malaria and other ailments apart from leprosy. In theory, the sick were supposed to be taken up to the local hospital. In practice, it proved to be a rough ride in the back of the truck, to be shovelled out at the other end and wait hours for an over-busy doctor. Other patients at the hospital did not like to be too close to the lepers. At one stage a doctor could only visit Mutoko once per week. Dr Luisa and the Sisters had visited the leper camp itself regularly twice per week and more. Now many preferred to be sick at home rather than face up to the ordeal of being 'taken' to the hospital. Mona Smith, an elderly retired nursing sister, still came to do bandages and to bath the women. The men were left to the attention of the orderlies.

To be fair to the orderlies – they had had no nursing training and were simply doing a job in an almost jobless society. They were probably also scared of leprosy. They and the Warden had no vocation like John, thus personal relations with the lepers were minimal unless they were in some way tribally related. Love and care were replaced by routine – the job.

John saw all this and the hurt went deep. As St Francis Xavier remarked, there is no greater suffering than to watch what one has built up for God being smashed down by man.

CHAPTER 50

'Piper's Vale'

A very kind white farmer erected a tin hut for John in a
secluded spot just outside of the camp. Pauline
comments, 'Back down the mountain again and into
"leagues and leagues of woe".' John lived first in a derelict
leper hut and subsequently in a tin rondavel

> ... shining silver circle
> Galvanised, of iron made ...

given him by a farmer friend and known as 'Piper's Vale'.
The unhappiness of those days was compounded by the
constant threat of police action should John enter the
leper compound from which he had been banned. John
was tormented and condemned as a madman; he had to
stand by and watch his weak and helpless old lepers
suffer, and he could do nothing to help them. Perhaps the
most difficult thing to bear was the forced departure of Dr
Luisa and the 'All Souls' Sisters from their devoted work at
Mutemwa clinic.

John liked his new tin hut since the acoustics were good
for his sung office and he could also stick poems and
pictures on the walls. At the beginning it was a solitary hut
in the wilderness. Later, with a donation, John built two
guest huts alongside, of simple rough brick and thatch. He
used these guest huts for lepers waiting to get into the
main camp or for lepers evicted by the Warden.

These sufferings of John and the build-up of tension caused by so many factions and persons form the backdrop to his untimely death.

John lived in that valley of Mutemwa with his gaze upon the camp, day and night. Nothing escaped his sensitive sight.

A few of the Rhodesian Leprosy Association paid regular monthly visits. John felt that these visits lacked real compassion. They were like inspecting the lines in army days. If anything was seen to be amiss it was attended to, but the 'Sergeant-Major' Warden saw to it that nothing that John knew to be amiss came to the notice of the RLA officer.

Relations between the Warden and John deteriorated as time wore on. John maintained that there were cases of violence done to the lepers. One such case was brought to court, but was dismissed for lack of evidence. I too heard these accusations when I came down to say Mass for the lepers. They spoke up at the Mass.

No complaint from John was ever accepted by the Committee. Friends of John involved the press, who came down to interview him. He had his say but was answered by people who really did not know.

John's agony was great – his lepers suffered, he was rejected, even deemed mad. St John Vianney, the saintly Curé d'Ars, was labelled in a similar manner. His bishop, Mgr Devie, said, 'I wish, gentlemen, that all my clergy had a touch of the same madness.'

On top of this, local Africans were puzzled by a white man living in such poverty. Perhaps he was mad, they thought. John put up with this too.

Moreover, everyone, including small African children, called him 'John'. He took this to be a mark of disrespect – at least he suffered it as such. I disagreed with him over this. Everyone calls you 'Baba' (Father) he would say, but I am just 'John' and what's more I'm a year older than you. Then he would laugh. Nevertheless it hurt – and to me it all added up to the experience of the rejection which Christ underwent.

Pauline comments:

John's position at Mutemwa was very unrewarding, humanly speaking, and few people understood it. Despite his ultimate concern for their comfort and well-being, he did not see himself as a father figure. He would go to endless lengths to ensure a Heavenly welcome for dying lepers, and he taught the people to sing hymns, say prayers and to pray the Rosary, but he never did any preaching or general teaching except by his example. Many of the old people depended heavily on him, Peter for example, a blind and helpless old man whom John bathed and cared for in many ways. There were others too but he had no sentimental ideas about his role there and never considered himself indispensable to them. In fact, he would often extol the lepers for their patience in putting up with him who blew up when they cut down trees, was intolerant of habitual hard drinking, and who often criticised their apparent lack of religious responsibility and fervour. Sometimes he longed to get away from Mutemwa and return to Jerusalem.

While he waited for Fr David Gibbs to come for Mass one day a couple of non-leper Massgoers appeared, chatting cheerfully and eating nuts. It took a moment for me to understand why John had exploded. Hardly had I called to mind the polite Shona greetings when John gave vent to his wrath: 'How could they come to Mass eating?' There was no expediency about John!

It is true he was occasionally disappointed in the lepers, but his righteous indignation was overwhelmingly tempered by his sorrow for their physical anguish, his respect for their deep spirituality and his great love for them. He used to say: 'If you need to storm Heaven, ask the lepers to pray; their prayers go straight there'.

There were always birds in John's life at Mutemwa: First the Auger Buzzard:

> Best park I know, blest King of Kings
> And all the worldwide verdent strand
> Is here: here auger-buzzard wings
> Wheel over green Mashonaland.

The owls nested amongst the great inaccessible boulders on the side of Chigona. John pointed out their busy comings and goings and we watched them through his little binoculars. Then there were the Hamerkops, returning each year to their ungainly stick nest by the river.

> ... nesting every year, in coil
> Of woven magic made to foil
> The would-be foes of chosen home ...

When we climbed Chigona we marvelled at the graceful antics of the crows which floated in the thermals above us. There were other creatures too. A chameleon took up residence at 'Piper's Vale': it climbed right onto the 'dome of St Peter' at the top of the Ark and stayed there for days on end, perched precariously! There were bees too, but never as many as John would have liked. All of the natural world was somehow charmed and transformed when appreciated with John.

CHAPTER 51

Sustaining Prayer

'There is a baptism I must still receive, and how great is my distress till it is over' (Luke 11. 47–54).

John needed a solid prayer life to sustain him through this agony of heart about the lepers. This valley between Mutemwa Mount and Chigona, once so bright in the dawn, witnessed the gathering of dark clouds yet again.

John's prayer was basically simple: 'We have no eyes for things that are visible, but only for things that are invisible, for visible things last only for a time, and the invisible things are eternal' (2 Corinthians. 4.18). Let us say that from Malaya onwards he had used the visible to lead him to the invisible – sadhus at prayer. Himalayan heights, eagles, bees, sunrise, sunset, all and more spoke to him of the invisible.

> O world invisible, we view thee,
> O world intangible, we touch thee,
> O world unknowable, we know thee,
> Inapprehensible, we clutch thee!

So wrote Francis Thompson, so believed John Bradburne. Like an ordained priest, though he was a layman, he had a routine daily prayer according to the rule of the Third Order of St Francis of Assisi, namely, the Little Office of Our Lady. One often heard him singing the hours. Then there was Holy Mass and the sacrament of Holy Commu-

nion – the Bread of Life. Apart from his Little Office book
he possessed a Bible, a missal and a little book entitled
The Cloud of Unknowing by an unknown author. He really
read nothing besides. Occasionally he might dip into
Shakespeare or read something short which one put into
his hand, otherwise Holy Scripture, the Divine Office, and
The Cloud were his only books.

> Like as the hart desires the water-brooks
> So pilgrim longs for fresh simplicity
> And total dispensation from the sands
> Of dry discursive thought and irksome books;
> But irksome not nor dry
> Is the Bible in the hands
> Of one who has at heart its lightsome Lord
> Who is the Key of David and the King
> Fit for unlocking every hidden thing
> Of Writ He'll bring to be a pasture broad.

His prayer included the sung praises of God. He loved to
play and sing before the Blessed Sacrament. He would rise
in the night to do so, and play during the day if he thought
no one was thus disturbed. He longed to see God, to dwell
in His house, to sing His praises:

> My soul is longing and yearning
> Is yearning for the courts of the Lord,
> They are happy, who dwell in your house,
> For ever singing your praise (Psalm 84).

The *Cloud of Unknowing* became more and more his
prayer of the inner soul. He loved *The Cloud* and he
longed to pierce its veil.

He believed that Walter Hilton, the author of the *Ladder
of Perfection* also wrote *The Cloud*, and compared the
two books in quite a deep research. Walter Hilton dates
back to the fourteenth century, along with St Julian of
Norwich.

The spiritual doctrine of *The Cloud of Unknowing* is
defined in Fr William Johnston SJ's excellent book *The
Inner Eye of Love*. He quotes from the (Pseudo-) Diony-
sius' *Mystica Theologia:*

Do thou, then, in the intent practice of mystic contemplation, leave behind the sense and the operations of the intellect, and all things that the senses or the intellect can perceive, and all things which are not and things which are, and strain upwards in unknowing, as far as may be, towards the union with Him Who is above all things and knowledge. For by unceasing and absolute withdrawal from thyself and all things in purity, abandoning all and set free from all, thou shalt be borne up to the ray of divine darkness that surpasseth all being (*Mystica Theologia*, 1, 1).

John might have put it in this way. There comes a time in one's search for God when nature – the mountains, the sky, the stars, the birds and the bees – can tell one no more about Him. Nor can the mind or the intellect. Thus the inner spirit reaches up and out into a cloud of unknowing, longing to see God. Yet on this earth, as the Book of Exodus 33, 20 tells us, 'You cannot see my face, for man shall not see Me and live.' Nature can tell us no more, the intellect can lead us no further, we are left in darkness knowing only with the inner eye. Let us listen to an extract from *The Cloud* for a moment.

Do not think that because I call it a 'darkness' or a 'cloud' it is the sort of cloud you see in the sky, or the kind of darkness you know at home when the light is out. That kind of darkness or cloud you can picture in your mind's eye in the height of summer, just as in the depth of a winter's night you can picture a clear and shining light. I do not mean this at all. By 'darkness' I mean 'a lack of knowing' – just as anything that you do not know or may have forgotten may be said to be 'dark' to you, for you cannot see it with your inward eye. For this reason it is called 'a cloud', not of the sky, of course, but 'of unknowing', a cloud of unknowing between you and Your God.

Fr Johnston notes that the anonymous author of *The Cloud of Unknowing* made some small but significant additions to the text of the *Mystica Theologia*, the most

significant being that the ascent into the realm of darkness, which transcends thought is accomplished by love.
In other words, we poor, frail humans with our finite intel-
lects can only comprehend the infinite Godhead by love
with our hearts. Hence a simple, uneducated peasant girl
like St Bernadette of Lourdes could know more about God
than many a great theologian.

The author of *The Cloud* put it in this way:

> The soul, when it is restored by grace, is made wholly
> sufficient to comprehend him fully by love. He cannot
> be comprehended by our intellect or any man's – or any
> angel's for that matter. For both we and they are created
> beings. But only to our intellect is he incomprehensible:
> not to our love.

In another chapter *The Cloud* continues: '[God] may be
well-loved but not thought. By love He can be thought and
held, but by thinking never.'

One noticed this aspect very much in John – he was
drawn by love. He was not a Pelagian-muscular Christian
who drew himself up to God by the sheer weight of his
penances, self denials and studied practice of the virtues.
The exciting thing about John was that he was in a sense
unmortified, he would let go, but was always drawn back
on to the path up to God by love. He was brought to sanctity, if one may use that term, not by hard discipline but by
his longing, his love for God. One might say that John's
big-hearted love covered a multitude of sins. The Lord left
him with enough 'failings' to keep him humble – pride,
anger, passion, all of which, incidentally, were used in
defence of the lepers. He was a lover 'par excellence', and
God brought him to that final act of supreme love when he
died for his little flock. It is all so encouraging since he was
never the bolt-upright 'saint' (if such a one ever existed).

One took him and his life so much for granted, but it
cannot have been easy to have lived in a tin hut amid the
heat of Africa with absolutely no facilities – no water, no
shower, no toilet. He was close to a vlei and the mosqui-
toes came out in their hundreds at night to invade and
torment:

A loathsome floating whining thing of blood
Which never is its own, a vile banshee
Disguised as an ephemeral, on flood
Of stinking base stagnation born, a glee
Of sanguinary pillage and a dire
Vampire diminutive that sucks and sets
Whole human beings lethally on fire,
A filthy blight loving the night that gets
Out of the light and hides at early morn
In corners! Wet with threat it winds its horn
While, somehow sweetly, it insinuates
Hatred's wing and deathsting at our gates,
Vibrant with bloodlust lingering it waits:
Unlucky flier, lier-low from dawn!

This was not all. He was alone in that hut, with a rickety old door and no glass in the windows: no protection at all either in peace or in war. Pauline has given us his diet sheet, which amounts to about a quarter of a meal a day. Yet when he came in to visit us at Silveira to live in comparative luxury with a hot bath, flush toilet and sheets, he was no sooner there than he longed to go back. Friend, he used to say, it is only in my hut that I find the spirit of home, of peace upon this earth. Yes, it was the spirit of love who led him to love what we should call poverty. He was so like St Francis of Assisi.

Moreover, he began to feel very awkward when he was away from his hut, his solitude. When on a visit, he would stand in front of the mirror in his room at Silveira and say to me: 'Gosh! I look awful – my teeth, wrinkles, hair.' Back in his hut in poverty he was never self-conscious.

John used the translation of *The Cloud of Unknowing* by Clifton Wolters. He underlined a few passages, given here at random.

Unite yourself to Him by love and trust, and by that union you will be joined both to Him and to all who like yourself are united by love to him – with Our Lady St Mary ...

Strike that thick cloud of unknowing with the sharp dart of longing love, and on no account whatever think of giving up.

Take a short word, preferably of one syllable ... with this word you will hammer the cloud and the darkness above you.

... you should have this blind out-reaching love to God himself, this secret love pressing upon the cloud of unknowing.

These passages illustrate his taste for the single word, silent prayer: 'El' and 'OM' were favourites with him.

When at Mutemwa Fr Michael Ivens SJ visited him and gave him *The Way of the Pilgrim* by a Russian mystic. He loved the Jesus prayer from that book and adapted it for his needs at Mutemwa. He wore a path from his hut when walking up and down reciting the Jesus prayer or one of his own composition – 'Jesus of Nazareth, King of the Jews, triumph through Juda' – a prayer which he said often in the last six months of his life.

Nevertheless, John was not a complete solitary. Fr Johnston, in his book we have already quoted from, mentions that the fruit of mysticism is a loss of self in God. This often moves one spontaneously and with great compassion towards the underprivileged, the poor, the sick and the imprisoned. John's long, solitary prayer led him to love the destitute poor and, above all, his beloved lepers. This love moved into the practical – the actual care of the lepers.Fr Johnston notes that St Thomas Aquinas also held that contemplation flows into action which is a sharing with others of the fruit gained in prayer. It is more like Christ, who prayed and then taught, preached, healed and lived an active life.

In many ways, too, John was like St Ignatius of Loyola, the founder of the Jesuits, who was able to find God in all things and all people. But John needed more solitude than most of these great men.

Finally, one must not forget John's poetry – this was prayer to him. Most of it went up on high and was inspired by his love of God and Our Lady. She had a special place in his poetical works.

Thus we see John at prayer with his sung office, we hear him in the chapel singing as he accompanied himself on the harmonium; watch him with his beads pacing his path by his hut or upon the heights of Chigona; observe him pondering the scripture in his hut; and finally composing poetry at his typewriter. All of this led him to a deep personal love of God and of his beloved lepezrs.

One great joy for John was his official clothing in the habit of St Francis. His old friend Fr Seán Gildea OFM was Superior of the Franciscans in Zimbabwe during John's latter days at Mutemwa. Fr Seán was deeply moved by John's truly Franciscan mode of living and his work among the lepers. Seán often used to say: 'John is more Franciscan than the whole lot of us put together.'

One day Seán arrived at Silveira House bringing his own habit. He asked me to clothe John in it when he next came in. I sent word to John and he came in on the African bus as usual. We then went together into our chapel. I could not find the prayer for the clothing ceremony and so I adapted a prayer for the blessing of a processional banner. It went something like this:

Lord Jesus Christ whose church is like an army set in battle array, bless this habit so that he who wears it in the name of the Lord God of Hosts, may through the intercession of St Francis of Assisi be helped to overcome in this life his enemies, visible and invisible, and after victory to triumph in heaven.

John was delighted with this prayer which he found very suitable to his circumstances in Mutemwa, enveloped as it was in war. He looked fine in his habit and wore it on all his journeys, with his head band and often bare feet.

The effect of such a prayer life upon others can be unknowingly deep. *The Cloud of Unknowing* remarks that those who engage in this work of contemplation are endowed with a discernment of the character and needs of others. They have the grace of being at home with those who seek them and the power to draw others safely home to God.

Without knowing it, John became a prophet for this, our twentieth century; a sign for the consumer society, this technological age, this era of materialism and disbelief. He was quite naturally supernatural with a gaiety and wit which enchanted all. He was a mystic, poet and music-maker all in one. His openness to God and easy converse with Him, both in his quiet, solitary prayer and through his poetry, and music, gave him a fullness, a fulfilment which others sadly lacked. He became a sure-footed pilgrim and cheerful guide to all seekers with inner faith. 'Never give up,' he used to say, while he, oblivious of the world and its ways, waited and longed for God to bring him safely home to the shores of truth and glory. Above all, he was an exemplar of faith, of trust in God's providence.

Fr George Carry SJ, a great friend and admirer of John, quoted a ballade written by John in a tribute to him after his death. The ballade entitled 'A Ballade of a Blithe Anticipation' gives a glimpse of John's spirit, with its wise advice to us all to think 'immortality'.

> To those who, loving little, live life not
> I make for death no deep apology;
> To those who look upon it as the cot
> Of rest in Christ till rising, I reply
> Duly with Alleluia; but, to die,
> Wait not till death: die to the deadly seven,
> Put on in time sublime eternity,
> Think immortality, link up with heaven.

CHAPTER 52

The War for
Independence

Then came the war. It took some time to reach the Mutoko area, but it came. The war put John in a dangerous position since it was not really possible to be neutral and survive. John hated both the oppression which led to the war and the violence which the war itself brought about. He lived for the day and for his work, which was to serve and watch over his little flock of lepers. The war hit Dr Luisa at All Souls Mission before it hit John. Her life became quite impossible.

John was much distressed when Luisa was arrested on 28 June 1976 for supposedly having treated a wounded guerrilla. She was thrown into a prison cell in Mutoko before being transferred to Chikurubi prison in Salisbury, not too far from Silveira House. John came in – he was worried. Luisa was released on bail. Somehow she thought they would hang her. After all, many Africans were hanged for supporting the guerrillas. We felt sure that they would deport her. However, after two agonising months her case was dropped. The wounded man turned out to be a villager caught in cross-fire. We were all delighted and relieved at Luisa's release.

The war crept forward. It was now all round John and Pauline, too, as it advanced towards Salisbury. It was a brutal war and the worst victims, as always, were the poor innocent villagers who were in the middle. The guerrillas were supported by the people since they had no supply drop from the air. The Rhodesian security forces tried to prevent the villagers from feeding the guerrillas by burning their granaries, burning their villages, beatings, and worse. They also extracted information from them as to the whereabouts of guerrilla hide-outs. Modern war knows no rules.

The guerrillas were assisted by mujibhas – village boys who acted as their eyes and ears. Any movement of soldiers or suspicious strangers was reported to the guerrilla hide-outs in the mountains. Gradually the mujibhas gained power. Some were even armed. Thus they greatly assisted the guerrilla advance and were often used to carry supplies and to seek out food. Wars are won and lost by gaining or losing supplies – food, arms and petrol.

The Rhodesian security forces were assisted by African Selous Scouts who aped the guerrillas. At first the people found it hard to know who was who, and thus unknowingly gave information to the wrong side. Later the security forces were assisted by auxiliaries who belonged to African political parties who opposed the guerrillas. Thus it leaves little to the imagination to comprehend the state of the poor who were caught in the crossfire from all of these different 'forces' making their separate demands.

The leper settlement, although semi-isolated, was nevertheless caught in 'the middle' too.

One ill wind which blew some good from the war was that Fr David Gibbs, based at All Souls Mission with Dr Luisa, was prevented by security forces from going out to the villages any more in his two-ton lorry, delivering Red Cross relief. It was said that this relief was only going to the 'Ters' (terrorist-guerrillas). He was confined to base at All Souls Mission and so he could now afford the time to go across to Mutemwa every week for Mass and to spend half a day with John and the lepers. David and John became heart friends. David helped John to do the shopping in Mutoko. John was wont to push a wheelbarrow the two miles into the village, buy supplementary rations for the lepers and push the full barrow back. David could now do all that for him in his truck. This was a boon for John, along with David's friendship. Few people ventured out to Mutoko now. It was too dangerous because of the war.

The second boon was Alistair Guthrie's acceptance on to the Leprosy Association Committee. Alistair had visited John over the years every month. Latterly, when fuel rationing came in, I went out with Alistair. Alistair was fearless and the Committee began to rely upon his visits to report back on the affairs of Mutemwa. He gradually persuaded the Committee to allow John back into the leper compound under his surveillance. This was granted and Alistair acted as a buffer between the Committee and John. It was not easy for Alistair. John demanded so much change. Alistair pleaded for time, especially over the dismissal of the Warden. Providence came to the rescue. When John was away with Luisa for a short break at Silveira House, the Warden was finally dismissed.

Was there to be a second spring? Not really, but things were better, as Pauline says: 'Somehow he learned to live with the situation, the war and Mutemwa, especially after the Warden was dismissed.'

He was happy again:

> The Piper is merry,
> Resilient very
> Is grace.

He loved to talk about *The Cloud of Unknowing* at this time, and also the *Way of the Pilgrim*. He was learning to say the Jesus Prayer as he sat under a mango tree and said it all the thousands of times a day the book tells one to do. 'It is a good cloud of forgetting', he would add, 'to prepare the way for the cloud of unknowing.' His prayer increased his concern for the lepers. He prayed much for their safety and peace in the land.

CHAPTER 53

Illness – Nearly unto Death

In August 1978 Luisa suddenly appeared at Silveira. This was not unusual. She often blew in after dark asking for five or six beds – two for lepers, four for very sick persons from All Souls Mission. This time she had John. He was semi-paralysed on one side of his face and jaw. He spoke with difficulty. It was late and so they put up for the night at Silveira. Next day Luisa put him into St Anne's Hospital in Salisbury under the care of the Irish LCM Sisters or 'The Blues' as we call them – lovely people whose vocation is to nurse the dying. Was John that bad? Luisa put John under the care of no less a person than Professor Gelfand, the top medical consultant in Zimbabwe, who was very fond of both Luisa and John. He diagnosed encephalitis, saying that a type of polio virus had attacked John. So it was serious. I visited him every day. He had too many visitors – he told me to write 'dead' on the door. He got worse and was hurriedly taken to the intensive care unit of the new Andrew Fleming Hospital. Even Professor Gelfand thought the end was near. Later I bumped into Professor Gelfand who said to me, 'I think the little beggar has stopped – John's better.'

He came to Silveira House for convalescence. We were lucky to have him. Each day he was out trying to ascertain whether he could see Mutemwa. An old friend, Fr Leonard Kennedy SJ, was invited out with maps and binoculars to try to establish whether a very distant feature on the horizon was in fact Mutemwa. At last the day came when Professor Gelfand grudgingly allowed him to return to Mutemwa, although he really did not think John strong enough to face up to the rigours of the life there.

What joy! Brother Fidelis took him back, with his green bag containing a toothbrush, his Little Office of Our Lady, and a spare pair of underpants. We had washed his habit and anything else we could find. It was late October 1978. Professor Gelfand attributed his complete recovery to the grace of God.

I managed to get out at Christmas but it was now becoming very dangerous. There was a daily convoy in and out of Mutoko but the times of its coming and going never suited our purposes. One flew down and flew back. John was in great form that Christmas. One of the orderlies was acting Warden of the camp and John got on with him well enough. No one visited him now due to the war except Pauline and, of course, Fr David Gibbs. They both went every week.

In January 1979, Alistair Guthrie, who had been ailing for a long time, was admitted to St Anne's Hospital in the last throes of cancer. I sent word to John who came in on the African bus. The bus was late so he walked seven miles at night in curfew through a danger area to reach Silveira House. He suddenly appeared out of the night, unannounced, oblivious of the danger. We got word early next morning that Alistair was dying. We rushed into town and were able to spend half an hour with him before he died. Both Alistair and Peter Donnelly, who had been such good friends of both John and the lepers, were now dead.

I was not able to get down at Easter 1979. It had become too dangerous and my Superior, who had lost seven Jesuits to the gun, was not keen for us to take risks. Luisa came in, however, with John not long after Easter. It was easier to judge at their end whether it was safe or not, but neither of them worried – after all, they were surrounded by both guerrillas and security forces alike.

This was the last time that they came in together. It was a great time, everyone pulling each other's leg. Luisa, from a high-born Italian family, was quite fascinated by John.

CHAPTER 54

Luisa's Death and the Parting of Lifelong Friends

Luisa paid us two more visits before her death. She was almost at the end of her tether trying to run a bush hospital with visits from the guerrillas at night and security forces by day. This was bad enough, but her staff would not stay. The last straw was when the faithful Sister Caterine had to go back to Italy for a spinal operation. Luisa was now alone but was helped by Fr David Gibbs who acted as 'matron' in the absence of Caterine. He was superb.

On 6 July 1979 Luisa came in to the Mutoko Hospital with a patient. She said a brief 'hello' which was 'au revoir' to John and then started back to All Souls Mission. She was checked through a police road block and proceeded on her way. The turn-off to the Mission is at a store 10 miles beyond Mutoko going north. There was a military security check going on, carried out by a security guard force. They waved Luisa and the truck in front to stop. She was in her ambulance clearly marked as such with a large green cross on each door and 'Ambulance' written at the front and back. She stopped while the truck was being checked. She must have thought that all was well since she started up the ambulance and slowly turned to the right, off the tar road on to her dust road to the Mission hospital. The guard force opened fire on the ambulance – about four shots were fired and one hit Luisa in the left leg just above the knee-joint line. It must have struck an artery. She bled to death before they could get her to hospital. The inquest report bore this final rejoinder: 'Security Forces must take great caution in situations where they wish to regulate the control of traffic to ensure that their intentions and requirements are manifest to drivers in order that such incidents may be avoided in the future.'

John came in by African bus for Luisa's funeral. It was on 10 July and both he, Fr David Gibbs and I were pall bearers, along with three close African friends of Luisa from All Souls Mission. The cathedral was packed for the Requiem. John knelt close to the coffin throughout the Mass. From early Mutemwa days, Elizabeth Tarira, an African girl now studying medicine, flew out from Rome with Dr Rosalba. After the funeral John was very anxious to be back at Mutemwa. 'Now we know *what* he hurried back for. St Luke writes of Jesus, 'now as the time drew near for Him to be taken up to heaven, He resolutely took the road for Jerusalem.' That was John's resolution too' [from the funeral oration].

My leave was due. I had booked to fly north on the Feast of the Transfiguration – 6 August 1979. John came in to say goodbye on 1 August. He stayed two nights. I tried to persuade him to be 'transfigured' as well. 'Can't make it,' he said, 'the Stock Exchange is not doing well!' He wouldn't leave Mutemwa.

Heather came out to Silveira House to see him, for the last time as it turned out. She comments:

John came to town one month before he was killed. I went to Silveira House straight after work to see him. We took a walk to the Grotto to look over the Chishawasha valley, the sun was beginning to set and the sky was a striking shade of red. I again suggested that John should leave Mutemwa because it was so dangerous in the Mutoko area. We talked about the possibility of his being killed. This thought put an end to our conversation and we walked quite a long way down to the Mission borehole in silence.

I remember thinking as we walked back that John was quieter and more serene than I had ever known him. A peace which I was quite unable to share. He was quiet and gentle and talked of God's love, continuously stressing the trust and faith that was possible if one accepted the completeness of God's love. I realised that John understood and embraced, with a serene joy and understanding, this love. With some sense of surprise I perceived that John the 'Joker' – John, self-acclaimed 'God's fool', was gone. In his place was a very holy man who, through his life of prayer and meditation, had reached some higher level of understanding. How imperceptive I was – listening with half my mind. This, I think, was part of John's sadness for me, for John always hoped that I would put, as he described it, 'my energies into the wish of God – and my intellect into the life of prayer'. So it was that, in a state of dullness induced by a mutual sadness, I said goodbye.

Driving home, I experienced a profound sense of loss which I could not and cannot define. I am sure that John had no doubts whatsoever. He understood and embraced God's love with a serene joy and true sanctity. I also understood with clarity that John had tried to share with me his perception of this Great Enduring Love which was indescribably beautiful and comforting and complete. That I lacked the grace or perception to understand saddened him for he kept saying, 'I will pray for you, Heather – and you pray too.' This was the last time I saw John.

Finally, he asked me, 'What shall I do if they come?' – meaning visitors in the night. I replied that he should give them what they ask for, adding, 'Don't die for five dollars.' 'Ah no,' he said, 'it is leper money. I will give them coffee.' I promised to look up his mother, his sister Mary and his brother Philip. Then, with his usual humility, he knelt in the road for a blessing. Disciple blessed guru – with that we parted, he back to Mutemwa with Fr David Gibbs in his two-ton lorry and I, sadly, to the north on leave.

PART X

THE END OF THE JOURNEY

Come sweet death
We are they
Fled to fight another day
But why, why should fight we still
When all was fought and won on Friday Hill?
(J.R.B.)

CHAPTER 55

The Second Wish

There had been a guerrilla attack close to Mutemwa where there is a reservoir fed from a nearby dam. They must have been fairly close to John but passed him by, even though he was quite alone at nights except for the two old lepers in the guest hut.

The guerrillas had passed him by. Was he, a lone white man and above all an outspoken prophet figure, safe? War knows no bounds. Many an innocent man and woman had gone to a cruel death due to false allegations at people's Courts – labels of 'sell-out', 'informer', 'traitor' – old scores being settled with enemies in neighbouring villages.

During all the time that John had been at the Leper Settlement certain people from neighbouring villages had shown hostility to him and the lepers. A good number of the lepers were diseased foreigners, expatriate farm labourers from Malawi, Mozambique, Zambia and elsewhere; others were from different tribes. They were not welcome to some of the local tribesmen who herded their cattle on to leper fields, stole firewood, broke the fences, pinched mangoes. It was alleged that leper rations and gift clothing went astray. John was the shepherd who did all he could to keep the wolves at bay from his battered flock. He impounded stray cattle and on occasion fined the owners, giving the money to the lepers. Moreover the orderlies were local people. Had not John taken the

African Warden to court at one time? Had he not condemned local mujibhas (village lads) for the murder of the old man who used to come to the leper Mass?

The odds were against John – enemies amongst the locals, enemies amongst the mujibhas, enmity with the white RLA. Even some whites in the security forces wondered how he had survived without helping the 'other' side in some way. The world had rejected John.

About two years after John's death some ex-guerrillas alleged that as the war intensified, with many more guerrilla bands in the area and many more secret meetings in the night, the locals held council. Why not abduct this menace, this white man, and take him to the guerrillas to meet his end? Once rid of the shepherd perhaps then they could scatter the sheep? The meeting was held at night near Mutemwa Mount. The stage was set.

It was at this time that John decided to move out of his tin hut into the middle hut of the three. He had some notion that his tin hut could be joined to the existing rondavel chapel to enlarge it. The hut into which he moved was a round brick hut with a thatched roof, having a few peep holes rather than windows. It had a wooden door and it was fairly dark inside but was much cooler than the tin hut. In the third hut there were the two old lepers waiting their chance to be given a hut in the compound. It was an eerie experience, especially at night. One could expect a visit at anytime.

In the daytime new 'birds', as he put it, could be seen over Mutemwa – helicopters. The situation was tense. Well-wishers urged John to leave. It was unthinkable. John said that, when the last leper had left Mutemwa, then, and then only, would he leave. He was also concerned about Fr David Gibbs since priests were vulnerable to all sides, although the guerrillas had been friendly to him.

Pauline describes her last Mass at Mutemwa with John on the Wednesday, some five days before he was abducted.

The little round church was crowded; the small congregation I had joined years before having, since then, nearly doubled. After Mass John and the lepers said the

St Francis peace prayer as usual, and then John helped the lepers who are unable to walk back to their huts. We went to John's house for breakfast – the last of so many treasured Wednesdays. My good cook, Stanley, had baked a cake for 'Baba' John, and we had the marmalade sandwiches. I counted heads: John, Fr David, my four children and me. Outside, sitting at the doorway of what should have been John's kitchen hut, were an old leper, his wife and a few friends of theirs. The old man, because of endless red tape, had been denied entrance to Mutemwa so John had given him shelter. I decided to give the sandwiches to the old man, and keep the cake for John and the rest of us. This 'unfair distribution' of the spoils so worried John that, not feeling in a position to reverse my decision, he changed places with me (I was wedged behind the door) to be out of sight of the people outside, rather than have them see him eating cake while they had only sandwiches! John's charity towards the old man had effectively robbed him of all privacy. He could not even draw breath without being observed, as the doors of the two huts were adjacent. This incident brought home to me the extent of John's poverty.

That was the last time I saw John. While we were packing to leave, he drew $\pm_M$ in the dust on the back window of our truck. A fitting farewell.

One day shortly before the end, John suddenly came up to Coletta to say that there was no longer any peace within his hut – he sensed evil. A type of red ant invaded his hut – an ill omen according to Coletta. John was forced to spend two nights in the chapel. The first day of September was a Saturday. He became agitated, taking a few things to the chapel for safety's sake. He asked prayers of Coletta and the lepers, implying that 'our fight is not against human foes but against cosmic powers, against the authorities and potentates of this dark world – superhuman forces of evil' (Ephesians 6).

On Sunday the second of September no priest came to say Mass. John held his usual communion service with lepers. Colleta says he preached about St Lawrence, the famous martyr of the early Church who suffered martyrdom at the hands of the Roman Emperor Valerian. He told the lepers that we should have the courage and forbearance of St Lawrence. He often used to quote from the prophet Jeremiah:

> So now brace yourself for action.
> Stand up and tell them
> All I command you.
> Do not be dismayed at their presence.
> I, for my part, today will make you
> into a fortified city,
> A pillar of iron,
> And a wall of bronze,
> To confront all this land.
>
> (Jeremiah 1. 17–19)

John's 'today' had arrived. He had been well prepared by grace for his 'hour.'

He refused to go back to his hut after the Mass, nor did he go for his usual climb up on to Chigona. He spent a good while in the chapel reading from the Book of Judith and about Esther. He kept asking Coletta to gather some lepers around him in prayer.

That evening a strange incident occurred. At the time of the evening prayer and rosary John developed an inexplicable, perhaps mystical, thirst. He ran to the water tap near the clinic. The water was turned off. He hurried back to Coletta and the lepers asking them for water – they had none. The Christ-like thirst eased as it came. This was the last that Coletta saw of him.

The two old lepers in the guest hut next to John's say that he retired there. In the night they heard voices at John's door speaking in English. They say John opened his hut door. Conversation ensued. There was a noise of departure and then all was silent. They were too afraid to leave their hut till the dawn.

The hour of darkness had arrived. It was a cunning plot. It is alleged that false information had been circulated that John had a transmitter radio – he was an informer. A kindly old woman, knowing this, had implored John daily to leave Mutemwa before it was too late. John was at a loss to know how to pacify this good woman. His inner spirit knew that he must stay. Then, one day before this fatal hour, he came down off Chigona mount and said that he had met a big Angel who inspired him to stay. Maybe the Angel of the agony?

Andrew Whaley, a playwright and screenplay writer, recently completed more research on John's abduction. He said that the area around Hunhu where John was taken was not so very far from Mutoko town itself. In fact, from the western edge one could see the outskirts of the township of Mutoko. The area was pocketed with granite hills and flat stone rocks which glowed eerily on a moonlit night. Even had Rhodesian security forces heard noise and carousing from this area, by 1979 they would have found it impossible to go in at night without coming to grief.

The whole of Hunhu, according to my investigations, appears to have been an area in which the guerrillas moved with great freedom and where the mujhibas held great sway. People were very reluctant to talk to a stranger, a white stranger at that, about the circumstances of John's death. One villager said it could become a 'police case'. It appears that a couple of the mujhibas held great influence in that area and were truly feared by local villagers, most of their parents and elders. During my enquiries I picked up two young people in their early twenties who told me, independently, that an elder brother and sister who had been mujhibas had been murdered by fellow mujhibas and left out on the hills above the kraals. They suggested that the mujhibas operated like a gang.

It was in this atmosphere that John Bradburne's abduction plot was hatched at the first meeting at Chimedza cave. Andrew Whaley's informants allege that John's captors consisted of a group of nineteen mujhibas who came from Chimedza cave near Hunhu village. This area, six or seven miles east of Mutemwa, was already liberated and enjoying independence since the Rhodesian Security Forces regarded it as a 'no go' area owing to its natural defences of rock features, caves and bush country. Moreover, it was of no real military significance to them since it was away out in the back of beyond. A number of them in the Hunhu area had made application to go to Mozambique to join the guerrillas proper. Up to this time their requests had not been heard.

They were now hearing stories about John Bradburne from disaffected people whose villages were in that area. They spoke of him as a white man and a spy. In fact, John had caught them and others stealing from the lepers and so they were anxious to be rid of him. This gave the mujhibas food for thought. What if they abducted John and took him to the guerrilla Area Commander on the charge that he was a white man and a spy? They heard that he had a transmitter and was sending messages to the Security Forces. Would not the Commander then allow them to go to Mozambique for training in reward for such a prize captive? Thus a great number of mujibhas held a meeting at the HQ Chimedza cave near Hunhu village on the day before John's abduction. They agreed to go ahead with their plan.

On the night of Sunday 2nd September 1979 John did not sleep in his tin hut, but in a cooler, thatched hut at the back. He usually had the camp radios and one record player with him for safe keeping. He put these out in the patients' compound during the day.

The group probably arrived before midnight, banging on his door and asking if he would come out to pray with them. They were armed with sticks and bazdas (hoes) and one of them had two hand grenades. They feared bumping into Security Forces on their journey. John got up and put on his Franciscan habit and red headband but was very reluctant to leave his hut. When they asked him to come out to pray he is supposed to have said that they could as well pray there. When he was persuaded to go a short way with them into the dark bush, he kept asking how far he must go to pray and for what purpose. The mujhibas hurried him on. It is said that they bound his hands and pulled him through the bush, causing him to stumble. He would argue with them: 'Is this the way you ask me to pray?' After a while, they apparently loosed his hands, but the struggle had tired him. He did not know how long it would go on. He kept saying that he must go back to Mutemwa and repeatedly asked them to get to the point; they had travelled far enough and could pray there, in the bush, instead of pulling him away from Mutemwa. They must have become irritated with his questions and his increasing breathlessness. One man said that Bradburne was not a fit man at the time. They took him first to Chimedza cave near Hunhu village just over six miles north east of Mutemwa. This was the power centre for the mujhibas and 30 or 40 were awaiting the arrival of the rest of the group. It was now the middle of the night (Monday 3rd September, 2 am approx.)

There was great rejoicing at Chimedza cave that they had brought a white man. John asked again when they would pray, but instead of prayer he was subjected to vile mockery. One creature asked him if he had ever eaten human excrement since he would soon do so. They even tried to force him to sleep with a village girl, a camp follower. John was politely strong in his refusals. Next they brought the record player and put on one of their pop tapes. They tried to force John to dance; he said that he could dance but not in their way. After they had had their fill of taunting and mocking, they brought him to a nearby village, bound him and put him in an empty hut. He was detained during the whole of Monday 3rd September.

Meanwhile the mujhibas called for the Chairman, lady Secretary and an Executive member of the local Zanu PF (Mugabe's political wing). They said that they knew John, a good man looking after poor black lepers. Others also came forward to speak up for him and they had seen him carrying a leper in his arms to the local Mutoko hospital. The mujhibas lied in saying that they would release him.

On the night of Monday 3rd September, John was taken (frog-marched, according to one account) by four mujhibas in search of the guerrillas. For security reasons, the guerrillas came and went and seldom stayed in one place for any length of time. They had no luck in their Chimedza cave area and so crossed into the Gwaze cave area which was under the control of a different District Commander.

They arrived at Gwaze cave at dawn on Tuesday 4th September. Opposite Gwaze cave there is a striking rock painting in blue of the figure of Christ with arms outstretched. When John saw this, he knelt in prayer. On entering the cave he caught sight of it again and knelt once more. Gwaze is not so much a cave as a rock shelter caused by the fall of a huge slab over an 'arbour' in the rock face. It has an entrance, highly concealed, and a small exit. It is dark and gives a sense of awe. (At this point Andrew Whaley's narrative ends).

This cave proved to be decisive in John's life-death narrative; he had written from London in 1961, asking if there was a cave in Africa where he could dwell. He had found his cave.

Another informant then alleged:

Untied by his captors, he sat down in the cave, exhausted. The District Commander of the guerrillas arrived after dusk with about 15 of his men. He first questioned the mujhibas as to why they had brought John, a man known to him and the guerrillas (one of them knew him personally), a harmless white man looking after the poor blacks. In reply, they said that John hated the war and so was not helping the struggle for liberation. Moreover, he prayed to *his* God, not to their ancestral spirits. The Commander became very angry with the mujhibas, rebuking them for bringing John, and questioned whether they had been followed. He observed that the 'transmitter', which had been brought from John's hut, was no more than a domestic radio. He decided to free John and send him back to Mutemwa.

Each guerrilla group had a comrade in charge of security; this comrade disagreed with the decision to release John. He had seen too much and his release would be a security risk. The Rhodesian Security Forces would press him for information, many people could be implicated and their safe cave HQ might be lost to them. After a heated discussion the Commander proposed to send John to Mozambique as a solution to the problem, but John would not accept the compromise, refusing to abandon his little flock. He was offered Tanzania or China, but was adamant that it was to be Mutemwa or nothing – in other words, death. Thus, Mozambique spelt life; Mutemwa death. They asked whether John was interested in their freedom. His response was to kneel in prayer. He prayed in Shona – *Baba vedu* (Our Father), *Kwaziwai Maria* (Hail Mary). It is said that they were all astonished at his profound peace and unconcern with regard to his fate.

The Commander treated John in a friendly manner, asking if he could eat their food or preferred tea and bread. After eating they all departed for a *pungwe*, a concientization of the local people. They went a mile or so in an easterly direction to a place where there was a large assembly of between three and five thousand people. John played no part in the *pungwe* but a lovely incident took place. A woman with twins came to sit next to John. She put the twins on his lap and they went to sleep. She stated that after a while John got up and gave the twins back to her, saying:

'Amai (mother), you will not see me again but I will pray for you.'

Then he knelt and, with arms raised, recited the *Our Father* in Shona.

After the *pungwe* the Commander told John that he could go free. He set off with the people who were leaving, to descend to the main road to Mutoko. Some of the villagers who accompanied the group said that John stopped to pray on two occasions when he heard a cock crow. There seemed to have been some tension due to the presence of the two guerillas, whose intentions were not apparent to those around them: the Commander had, after all, set John free to return to Mutemwa.

It is alleged that after reaching the main Mutoko – Nyamapanda road a gunman emerged and edged John off the road to a little stream which flowed under a culvert. John knelt in prayer and as he rose the gunman emptied an AK magazine into his back. An old man said that John fell upon his knees and then sank gracefully to the ground. He died like a *hwayana* (a lamb): silent, without complaint.

The old man alleges that the whole group then became

very agitated – if the white security forces find John's body here they will kill us and all the villagers around and about. They decided to carry the body hurriedly back over the main road to the rocky terrain on the far side. There they would hide John's body so that it would not be found.

Quite extraordinary happenings took place. The old man stated that as they were crossing the main road they heard people singing. They dropped the body of John and ran. After a while they calmed down and crept back to the road. The singing was louder than ever. They fled again.

Fear of discovery of the body by the security forces urged them to return to the body. The old man said that they saw something never seen before. A strange, large white bird hovered over John's body. It moved up and down over the body seemingly to guard it. They retreated again in alarm, but they were torn between fear of these phenomena and fear of the security forces. They lay low for quite a while and then plucked up courage to go back to the road for the third time. They were overawed on arrival at the sight of what appeared to be three beams of light ascending from the proximity of John's body, meeting at a height and descending as one beam. The colours seemed to be blue and red and white. They fled, not to return again.

Voices singing? – how John longed to hear the choirs of heaven. A very large white bird – the Holy Spirit? Finally three beams of light joining and forming one. John so loved the Holy Trinity. Whatever the explanation, one thing seems sure. The Lord, whom John had loved and served all his life, desired that the body remain on the road to be safely carried away by loving hands. It was about three a.m. Thus John's body remained alone in the dark, awaiting the dawn.

The phenomena described were beyond the invention of people of a vastly different religious culture. The old man was not a Christian; he honoured his ancestral spirits in a traditional manner. Thus the symbolism of the phenomena had no meaning to the group: the sweat of the agony coupled with the three kneelings in deep prayer by John, the great white bird, and the three in one beam of light. This was all beyond their comprehension. They only experienced fear and bewilderment.

Dawn broke and the two old leprosy patients cautiously left their hut to find John gone.

Gone home through the cloud of unknowing – migrated like the birds he so loved, his pilgrimage over, his tent folded.

The Third Wish

Come, sweet death, on Wednesday
If you will and if you may ...

(J.R.B.)

Fr David Gibbs reports:

At about 1.30 p.m. on Monday, 3rd September, 1979, Brother Athanatius returned from Mutoko to All Souls with the news that John Bradburne had been abducted from his hut at Mutemwa Leper Camp some time during the early hours of the 3rd of September. I immediately drove from the mission to Mutemwa where I questioned several people but nobody had any further information to give me. I then went to John's hut but found it locked so I drove up to Mutoko Police Station where I was told that the keys to John's hut were being kept at the JOC [Joint Operations Command] Mutoko:

I went at once to the JOC where I was given the keys and returned to Mutemwa. I entered John's hut and found that only a camp record-player was missing – everything else appeared to be intact. On my way back to Mutoko I met Pauline Hutchings and returned with her to John's hut where we collected his prayer-books which Pauline took home for safe-keeping. I then gave back the keys to the Member-in-Charge and returned to All Souls, reaching the mission just before curfew.

On the next afternoon [Tuesday] Father Mhishi, the Mission Superior, went into Mutoko to see if there was any more news of John. Father Mhishi returned with no further news. Extensive enquiries around the mission also revealed nothing.

At about 6.15 a.m. on Wednesday morning, 5th September, I left the mission in the mission ambulance to go to Mutemwa. About one mile from the mission I met a friend who told me that a European had been killed. I questioned him closely but he did not know the name of the European. I continued on towards Mutoko and about twenty minutes later came across John lying on the main Mutoko-Nyamapanda road.

John was lying half-on and half-off the tarmac on the left-hand side of the road, dressed only in his underpants.He had wounds in his legs and the lower part of his chest. The upper part of John's chest, his arms and his head were unmarked. He was lying on his back, his eyes were open and his right hand was under his head, with his left hand by his side. I closed John's eyes and spent a short time in prayer by his side.

Another eye witness said that John's head and body were on the tar and his legs were on the sand at the side of the road. The sand was soaked with blood. There was a long gash-like wound in the abdomen which made people believe that he had been bayoneted to death. In fact he had been shot from behind. The entrance wounds in his back were small but the exit wounds were large, which is normal with AK bullets. It was reported that 24 spent cartridge cases were found at the scene.

David Gibbs continues:

I then put John's body into the ambulance and drove straight to the Military JOC H.Q., Mutoko, the only place in Mutoko where there was a fridge for keeping bodies. I left John's body at the JOC and, after putting it into the fridge, I drove to Mgwaalati farm, the home of Pauline and Tony Hutchings. Tony was away but I broke the news of John's death to Pauline and together we went to a small cave in the hill behind the house where I said

Mass for John. After Mass I returned to Mutoko and drove to Mutemwa. There I spoke to all the lepers, told them about John, and then celebrated Mass in the Mutemwa Chapel. After Mass I returned to All Souls with the news of John's death.

Pauline gives her account:

Father David Gibbs came to our farm after leaving John's body at the Army H.Q. Shocked and grief-stricken we climbed up the kopje to our cave and there in view of Mutemwa mountain Fr David said Mass. That day a heavy pall of veld smoke settled over Mutemwa and the mountain was not visible again from here for over a month. It reminded me of Moses in the desert and the Cloud which covered the tabernacle. I felt it almost as an injunction to me: 'While the cloud covers Mutemwa, stay quiet in your grief, paying worship to Yahweh and giving thanks to Him for his beloved servant John.'

I was away at the time and so Fr David Harold-Barry took over all the arrangements for John's Requiem and burial. David gives the full account:

What remains is for me to give some account of John's death and burial. The news first came to me on Tuesday, September 4th, 1979 at about 11.30 a.m. Pauline Hutchings rang me to say John had been abducted early the day before and that she was going to Mutemwa to save what she could. I had been thinking of John that weekend, 1–2 September. Normally, when John Dove was at Silveira, I did not see it as my responsibility to keep in close touch with him. But that weekend I got together his monthly rations of Lactogen, brown sugar, cheese and chocolate and enclosed a postcard of an Irish cottage illustrating where John Dove was. I was going to send the parcel with one of the young people from the Youth Congress but heard that Fr Mhishi from All Souls was coming early the following week. Alas, I never sent the parcel.

After Pauline's call, the Archbishop, Fr Wardale (the

Jesuit Provincial) and I tried to contact Fr Dove and ask him to contact John's family. As it turned out it was not until the next day that contact was made with the remote Irish cottage where John Dove was staying and the message by that time was that John was dead. His body had been found on the Mutoko Road by Fr David Gibbs and a nursing Sister at about 7.00 a.m. that morning. It was a sad, sad day at Silveira – the home of John for many years and where he often stayed from Mutemwa. All the staff heard the news as they came and went about their daily work. We had a Vigil Service of prayers in the evening.

Gradually we had to face the reality that John was dead. The Archbishop invited us at Silveira to arrange the funeral – a Mass of the Resurrection which was fixed for 10.00 o'clock on the 10th September. Archbishop Patrick Chakaipa himself would be the celebrant and I was to preach the funeral oration. Great friends of John's and ours, Kit and Arthur Law, helped to plan the service and Kit was the organist. At the entry she played Pachelbel's Ciaconna, one of John's favourites. The Kyrie, Gloria and Gradual were sung in Shona by the Silveira choir, whilst the Rhodesville choir sang Mozart's Ave Verum, the Nunc Dimittis and other hymns. The bidding prayers were led by Fr Seán Gildea OFM, Agnes Mapfumo of Silveira, Heather Benoy (a long-time friend of John's), Sister Bonaventura, the cook at Silveira House, and others. The Offertory, Sanctus and Agnus Dei were sung in Shona by the Silveira choir. The absolutions were given by Archbishop Markall.

At Communion time three lilies were laid on the coffin at the request of John's dear friend, Mrs Ann Lander. And at that very time drops of blood were seen to fall from the coffin.

I asked Ann why she had sent the three lilies. She replied quite simply that they were a memento of John's great love of the Trinity and then went on to add:

On hearing of his death I felt totally bereft and very distressed. All that night I hardly slept and, on rising early the following morning, I simply knew with a

conviction that I had to place three white flowers on
his coffin. As I was going overseas the next day I asked
a friend of mine to do this for me in my absence and I
wrote a little card with the words 'Three-in-One' on it
and asked her to place it with the flowers on his
coffin. Having been given the exact time of the Service
I was able to be with the mourning congregation in
spirit. My friend who took the flowers up said that, as
she placed the flowers on the coffin, she felt as if she
had been caught up in a 'spiritual whirlpool'. It was
very shortly after their placement that the three drops
of blood became evident. During the time of the
service I felt so close to John and was able to share
with him a spirit of gladsome fullness and joy.

John was a man who gave more than he ever
received and his longing for God must have been
often painful and anguishing. He saw God in men and
all creation and situations and his joy in doing so was
apparent to those he was with. And yet his longing for
God the Father, God the Son, and God the Holy Ghost
was what I felt whenever we came together. It was the
certainty that John had reached his union with the
Trinity that helped to ease the ache and pain for me.

To have known him is a gift from God that I will
treasure all of my life.

David Harold-Barry continues:

I first noticed the blood when I saw Fr Michael O'Halloran go down and put a clean purificator cloth over one
drop. At that point I saw another drop fall. I thought
someone must have cut their finger somehow and did
not take much notice. After Mass was over Michael asked
if I had noticed the blood and I said that I had, and we
discussed it a little and felt it was extraordinary. Gradually the Press got to hear of it and I remember feeling
annoyed at their 'going for the sensational'. But then I
realised I was instinctively trying to block out the event
from my mind, whereas in fact the truth was that it was
sensational.

Simbarashe Muzuva and Sister Felicitas LCBL also saw

the blood fall from the bottom of the coffin. No one saw more than three drops.

Three drops forming one pool is certainly a symbol of the Trinity. It was this little pool which enabled John to get his final wish – to be buried in the Franciscan habit. It was the cause of the re-opening of the coffin and subsequent clothing of John's body in the habit of St Francis. It was an underscoring, too, of his whole life. A sign, a seal from God upon a life dedicated to the Trinity and God's poor.

In the meantime, the World Press picked up the story. John became news overnight. Judith Countess Listowel, a good friend of John and his brother Philip, spoke of him on the BBC. Reporters began to contact me.

The Undertaker's report to this extraordinary event is interesting:

The late Mr Bradburne was removed from the Mortuary at Mutoko on Friday the 7th September, 1979. The remains were transported by hearse to our Mortuary at 161 Salisbury Street, Salisbury, Zimbabwe.

When the remains arrived at our Mortuary, our Mortician Mr R.R.M. Bury removed the remains from the stretcher and placed them into a casket for burial, covered with a calico robe. All wounds were checked and covered with cotton wool as a matter of formality.

At this stage, observations were made but not considered relevant at the time; (They were recalled because of the subsequent events).

1. The remains were frozen.
2. The state of the cadaver was seen to be 'excellently preserved' with no putrefaction.
3. No skin slip.
4. No decomposition at all.
5. Wounds were clean, clear and dry (no blood was seen).
6. No discoloration.

On Monday 10th September, 1979, the casket was removed from the cold room and placed in the hearse. The hearse then left for the Catholic Cathedral where the Concelebrated Requiem Mass of the Resurrection was to take place commencing at 11.00 a.m. At the Cathedral the casket was removed from the hearse, placed on a trolley in the portal and preceded by the Priests and the two Archbishops. The trolley was wheeled to the front of the Cathedral and was placed in exactly the same place as Mr C.W. Hamer-Nel and his father before him had placed caskets for Funeral Services in the Cathedral, for the past twenty-five years.

At approximately 12.10 p.m. Mr C.W. Hamer-Nel and his Funeral Assistant, Mr C. Nel, proceeded to the front of the Cathedral and stood a short distance away from the casket as the Mass was due to end.

Just before the Archbishop, Patrick Chakaipa, and his assistants were due to come down to give the final blessing, Fr O'Halloran, one of the priests involved in the Concelebration, placed a white cloth (Chalice Purifier) under the casket. This was a deviation from the normal service and had never been observed before.

When Mr C.W. Hamer-Nel and Mr C. Nel walked towards the casket after the final blessings were given, Mr C.W. Hamer-Nel observed a blood stain on the Chalice Purifier; he was deeply shocked by this. Mr C.W. Hamer-Nel genuflected next to the casket, picked up the Chalice Purifier and placed it on top of the casket next to the flowers. While doing this he observed that the blood on the Purifier was crimson and looked fresh. In view of what he had seen, Mr C.W. Hamer-Nel checked the aisle on the way out of the church in case any spots of blood might be there. He observed no blood in the aisle. He did this because he was concerned that seepage might have occurred. At this stage he had not seen the remains and did not know what state the remains were in. It should be noted that no blood was observed by Mr C.W. Hamer-Nel or anyone else when the casket was wheeled into the Cathedral. If it was there, it would have been observed because the blood which was seen, was in approximately the same place where Mr

C.W. Hamer-Nel genuflected before turning to place the casket in position between the candles.

The casket was then placed in the hearse and brought back to the Funeral Parlour at 161 Salisbury Street; Fr Riederer arrived at Doves-Morgans Funeral Parlour within a few minutes after the hearse arrived back. Fr V. Riederer requested that the casket be opened as he wished to examine the remains. The casket was opened in the presence of Mr C.W. Hamer-Nel, Mr R.R.M. Bury and Fr V. Riederer. It was at this stage that Mr C.W. Hamer-Nel was surprised to note the perfect preservation of the remains, there was no seepage. Fr Riederer examined the casket by wiping his hand inside and underneath. No blood or dampness was present or observed. All wounds were inspected and seen to be dry. Fr Riederer then took the Chalice Purifier, which was placed in an envelope, back to the Cathedral.

Later in the afternoon Fr Spence and Sister Margaret examined the remains. Sister Margaret then enquired why the remains were not dressed in the Franciscan Habit. (This had been one of John Randal Bradburne's wishes). We advised that no habit was given to us for this purpose. Fr Desmond O'Malley later delivered a Franciscan Habit.

At this stage the burial was to take place at Mutemwa Leper Colony near Mutoko. Fr Spence cancelled these arrangements. The burial was then arranged to take place at Chishawasha Mission on Wednesday, 12th September, 1979.

At approximately 8.30 on Wednesday the 12th September, 1979, Fr Spence and Dr Lamplugh came down to the Funeral Parlour Mortuary and saw Mr Bury the Mortician to obtain a sample of blood. A sample was taken from the leg with great difficulty, near a leg wound.

The casket was closed by Mr Bury in their presence and then placed in the hearse. Mr C.W. Hamer-Nel and Mr Bury then proceeded to Chishawasha Mission for interment.

Please note if there had been any blood on the

Cathedral floor before the service, the Priest's robes would have smeared it all over the floor and carpets around the altar.

As you are well aware what happened was most upsetting and we have no explanation for it.

These are the facts arising before the interment took place and are true as detailed.

The report was signed by the witnesses.

Later in private conversation with the Undertaker, Mr Hamer-Nel, he said to me: 'Father, that blood on the cloth was crimson, bright and fresh. Blood is never like that from a dead body.' I asked him if it could not have been blood from someone's finger or even red juice from the flowers. He was emphatic that it was no such thing. They had examined the coffin thoroughly and there was no sign of a drip 'run' from the top, down the side, or underneath the coffin. He would certainly have noticed anything of that sort. He went on to tell me that his own reaction inside the Cathedral had been quite dramatic. He had wished the ground beneath him to swallow him up. He foresaw the end of his business – a bad clean-up job leading to bad publicity. He was itching to get out of the Cathedral to vent his rage upon his assistants. He went on to say that, when Father Riederer arrived at his Funeral Parlour, he himself was sitting with his head in his hands and refused to go anywhere near the coffin. Eventually Father Riederer persuaded him to go with him to the cold room. He went, examined the body and left mystified. Like St John after entering the tomb of Christ, he gradually began to believe that an extraordinary happening had taken place.

Fr David Harold-Barry concludes:

John's body was to have been taken to Mutemwa that night for an all night vigil but Fr David Gibbs, who had returned immediately after the funeral to Mutemwa, phoned to say it was not safe to do that. In the end the body was kept in Salisbury until the folowing Wednesday and then it was buried in the Chishawasha Mission Cemetery next to those of the other Dominican Sisters,

Jesuit priests and Brothers who died at their posts during the war.

The Archbishop said a few words at the graveside and I remember him saying:

'John reminds us so much of Christ.'

Afterword

Since John Bradburne's death there have been many signs of his sanctity – visits by bees and eagles, claims to cures and many strange answers to prayer. Moreover, latterly, there is evidence that Mutemwa has become a Marian Centre due to John's extraordinary love of Maria the Mother of God. Many signs indicate this fact. Thus pilgrims are now coming from all over Zimbabwe and South Africa to seek help from John and his beloved Maria The Mother of the Lord.

In addition, a new Community has emerged. The Mother of Peace Community has given its all to care for small, abandoned children with Aids. Made up of a small group of extraordinarily dedicated people, both white and black, who live on land adjoining Mutemwa, the Community share in the great spirit of John and his love of Our Lord and His Holy Mother Maria.

It is evident that John's heroic love of the poor, coupled with his great holiness, is bringing many back to seek God as he sought Him throughout his life. Moreover, just as he brought the kingdom of joy and love to the unloved and rejected lepers, so now he is inspiring many far and wide to seek that same kingdom which leads to joy and peace.

Strange vagabond that knows not what to seek!
The rest you lack lies not this far afield:
Much babel tumult makes your hearing weak,
And all replete with sights your eyes are sealed.
Far out you've strayed to find your inmost soul
But souls their eloquence in stillness find:
Be still then! let God's silence make you whole,
For He alone can calm your troubled mind.

Your heart's desire is nearest, though unseen,
Your haven of perfection close at hand;
And that drear quest was as a fevered dream;
God's love within you is your native land.
So search none other, never more depart,
For you are homeless, save God keeps your heart.

J.R.B.

John Bradburne Memorial Society
PO Box 32
Leominster, Herefordshire HR6 0YB
England